Making Machu Picchu

Making Machu Picchu

The Politics of Tourism in Twentieth-Century Peru

Mark Rice

The University of North Carolina Press CHAPEL HILL

This book was published with the assistance of the Authors Fund of the University of North Carolina Press.

The University of North Carolina Press has been a member of the
Green Press Initiative since 2003.

Library of Congress Cataloging-in-Publication Data
Names: Rice, Mark, active 2012– author.
Title: Making Machu Picchu : the politics of tourism in twentieth-century Peru /
    Mark Rice.
Description: Chapel Hill : University of North Carolina Press, [2018] |
    Includes bibliographical references and index.
Identifiers: LCCN 2018013222| ISBN 9781469643526 (cloth : alk. paper) |
    ISBN 9781469643533 (pbk : alk. paper) | ISBN 9781469643540 (ebook)
Subjects: LCSH: Tourism—Peru—Machu Picchu Site—History—20th century. |
    Tourism—Political aspects—Peru—Machu Picchu Site. | International travel—
    Peru—Machu Picchu Site—History—20th century. | Peru—Symbolic
    representation—History—20th century.
Classification: LCC F3429.1.M3 R524 2018 | DDC 985/.37—dc23
    LC record available at https://lccn.loc.gov/2018013222

Cover illustrations: front, by Steven Garcia (© 2018 Anderson Design Group, Inc., all rights reserved, used by permission; see the entire collection at http://www .ADGstore.com); back, photo of Machu Picchu (detail, JM-0026, Coleccion Jorge Muelle, Archivo Historico Riva-Aguero, IRA-PUCP).

A portion of chapter 4 was previously published in a different form as "Generals, Hotels, and Hippies: Velasco-Era Tourism Development and Conflict in Cuzco," in *The Peculiar Revolution: Rethinking the Peruvian Experiment under Military Rule*, ed. Carlos Aguirre and Paulo Drinot (Austin: University of Texas Press, 2017), 295–318.

For 未来

Contents

Illustrations, Maps, and Graph

Acknowledgments

If writing a book can be considered a journey, then I often felt like a lost tourist. Fortunately, just like the hikers on the Inca Trail to Machu Picchu, I could rely on experienced guides who knew the territory and patiently helped me reach my destination. Unfortunately, the constraints of space (and available ink) limit my acknowledgments to only a few of the many who have directly helped me with this book. For those not formally mentioned in these acknowledgments, you know who you are, and you have my thanks.

I must thank the talented people working on the history of Peru and Peruvian tourism who welcomed me into their scholarly community and offered invaluable advice on the research and writing of this book. Out of the many individuals in this group, I would like to especially mention Magally Allegre-Henderson, Ying-Ying Chu, Paul Firbas, Norma Fuller, Christopher Heaney, Jaymie Heilman, Willie Hiatt, Cameron Jones, Adrián Lerner, Rory Miller, Martín Monsalve, Elizabeth Montañez-Sanabria, Javier Puente, José Ragas, Gonzalo Romero, Natalia Sobrevilla, and Charles Walker.

Many other scholars and friends provided support, insights, critiques, and sometimes a much-needed dose of encouragement. I would like to thank in particular Eron Ackerman, Jennifer Anderson, Juan Pablo Artinian, Marisa Balsamo, Michael Barnhart, Ashley Black, Adam Charboneau, Ray Craib, Brenda Elsey, Froylán Encisco, Andrés Estefane, Brian Gebhart, Carlos Gomez, Young-Sun Hong, Sung Yup Kim, Ned Landsman, Choonib Lee, Clive Linssen, Gary Marker, April Masten, Elizabeth Newman, Timothy Nicholson, Mary Beth Norton, Nicholas Ostrum, Raquel Otheguy, Raymond Pienta, Glen Short, Carmen Soliz, María-Clara Torres, Kathleen Wilson, Kevin Young, Aihua Zhang, and Cristóbal Zúñiga-Espinoza.

I also want to thank organizers and attendees at panels and meetings where I was able to present early drafts of this work and receive important feedback. This includes participants at meetings of the American Historical Association, the Conference on Latin American History, and the Latin American Studies Association, as well as the New York City Latin American History Workshop. Two conferences on the Velasco military government provided forums to contextualize my work on tourism during that era. One was hosted at the Institute of the Americas at University College London.

Martín Monsalve, Norberto Barreto-Velásquez, the Instituto Francés de Estudios Andino, and the Universidad del Pacífico also were generous in allowing me to present my work on the Velasco government. I would like to thank the history students at the Universidad Nacional de San Antonio Abad del Cusco who invited me to talk about my research; their enthusiasm predicts a bright future for the study of Cusco's history.

I was fortunate to write this book as a member of the Department of History at Baruch College of the City University of New York. T. J. Desch-Obi, Vincent DiGirolamo, Bert Hansen, Elizabeth Heath, Thomas Heinrich, Martina Nguyen, and Andrew Sloin provided advice on the preparation of the manuscript. The department's collegial environment owes much to the work of Katherine Pence, who served as chair for most of the time I was writing this book, and department administrative assistant Ana Calero. However, I owe all of my departmental colleagues my gratitude for creating an engaging and supportive place to both write and teach. I am also grateful to my students, especially those from my spring 2017 history seminar on tourism, who kept me inspired and challenged me to think about my work in new ways.

The PSC-CUNY Research Award Program provided an important source of funding for the completion of this book, and I would like to thank the staff of Baruch College's Office of Sponsored Programs and Research for their help. The Tinker Foundation and the Bernard Semmel Award also provided funds to conduct research. My research was aided by the staffs of many archives and libraries. In particular, I want to thank the staff of the Archivo General de la Nación del Perú, Archivo Histórico Riva-Agüero, Biblioteca Central "Luis Jaime Cisneros" de la Pontificia Universidad Nacional del Perú, Biblioteca Nacional del Perú, Biblioteca de la Universidad Nacional de San Antonio Abad del Cusco, *Caretas*, Centro Bartolomé de las Casas, Manuscripts and Archives Department of Yale University Library, Martín Chambi Archivo Fotográfico, Newman Library at Baruch College, New York Public Library, the United States National Archives, and the Biblioteca Municipal del Cusco for the use of their hemeroteca (newspaper archive) and the Archivo Municipal del Cusco stored in their collection. I want to especially thank the employees of MINCETUR and the Ministerio de Cultura (both the Lima and Cusco offices). Lacking official archivists, staff in these ministries generously offered their limited time (and equally limited desk space!) so I could access many important and never-before-researched collections.

The history of tourism is a new field in Peru. In order to locate archives, collections, and interviews, I often sought the help of individuals whose own careers were closely linked to tourism and Machu Picchu. I would particularly like to thank Donato Amado, Beatriz Boza, Jorge Flores Ochoa, José Koechlin, Vera Lauer, Mariana Mould de Pease, José Tamayo Herrera, and Roger Valencia. These individuals, representing diverse (and sometimes conflicting) perspectives, all gave generously of their time in helping me track down people and archives so I could trace Machu Picchu's modern history. These individuals, along with others who agreed to be interviewed for this book, provided much-needed information that was often left out of archives.

I thank the individuals who read the entire manuscript or large parts of it. Deborah Poole offered key insights on Cusco's history. Eric Zolov lent his expertise to many areas of this book, especially in regard to U.S.–Latin American relations and the history of counterculture. Brooke Larson helped in countless ways, and the framing of the book's argument in the larger social and political history of the Andes is thanks largely due to her advice. Carlos Aguirre, Paulo Drinot, and anonymous reviewers at the *Radical History Review* also improved the manuscript through their advice on other research projects related to tourism in Peru. It is impossible to list all the ways Paul Gootenberg's insights improved this book. All I can say is that I owe him a tremendous debt of gratitude for his help, his mentoring, and his friendship. The revision of this manuscript benefited tremendously from the advice of two anonymous reviewers (one who revealed himself to be Paulo Drinot). Their constructive feedback helped hone this book's arguments, especially in regard to engagement with tourism theory and questions of state formation and social change in Peru. Barbara Goodhouse meticulously copyedited the manuscript. Elaine Maisner, my editor at the University of North Carolina Press, guided this entire process with the patience and aplomb that made the writing of this book intellectually stimulating and rewarding. I owe great thanks to everyone at the University of North Carolina Press for their helpfulness and patience with the preparation of the manuscript, images, maps, and book cover.

No acknowledgments section is complete without thanking loved ones. I have relied on the friendship of Aditya Didolkar, Danielle Liebling Tepper, and Jacob Tepper. My parents, Anna Marie and Charles Rice, have always been a source of steady and loving support. I thank my wife, Weilai, whose intellectual talents and love have supported this project from the very start. This book is dedicated to her not just as a token of my gratitude, but as a reflection of the central role she has played in its completion.

The findings of this book are a credit to the help of all those listed here and many more who have lent their advice over the years. Of course, any errors or omissions are entirely the fault of my daughter, Sally. I blame her for two reasons. First, she is two years old and really can't defend herself from such accusations. Second, Sally was born while I was writing this book and immediately surpassed it to become my favorite new project. I wouldn't want it any other way.

Abbreviations in Text

APRA   Alianza Popular Revolucionaria Americana, American Popular Revolutionary Alliance

CANATUR   Cámara Nacional del Turismo del Perú, National Tourism Chamber of Peru

CCPT   Comité Central de Propaganda Turístico, Central Tourism Propaganda Committee

CIAA   Coordinator of Inter-American Affairs

CNT   Corporación Nacional del Turismo, National Tourism Corporation

COPESCO   Plan Turístico y Cultural Perú-UNESCO, Peru-UNESCO Tourist and Cultural Plan

CORPAC   Corporación Peruana de Aeropuertos y Aviación Comercial, Peruvian Corporation of Airports and Commercial Aviation

COTURPERU   Corporación de Turismo del Perú, Peruvian Tourism Corporation

CRYF   Corporación de Reconstrucción y Fomento del Cuzco Reconstruction and Development Corporation

DGTUR   Dirección General del Turismo, General Office of Tourism

ENAFER   Empresa Nacional de Ferrocarilles del Perú, National Railroad Company of Peru

ENTURPERU   Empresa Nacional del Turismo, National Tourism Company

FOPTUR   Fondo de Promoción Turística, Tourism Promotion Fund

ICPNA   Instituto Cultural Peruano-Norteamericao, Peruvian–North American Cultural Institute

IDB   Inter-American Development Bank

INC	Instituto Nacional de Cultura, National Institute of Culture
INRENA	Instituto Nacional de Recursos Naturales, National Institute of Natural Resources
MICTI	Ministerio de Industria, Comercio, Turismo, e Integración, Ministry of Industry, Commerce, Tourism, and Integration
MINCETUR	Ministerio de Comercio Exterior y Turismo, Ministry of Foreign Commerce and Tourism
OIAA	Office of Inter-American Affairs
PMP	Programa Machu Picchu, Machu Picchu Program
TACP	Touring y Automovíl Club del Perú, Touring and Automobile Club of Peru
UNSAAC	Universidad Nacional San Antonio del Abad del Cusco

Making Machu Picchu

Introduction

Speaking at a National Geographic Society gala in 1913, Hiram Bingham, the explorer celebrated for uncovering the famed "lost city" of the Andes less than two years earlier, confessed that Machu Picchu "is an awful name, but it is well worth remembering."[1] For over a century, it appears that millions of travelers have followed Bingham's advice. When Bingham first arrived at Machu Picchu in 1911, the site was an obscure ruin. Now, Machu Picchu serves as the focus of a burgeoning tourism economy centered on the Cusco region of Peru. In 2017 alone, 1.5 million tourists visited Machu Picchu. It is the key attraction of a tourism industry that contributes $7.6 billion annually to the Peruvian economy and forms 3.9 percent of Peru's national GDP.[2] As Machu Picchu has evolved into a travel destination, so has its cultural prominence. Once considered a forgotten city, Machu Picchu is now known on a global scale. Spurred by tourism, Machu Picchu has become the central subject in numerous outlets that range from serious scholarly inquiries to television commercials marketing mobile phones. Machu Picchu's increased touristic prominence has led the site to acquire its most important contemporary role: it serves as a powerful symbol of Peru that directly links its national identity to an Andean and Inca past. This book tells the story of how Machu Picchu came to occupy such a prominent place in Peruvian national identity and of the role tourism has played in its transformation.

It is tempting to think that Machu Picchu's emergence as one of the world's most famous tourist destinations was predestined from the moment Bingham arrived at the site in 1911. The tourist industry, which specializes in the fashioning of certain sites as sacred and fantastic, certainly has helped create the mythologized image of Machu Picchu as a lost city untouched by time. Yet, as historian Donna Brown reminds us, "Tourism is not destiny, imposed on a community or a region."[3] Even the development of most sui generis sites, including Machu Picchu, depended on pragmatic decisions to build political consensus, construct infrastructure, and create a cultural meaning attractive to travelers. Hal Rothman, analyzing tourism development in the U.S. West, observed that even the Grand Canyon "would remain no more than a remote geologic oddity" without the actions of developers, locals, and the state that transformed the site into a tourism destination.[4]

Although tourism promises travelers an escape from the banality of labor, politics, and financial decisions, its success or failure is determined by these same activities. This book, by revealing the narrative of how locals and their global allies made modern Machu Picchu, will highlight the substantive role tourism has played in the creation of national symbols in the twentieth century.

Although its rise reflects the narrative of other famous sites, in many ways Machu Picchu is a unique case study when compared to other global cultural attractions. First, Machu Picchu's rise from near-total obscurity to global renown is remarkable. Unlike most historic sites visited by tourists, Machu Picchu is defined not by its prominence but by its relative absence in Peruvian history over three centuries. Indeed, Machu Picchu is arguably more famous for being "forgotten" than known. Even when most Peruvians became aware of its existence after 1911, few felt a direct connection to the Inca past symbolized by Machu Picchu. Second, Machu Picchu's singular dominance as a representation of Peru is also unique. Machu Picchu is far from the only historical site in Peru, and international tourists do visit other areas, but none enjoy the same prominence. The status of Machu Picchu in Peru would be comparable to an alternate universe where all international attention and travel related to Great Britain centered solely on Stonehenge while considering sites in London or Scotland as afterthoughts. This status is even more surprising when one considers that, at the start of the twentieth century, most Peruvian leaders hoped to discard signs of the nation's indigenous past, seeing them as incompatible with their vision of a modernizing country.

How, then, did Machu Picchu transform from a site so obscure that few, if any, remember its original name to such a powerful representation of Peru? Additionally, how did the national state decide to embrace a symbol representing Peru as an indigenous Andean nation? The answer lies in understanding the historical importance of tourism in Machu Picchu's rise. Recent scholarship on Machu Picchu has mostly focused on the archeological and cultural factors that have aided Machu Picchu's rise to global renown.[5] These works have largely assumed that tourism emerged as a result of Machu Picchu's growing fame. However, this book argues that tourism development at Machu Picchu was not a consequence of its rise to prominence. Instead, tourism played a central role in the modern remaking of Machu Picchu from the very start.

In order to understand why tourism played such an important role in Machu Picchu's rise, we must highlight the transnational actors that guided its development. These transnational actors, best described by Micol Seigel as "units that spill over and seep through national borders, units both greater and smaller than the nation state," played a key role in the development of Machu Picchu as both a tourist site and a symbol.[6] As we shall see, tourism in Cusco relied on political, economic, and cultural links between locals and actors that transcended the frontiers of the Peruvian state. Sometimes such links were forged by powerful transnational institutions like UNESCO or investment banks. At other moments, personal friendships, cultural movements, and even hippie backpackers played important roles in promoting tourism at Machu Picchu. What remained constant through Machu Picchu's modern history was the presence of transnational institutions and ties that often acted independently of the national state.

In fact, this book traces how the transnational character of tourism played a central role in encouraging the national state to embrace Machu Picchu and the indigenous culture it represents. A key reason few predicted that Machu Picchu would become a travel destination stemmed from the fact that national leaders of Peru at the start of the twentieth century saw few political, economic, and cultural possibilities in their nation's Andean regions. For these observers, Peru needed to shed its Andean and indigenous past in favor of modernization, urbanization, and industrialization based in its Pacific coast cities, especially Lima.[7] However, as the tourism industry promoted Machu Picchu as a site of international interest, the national state became more willing to embrace signs of the Andes and the Inca as national symbols. In many ways, tourism became the most important force in transforming Machu Picchu into what Mary Louise Pratt has theorized as a "transnational contact zone"—essentially, a place where global and local notions of "Peruvianness" intersected, imbued Machu Picchu with meaning, and elevated it as a national symbol.[8] This transnational contact zone not only affected the nature of tourism in Cusco, but also contributed to the spread of Machu Picchu as a symbol employed for numerous purposes both within and outside of Peru as a representation of its Andean culture.

The role tourism has played in elevating Machu Picchu as a national symbol of Peru raises important new questions regarding the intertwined nature of nationalism and transnationalism. When scholars led by Eric Hobsbawm, Benedict Anderson, and Pierre Nora began to critically examine the origins of nationalism and national symbols, they looked primarily to domestic political and market forces. They argued that the "imagined community" of nationalism emerged from the construction of modern domestic structures of politics, state building, and economics.[9] Following this logic, societies that lacked these institutions often faced difficulty in creating a strong nationalism. Thus, postcolonial nations like Peru whose politics and economic development were dominated by foreign or imperial powers have faced considerable obstacles in the creation of national identity.[10] In fact, historians have often used the example of Peru to illustrate how the lack of inclusive political and cultural institutions has thwarted the construction of a strong sense of nationalism in Latin America.[11] However, others have argued that in Latin America, transnational forces and contact zones can prove influential in the construction of nationalism.[12] The story of Machu Picchu lends support to this interpretation by highlighting the close relationship between tourism and the construction of national symbols in Peru. In fact, the remarkable rise of Machu Picchu suggests that transnational forces can bypass or shortcut traditional domestic obstacles in the creation of national identity.

In the case of Peru and Machu Picchu, we must also consider the role of region as part of this process. Like nationalism, regional identity is not just a geographic but also a cultural and political creation forged through performance and invention.[13] As we shall see, Cusco's regional identity was often formed in contrast to Peru's capital, Lima. As national economic and political power became centralized in Lima, Cusco's regional leaders asserted their Andean identity as the "true" Peru. These efforts were aided by tourism and the rise of Machu Picchu. Ironically, the disinterest on the part of national elites in the tourist economy left the opportunity for regional leaders of Cusco, working with transnational cultural and financial links, to use tourism to assert their regional identity as the representation of Peru. However, reliance on tourism posed risks for Cusco. If international tourism has popularized Cusco's heritage, it has also forced locals to create and alter narratives to make them appealing to global markets and travelers. Transnational global capital and cultural forces of tourism have increasingly commodified Machu Picchu to represent not so much Cusco, but an image of Cusco believed to be appealing to tourists and visitors. By doing so, the symbolism of Machu Picchu has morphed into what John L. and Jean Comaroff have termed "Ethnicity, Inc.," that is, identity marked not only by history but also by its ability to be commodified and consumed in the era of globalization.[14] Tourism has made Machu Picchu into a famous site, but, as this book examines, one that has become increasingly unmoored from the social and cultural realities of the region and nation it represents.

It is tempting to identify the rise and commodification of Machu Picchu as a product of the economic patterns of globalization and neoliberalism since the 1980s and 1990s. However, as this book illustrates, the story of the making of Machu Picchu extends over a century, and the process was rarely motivated solely by a search for profits. In fact, I argue that the cultural influence of tourism has played an equal, if not more influential, part in the remaking of Machu Picchu. As we shall see, Machu Picchu's emergence as a problematic national symbol makes it no less powerful or less important to understand. Highlighting the role that tourism has played in the modern invention of Machu Picchu helps us understand its rise to global renown. Even more importantly, the story of Machu Picchu's transformation highlights the previously overlooked role that tourism in particular, and transnational forces in general, have played in altering notions of Peruvian national identity. The historian Alberto Flores Galindo once observed that Peruvians are often "in search of an Inca" to forge symbols of a new Peru.[15] Perhaps it is time we lent attention to the influence of tourists also in search of an Inca in the making of Machu Picchu and Peruvian national identity.

Machu Picchu's Place in Modern History

This book uncovers the previously unknown history of Machu Picchu's transformation into a global travel destination and national symbol of Peru. Machu Picchu has certainly served as the subject of numerous publications.[16] These studies tend to fall into two categories. The first set examines the site's archeological past. The second, much larger category includes diverse publications directed mainly at interested travelers and casual readers that showcase the site's present-day beauty, appeal, and ecological setting. Although most of these works provide valuable information, they overlook the important history that lies between Machu Picchu's pre-Columbian era and the present day. Recently, excellent scholarship has revisited the complex legacy of Bingham and his expeditions to Machu Picchu.[17] Bingham certainly plays an important role in Machu Picchu's history; however, focusing our attention only on him, even critically, risks echoing the false touristic narrative that portrays him as the only protagonist in the site's rise to fame.[18] Drawing on previously unused archives located on two continents, this book highlights the fact that Bingham's activities formed only part of a fascinating historical narrative played out on the local, national, and global stage. More importantly, Machu Picchu's modern history helps us trace larger political and cultural shifts in Peru's southern Andes and beyond.

In addition to uncovering the modern history of Machu Picchu, this book makes several important contributions in multiple disciplines studying themes related to tourism, Peru, and Latin America. First, this book contributes to the global field of tourism studies. Some of the first scholarly critiques of tourism largely dismissed it as crass consumerism that distorted and commodified history or, at best, was a poor cousin to the rich "Grand Tour" travel narratives of the nineteenth and early twentieth centuries.[19] Beginning in the 1970s, however, the sociologist Dean MacCannell argued that the consumerism of tourism did not make the meanings it created less important. Tourism studies asserted that modern travelers' search for authenticity and the efforts by the tourist industry to present, craft, and sell to these desires were critical to understanding the postmodern and postindustrial world.[20] Work by other sociologists led by John Urry and anthropologists like Valene L. Smith continued to examine ways in which meaning and narrative are contested, presented, and imagined in modern tourism economies. These studies found that although tourism symbols and narratives were invented, they still held tremendous influence on how both hosts and travelers viewed themselves.[21] Considering the growing influence of tourism economies in the Americas, it is no surprise that Latin Americanists have examined the effects of international travel on the region's society and culture.[22] The Andean region has also provided rich ethnographical case studies on the local effects of tourism.[23] However, these studies overwhelmingly focus on the contemporary consequences of tourism. This book will complement the ethnographic research on tourism in the Andes by providing a deeper historical perspective.

Second, this book contributes to the rapidly growing field of the history of tourism in Latin America. Cuba, Mexico, and the Caribbean were home to some of the first significant tourism booms and have thus attracted the bulk of attention from historians of travel in Latin America.[24] The historical development of tourism in the Andes, on the other hand, has received little attention. In addition, historical studies on tourism in Latin America have mainly analyzed its growth through the lens of the nation-state. This is largely due to the fact that, in many Latin American republics such as Mexico and Cuba, tourism did in fact emerge as a national cultural or political project. These studies have not ignored transnational factors, particularly the growing economic and political influence represented by the United States. However, little scholarly work has analyzed the historical development and influence of tourism on a regional level. Historians of travel in the United States have argued for the importance of examining how tourism has influenced regional identity, politics, and economics.[25] Only recently have historians begun to examine tourism's effects on a regional level in Latin America.[26] Decentering the state, this book looks to the connections between the regional and the global to examine the effects of tourism in the southern Andes.

A third contribution of this book is its examination of the relationship between regionalism and transnationalism. Scholars have called our attention to both the history of regional identity formation and the importance of understanding the tension between region and nation in Latin America.[27] Fortunately, Cusco's regional history has long attracted the interest of scholars. One key question for historians of Cusco has included the formation of regional politics and identity following independence.[28] Historians and historical anthropologists have investigated the burst of regional cultural movements and folklore projects, especially *indigenismo*, in Cusco during the early twentieth century.[29] Cusco has also proved to be a case study for analyzing the challenges of political change and development in Peru's southern Andes.[30] This book provides a key regional perspective on the history of the economic and cultural effects of tourism that have become one of the most important forces in twentieth-century Cusco. By doing so, this book also contributes to a growing field of scholarship that has called attention to understanding the relationship between regional and global forces in the Andes.[31] The story of tourism in Cusco illustrates how the formation of regional identity is not just a local process but also a transnational one.

By looking beyond the frontiers of the Peruvian state, this book does not ignore its importance. The final contribution of this book is to use tourism to examine the shifting policy and structure of the Peruvian national state in the twentieth century. Although the Peruvian state has usually exercised less influence over tourism than many of its Latin American peers, it has never been absent from such development. In fact, the history of tourism in Cusco has often reflected or reacted to political and economic changes in Lima. Tourism policies can illustrate these larger shifts in regard to regional politics in Peru. Examining them also helps broaden our understanding of the historical rivalry between Cusco and the national capital over the place of indigenous culture in Peru. Studying the tools and strategies used by the Peruvian state to encourage tourism in Cusco can also help us trace national economic shifts from liberal orthodoxy to state-led development and ultimately, to neoliberalism. Additionally, as histories of tourism in Europe have shown, the state is often aware of both the potential and the threat posed by international travel in debates over national identity.[32] The case of Machu Picchu expands on this work to show the influence of tourism on nationalism in Latin America.

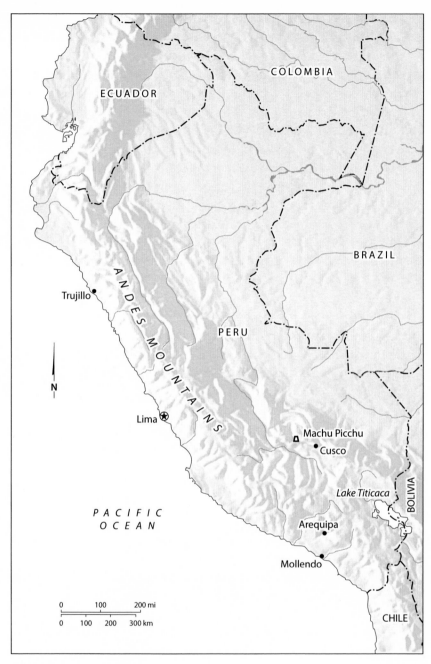

Peru and the Cusco Region

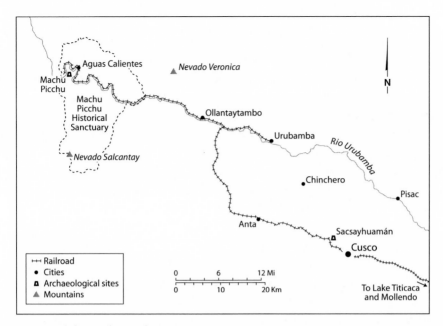

Cusco and the Machu Picchu area

Cast of Characters

The modern history of Machu Picchu is complex and features a large cast of historical actors. Before diving into this narrative, it is important to provide a short introduction to a few people and places that feature prominently in this story.

Machu Picchu

The Inca archeological site known as Machu Picchu lies roughly eighty kilometers northwest of the city of Cusco. It sits at 2,430 meters above sea level in the *ceja de selva* (literally translated as "eyebrow of the jungle") climate. This environment is a temperate highland jungle that lies on the eastern flank of the Andes in Peru between 1,000 and 3,600 meters above sea level. It occupies a climatic niche between the higher and more arid altiplano grasslands to the south and west and the lower rain forest of the Amazon Basin lying to the north and east. The Urubamba River cuts through Cusco's ceja de selva, forming the fertile Sacred Valley. The archeological complex of Machu Picchu sits about 450 meters above a horseshoe bend of the Urubamba River and is centered on a small plateau between two mountains. The first mountain is named Huayna Picchu, translated as "young peak" in the Quechua language. This peak, rising dramatically to the north of the site, appears in most photos of Machu Picchu. The second, taller mountain rises to the south of the archeological complex and is named Machu Picchu, or "old peak."[33] The historian José Tamayo Herrera argues that Machu Picchu's likely name in Quechua was Willkallaqta. However, in modern times Machu Picchu has taken its name from the neighboring mountain because there is little agreement about the original name of the site.[34]

Many aspects of Machu Picchu's pre-Hispanic history remain the subject of debate. The first theories proposed by Bingham bestowed an almost mythic status on Machu Picchu. He believed that Machu Picchu was Tampu Tocco, the fabled birthplace of the Inca civilization; that the site was also Vilcabamba, the last capital of the empire after its leadership fled Cusco and the Spaniards in 1536; and that the site served as a home for an Incan version of the Vestal Virgins.[35] Archeologists have debunked all of these theories. Instead, they believe that the first construction at Machu Picchu occurred around 1450 A.D. during the rule of Pachacuti, a leader who greatly expanded the economic and political reach of the Inca. The site likely was a royal estate, that is, the property of the Inca leadership. Based on its location, architecture, and layout, Machu Picchu likely served an administrative and ceremonial role in the Inca Empire. Machu Picchu remains a key example of Inca architecture and urban design from an era when the empire reached the peak of its political and cultural influence, and its Intihuatana stone, a ritual marker of the sun's movements, is one of the best preserved in Peru. However, Machu Picchu was far from the most historically important site in the Inca realm. Machu Picchu remained inhabited until the 1550s. After that, depopulation due to disease and Spanish efforts to resettle the area's population in new towns left Machu Picchu largely abandoned. However, rural settlement and use of the site persisted throughout the colonial era and into the twentieth century.[36]

Hiram Bingham

Despite the efforts of archeologists to dispel the myths of Machu Picchu, many of Bingham's theories persist in the tourism narrative. Another oft-repeated claim of Bingham, that he discovered Machu Picchu after centuries of abandonment, is also false. The area around Machu Picchu was inhabited by longtime residents who were familiar with the site. There is significant evidence that foreign cartographers and travelers had visited and mapped Machu Picchu long before Bingham's arrival.[37] None of this mattered to Bingham, whose personal ambition played a key role in elevating Machu Picchu (and himself) to fame following his 1911 expedition to the site.

Hiram Bingham III was born in Hawaii in 1875 to a prominent family of Christian missionaries who had lived on the islands since the early 1800s. He earned a bachelor's degree from Yale University in 1898, where he lost interest in the missionary tradition of his family in favor of exploration and history. He earned postgraduate degrees from the University of California at Berkeley and Harvard University, where he emerged as a backer of U.S. imperial expansion and the ideals of the strenuous life. Bingham married into the wealthy Tiffany family in 1900 and likely used its prominence to secure a position as a lecturer at Yale University in 1907. The following year, Bingham made his first trip to South America and attended the First Pan-American Scientific Conference in Santiago, Chile. He first visited Cusco during his return voyage to the United States. Bingham hoped to achieve fame by discovering Vilcabamba, the lost final capital of the Inca, where the empire's leadership fled after a failed rebellion against the Spanish in 1536. Bingham organized an expedition to Peru in 1911 sponsored by Yale and funded by a smattering of private donors. During this trip, Bingham arrived at Machu Picchu on July 24, 1911, and quickly used the discovery to bring attention to the site and his efforts. Bingham returned to Peru for two additional expeditions with the backing of Yale and the National Geographic Society; one took place in 1912, and another in 1914–15. Ultimately, Bingham left Peru under a cloud of criminal accusations in 1915 and would not return for over three decades.

Following his departure from Peru, Bingham pursued other interests. He joined the military and served in World War I, where he commanded an aviation unit of the U.S. Army. For the remainder of his life, Bingham advocated for the advance of aviation in travel and military fields. He entered Connecticut politics and eventually became a U.S. senator in 1924. In the Senate, Bingham was censured in 1929 for having a lobbyist serve on his staff. The incident damaged his political career, and he lost a bid for reelection in 1932. For the remainder of his career, Bingham kept a low profile and worked in the private sector. Only in the 1940s, thanks to tourism promotion efforts based mainly in Peru, did Bingham begin to capitalize once more on his connection to Machu Picchu. He published about the Inca and his expeditions once more and even returned to Peru in 1948 to promote travel. At the time of his death in 1956, Bingham was increasingly known to the public as the explorer who discovered Machu Picchu.[38]

Cusco

Machu Picchu is located in the region of Cusco in the southern Peruvian Andes. The region's capital city and largest urban area, also named Cusco, is about 575 kilometers southeast of Lima and sits at 3,339 meters above sea level. Cusco was the capital of the Inca Empire, which ruled most of modern-day Peru, Bolivia, and Ecuador as well as significant areas of Argentina, Chile, and Colombia. In 1533 the city and the Inca Empire fell to the invading Spaniards. With the establishment of Spanish rule, the political capital of Peru moved to Lima on the Pacific coast. Cusco retained a vibrant economy that entered into decline only in the late colonial period of the 1700s when Spain enacted a series of administrative and economic reforms that isolated the region from lucrative trade routes and raised taxes. These changes provoked a massive anticolonial rebellion that devastated the region in the 1780s. After Peru gained its independence in the early nineteenth century, Cusco remained a largely agricultural region, while political and economic power increasingly became concentrated in Lima and other coastal cities.[39]

The majority of Cusco's inhabitants, called cusqueños, have been, and continue to be, employed in an agricultural economy. Farming in the semi-arid altiplano plateau areas in the region's central and southern zones is dedicated mainly to the harvest of potatoes, barley, and quinoa. Livestock grazing, particularly of llamas, alpacas, and sheep, is also common in these areas. In the northern areas of Cusco, which occupy lower elevations in the humid ceja de selva climate, agricultural activity specializing in the production of coca, sugarcane, coffee, and fruit emerged in the late 1800s. A small but powerful elite dominated Cusco's regional politics during most of the nineteenth and twentieth centuries. These elites drew their political power from their ownership of large rural estates called haciendas. The elites often had residences in the city of Cusco, and some also owned homes in Lima. Besides their ownership of haciendas, Cusco's elites used their resources to invest in other financial and commercial endeavors. The majority of Cusco's population at the start of the twentieth century was composed of indigenous Quechua speakers. Originally called "Indians," Cusco's indigenous Quechua-speaking population increasingly identified as "campesinos" in the years leading up to and following the 1969 agrarian reform. These residents either made their living mainly working as peasants on the haciendas or were small landowners or inhabitants of indigenous villages scattered throughout the region. Conditions on haciendas were often harsh for workers, and indigenous villages and small farmers often faced a precarious existence at the whims of unsympathetic authorities who often acted in the interest of the elites and their estates.[40] The city of Cusco was the region's main urban and market center. At the start of the twentieth century small industry and commerce had emerged in the city. According to a census taken in 1912, the city had a population of nearly 20,000, of which 22 percent were white, 23 percent indigenous, and 50 percent of mestizo, or mixed race, ethnicity. Half of the city's population remained illiterate.[41] Like many Latin American cities, during the twentieth century Cusco's urban center grew, reaching a population of almost 55,000 in 1940 and just over 350,000 by 2007. Peruvian national censuses documented 486,592 residents of the region of Cusco in 1940. By 2007 the regional population had risen to 1,171,403.[42] Despite these changes, including the growth of tourism, the historic tension between the region's traditional landed elite and the vast majority of rural, indigenous residents remained a key historical factor in its development in the twentieth century.

Tourists

Unlike migrants or other travelers, tourists are motivated by a pursuit of leisure and undertake their journeys voluntarily. Valene L. Smith identifies tourism as travel defined by three characteristics: leisure time, discretionary income, and positive local sanctions.[43] These elements have distinguished tourists in Cusco from travelers who arrived in the region not for leisure but to complete writings or scholarship. In addition, this book focuses primarily on international tourists to Cusco. This does not signify the absence of domestic tourism in Cusco. However, this book argues that, from the beginning, Cusco's tourism was uniquely oriented toward serving an international market. Historically, elite and middle-class Peruvians who composed the market for domestic travel spent vacations along the Pacific Coast, which was more convenient to reach from the major urban centers where most of them resided and worked. Consequentially, international tourists have often outnumbered domestic visitors to Cusco. More importantly, the influence of international tourism had a disproportionally larger economic and cultural influence in the eyes of both cusqueños and the Peruvian state. Many Peruvians have made trips to Cusco and Machu Picchu, especially in recent years as the middle class has grown and the sites have emerged as national icons. Yet, the status of Machu Picchu and Cusco continues to be largely legitimated by their appeal to international travelers. This book will examine why this continues to be the case.

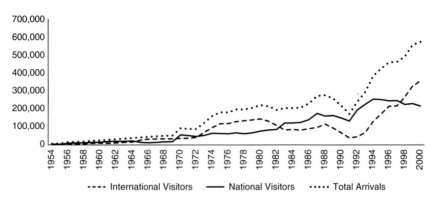

Tourism arrivals to Cusco, 1954–2000

Legend: - - - - International Visitors   —— National Visitors   ••••• Total Arrivals

Scope and Style

The narrative of this book covers roughly one century and traces the development of tourism at Machu Picchu. As we shall see, far from being predestined, Machu Picchu's modern transformation followed a long historical path with many turns and, at times, dead ends. Instead of following a set model, Cusco's tourism economy was often influenced by the grafting of successive visions of development and cultural politics over time. Although unlikely, this process was not unpredictable and often reflected local responses to national and global change. This book tracks these changes to gain a broader understanding of tourism, Machu Picchu, and their influence on Peruvian national identity. Tourism in Cusco passed through three general eras. In the first period, from 1900 to 1948, covered by chapters 1 and 2, tourism served the interests of cultural politics to validate Cusco's modernity and indigenismo folklore. The second era, between 1948 and 1975, is covered in chapters 3 and 4. In these years, tourism continued to be seen as a positive, modernizing force. However, locals and the national state increasingly embraced tourism as a tool for needed economic development and reform in Cusco. The final period, from 1975 to 2011, is documented in chapter 5 and the epilogue. Machu Picchu emerged as Peru's key travel destination and symbol. However, rather than represent a modernizing force, Machu Picchu increasingly symbolized the exotic and adventurous. Simultaneously, control over tourism shifted from locals and the state to private, increasingly outside interests.

On a final editorial note, all translations (unless indicated otherwise) are mine. The names of places and archeological sites in Peru have often changed over time. For clarity, I use the most common contemporary terms to refer to the city of Cusco and the archeological site of Machu Picchu (instead of other historically accepted spellings such as Cuzco, Qosquo, Machupijchu, or Machu-Picchu). However, in direct quotes and cites, I have maintained the original spelling contained in the source material. I follow the same policy with other names for which multiple spellings have been used, including Inca, Sacsayhuamán, Coricancha, Ollantaytambo, and so on. The town at the base of Machu Picchu and the seat of the local government, Machu Picchu District, has also featured numerous names over the past. While locals have increasingly called the settlement Machu Picchu Pueblo, I refer to it as Aguas Calientes, which reflects the dominant name used during most of the twentieth century and avoids confusion with the actual archeological site. The same shifting terms apply to the status of Cusco's regional government. For most of its history, Cusco and its regional government were considered a department. During a flawed reform of regional government in the 1980s and 1990s, Cusco was merged with the departments of Madre de Díos and Apurímac to form the Inka Region. The Inka Region was eventually dissolved in the early 2000s. Since 2002, Cusco, along with most of Peru's twenty-four former departments, has been called the Cusco Region. This region's boundaries are the same as the former Cusco Department. Thus, my references to the Cusco Region correspond to the boundaries of the current region and those of the former Cusco Department.

CHAPTER ONE

Making the "Modern" Destination, 1900–1934

Returning from his first visit to Peru in 1909, Hiram Bingham reported, "Cuzco has, in fact, long been notorious as one of the dirtiest cities in America; and it justifies its reputation."[1] It appears strange that Bingham, whose exploration of Machu Picchu in 1911 is widely credited for establishing Cusco's tourism economy, introduced the region to North American readers in such disparaging terms. However, as this chapter shows, Bingham echoed a common sentiment about Cusco held by Peru's national political and intellectual leaders based in Lima in the first decades of the twentieth century.[2] In fact, for many Peruvians and foreign travelers, Cusco and its indigenous heritage served as a representation of an Andean society incompatible with the modern world. These factors, as well as Bingham's controversial actions taken during his expeditions to Machu Picchu, thwarted early attempts to promote travel to the archeological site. However, we shall see that these challenges did not prevent cusqueños from pursuing the development of tourism in their region. In fact, cusqueños embraced tourism because it allowed them to recast Cusco's indigenous heritage as compatible with the modern world. Long before tourism became a question of economic development in Cusco, it gained popularity because locals could employ the language of modern travel to assert their region's importance to the nation.

Local support for tourism in its early years often proves to be critical in determining its future development.[3] Cusco's early embrace of tourism certainly follows this pattern. While other regions of Latin America often viewed international tourism suspiciously as a source of corruption or vice, it enjoyed broad support in Cusco.[4] The key reason for this strong local support was cusqueños' recognition of the power of tourism in the creation, or recasting, of regional identity. While some scholars have dismissed tourism narratives as commercial, and often crass, inventions, other historians have illustrated how certain places, ranging from the Rhineland to New England, have employed tourism to define and popularize a specific vision of their historical past and regional identity. In fact, central aspects of tourism— guidebooks, staged imagery, planned itineraries, and coordinated ceremonies—have proved uniquely useful in the creation of an official narrative of regional culture, identity, and history.[5] Cusqueños realized that the tools of tourism could be employed to create an official historical and cultural narrative that emphasized their region's importance to Peruvian debates over national identity.

Central to this effort was the role that indigenous culture would play in Cusco's tourism narrative. These efforts in Cusco reflected a hemispheric embrace of indigenismo, a broad cultural and political movement that asserted the centrality of indigenous culture in Latin American nationalism.[6] Cusco's indigenistas engaged with these efforts in varied and complex ways. On one hand, the indigenistas looked to assert their belief that Andean culture had a place in the modernizing national project in Peru. On the other hand, however, these same indigenistas also had to resolve fierce tensions between grassroots political demands of Indians and the interests of regional elites and the state, who, while embracing indigenous culture, stood against broader social change.[7] Studies of indigenismo in Cusco have largely overlooked the role tourism played in this important cultural movement.[8] This chapter analyzes how Cusco's indigenistas employed the discourse of tourism to elevate their vision of indigenous culture over competing movements on the local and national levels. The ultimate goal of Cusco's indigenistas was to use tourism to produce an idealized image of Indian culture while promoting their region's importance in a modern Peru.

A second important trend that proved influential in early tourism efforts in Cusco was its inherently transnational character. Of course, Cusco was not the only region to use tourism to forge and alter global perceptions of nations and regions both inside and beyond Latin America.[9] However, even when compared with other regions, Cusco's early use of transnational networks stands out as a unique case. Bypassing the largely uninterested national government, early local tourism promotion relied on transnational actors who served as interlocutors between Cusco and the world. More important, Cusco defined itself as a potential tourist destination based on the region's appeal outside the national frontiers of Peru. Long before international travel became an economic project in Cusco, it served as a critical influence in debates regarding the region's place in Peruvian nationalism. In fact, Cusco's legitimacy as the true representation of Peruvian national identity stemmed largely from its claims to be able to attract the interest of international travelers. The outsized role played by transnational forces in promoting Cusco's regional identity in Peru in the first decades of the twentieth century began a process that would define the narrative of tourism in the Andes.

Finding and Forgetting Machu Picchu

Although Bingham depicted Cusco as a backward city in his 1909 accounts, the first decades of the twentieth century were marked by dramatic economic and social change for Peru's southern Andes. Less than a year before Bingham arrived in Cusco, the city celebrated the arrival of the Southern Peruvian Railway on September 13, 1908. The inauguration of the railroad marked what cusqueños hoped would become a major turning point in what seemed to many the region's long political and economic decline. Once the seat of the mighty Inca Empire, Cusco found its influence eclipsed with the foundation of Lima as the administrative center of Spain's South American colonial system. For most of the colonial era, Cusco boasted a dynamic economy based on agricultural and textile production for regional consumption and markets in Arequipa, Lima, and the booming mining region of Potosí.[10] In the eighteenth century, Spain's new Bourbon dynasty rulers introduced administrative and economic reforms that severed Cusco's links with the lucrative Potosí market, saw the region's domestic economy erode, and angered its rural indigenous population with increased taxes. Under these pressures, Indians violently rose up against colonial authorities in 1780 under the leadership of a local indigenous leader named José Gabriel Condorcanqui. Adopting the name Túpac Amaru II, he hoped to reestablish a form of the Inca Empire and cast out the hated and abusive Spanish colonial officials.[11]

The Túpac Amaru rebellion was one of the largest in Latin American history, and historians have fiercely debated its political aims, socioeconomic origins, and historical legacy. Recent historical work has emphasized the tremendous violence of the rebellion. The uprising and its suppression under Spanish forces resulted in nearly 100,000 deaths and devastated Cusco's economy.[12] These new studies have also emphasized the severe repression against Andean and indigenous culture that was unleashed in the wake of the rebellion. Colonial authorities who previously had tolerated and acknowledged symbols of the Inca and indigenous culture violently attempted to erase signs of Indian political and cultural activity.[13] Cusco's fortunes failed to improve after independence, when, despite regional attempts to counter Lima's influence, economic and political power continued to be concentrated on Peru's Pacific Coast.[14] This trend accelerated with the rise of the Peruvian "Aristocratic Republic," in the final decades of the nineteenth-century, when control over Peru's lucrative exports increasingly concentrated wealth and power in the hands of a small group of coastal elites. The gap between the modernizing coast and the seemingly backward Andes only appeared to grow with the dawn of the twentieth century.[15]

The arrival in 1908 of the railroad, which would connect Cusco to the Pacific Ocean port of Mollendo, promised to reverse the region's economic decline. As early as 1895, Cusco's regional economy had begun to grow and diversify. Electrical service was inaugurated in December 1914. Although not a manufacturing powerhouse, by the end of the 1920s Cusco boasted a robust textile sector and had even surpassed Arequipa in terms of industrial output. Equally important, economic modernization created a new industrial working class as well as a small but influential middle class of clerks and professionals. Over fifty new newspapers circulated in Cusco during this era. New civic associations began to participate in local politics, and they were joined by artisan societies of skilled workers and more proletarian labor groups. Yet, colonial era concepts of race and ethnicity remained stubbornly powerful, and indigenous communities remained largely excluded from these new groups. Despite this, by 1930 most observers concluded that Cusco had experienced a period of dramatic economic and social change.[16]

As Cusco's elites pinned their hopes on new access to the Pacific, they also expressed interest in expanding economic links into the region's interior valleys to the northwest. Starting in the 1880s, rising global demand for rubber and other tropically grown commodities motivated Cusco's economic elite to explore the humid valleys north and west of the city located in the ceja de selva climate. Cusco's elites, hoping to expand their investments beyond the traditional, but relatively arid, agricultural altiplano zone, believed that their region's future prosperity lay in exploiting land in these verdant valleys.[17] Growing interest in the ceja de selva valleys near Cusco led to the creation of the Centro Científico del Cuzco (Cuzco Scientific Center) in 1897. Although the institute operated for only ten years, it published several geographic surveys of the Sacred Valley area in the hopes of encouraging the construction of a new railway.[18] These efforts proved successful in 1910 when the Peruvian government approved the construction of the Santa Ana Railroad, which would connect Cusco with the fertile valley of La Convención by traveling through the Sacred Valley. The path of the railroad would travel directly below the site of Machu Picchu. By 1900 significant clearing had begun in anticipation of the route.[19] Thus, by 1911 the environs of Machu Picchu were not the uncharted wilderness described in Bingham's accounts but a key economic frontier of Cusco.

On the eve of Bingham's arrival in Cusco, the region also experienced an era of tremendous intellectual change. New literary works began to challenge the dominant national discourse that disparaged regions like Cusco as part of the nation's *mancha india* (Indian stain) dismissed as incompatible with a modern nation. Literary works sympathetic to the plight of Peru's Indian population appeared as early as 1848 when Narciso Aréstegui published *El Padre Horán*.[20] However, at the start of the twentieth century, interest in the condition and cultural background of Peru's Indian population began to increase, led by the Lima writer Manuel González Prada. Writing in the wake of Chile's victory over Peru in the War of the Pacific between 1879 and 1884, González Prada blamed the defeat on the unwillingness of national elites to incorporate Indians into Peruvian nationalism. One of González Prada's students, a Cusco native named Clorinda Matto de Turner, authored what many literary critics believe is the first indigenista literary work, *Aves sin nido* (*Birds without a Nest*), published in 1889. Echoing González Prada, Matto de Turner's work documented the suffering of Peru's indigenous population and called for their incorporation into national politics and culture.[21] Although early indigenista works remained an urban-based movement, the works of González Prada and Matto de Turner raised intellectual awareness of Indian culture and history in Cusco.[22]

These intellectual shifts affected Cusco's primary learning institution, the Universidad Nacional de San Antonio Abad del Cusco (UNSAAC). The governing structure and curriculum of UNSAAC had remained largely unchanged from the colonial era until May 1909, when students began a strike to call for a democratic university administration, a modern curriculum, and lower tuition. The students won the support of the local press and influential sectors of the regional political elite, and the national government led by President Augusto Leguía acceded to their demands.[23] In 1910 Leguía appointed a twenty-seven-year-old educator from Philadelphia named Albert Giesecke as the new university rector to reform and modernize UNSAAC.[24] To the surprise of many, the new rector successfully won the approval of the student strike leaders, local elites, and educators. In addition to acting as rector of UNSAAC between 1910 and 1923, Giesecke also served in city government and as mayor between 1920 and 1923.

Giesecke would lay the foundation for the development of cultural tourism in Cusco. First, the education reforms instituted by Giesecke at UNSAAC aided the formation of a generation of scholars and political leaders known as the "Generation of the Sierra." Giesecke and the young members of the Generation of the Sierra—including José Gabriel Cosío, Luis E. Valcárcel, José Uriel Garcia, and Francisco Tamayo—would play a central role in promoting folklore, indigenismo, and archeological studies of Cusco in the twentieth century.[25] Second, Giesecke's familiarity with North American learning and political institutions guaranteed that UNSAAC and Cusco could establish critical academic and cultural links beyond Peru.

Giesecke's connections with the United States helped link Bingham with Machu Picchu. Giesecke, eager to foster cooperation between UNSAAC and U.S. academic institutions, aided Bingham during his first expedition in Peru in 1909. Bingham returned to Cusco in 1911 on an expedition to locate Vilcabamba, the last refuge of Inca resistance, which fell to Spanish forces in 1572. Through research in the United States and Lima, Bingham knew that the unmapped Vilcabamba lay in the ceja de selva in Cusco's northwestern valleys. With Giesecke's help, Bingham talked to hacienda owners, regional authorities, and UNSAAC students to learn more about potential Inca sites in the Sacred Valley.[26] Giesecke, along with numerous local authorities and landowners, suggested to Bingham that he inspect a ruin that lay between the twin peaks of Huayna Picchu and Machu Picchu.[27] In fact, maps identifying Inca ruins at Machu Picchu dated back to the 1860s.[28] Traveling down the Sacred Valley was difficult but far from impossible considering that most of the route was being cleared in anticipation of road and rail projects. Arriving at the base of Huayna Picchu just west of present-day Aguas Calientes, Bingham and a Peruvian military sergeant named Carrasco encountered a local, Melchor Arteaga, who confirmed the existence of a ruin on the summit above and accompanied them on their ascent to the site on July 24, 1911. Much to Bingham's surprise upon arriving at the summit, he found a family named the Richartes living and cultivating crops adjacent to the ruin. One of their young sons, reportedly named Pablito Richarte, guided Bingham through the ruins of Machu Picchu for several hours.[29] In light of these facts, Bingham's reputation as the sole discoverer of the lost city of Machu Picchu proves tremendously false. Pablito Richarte, however, could at least claim the honor of being the first of many future tour guides at Machu Picchu.

Despite the fact that cusqueños had known of, and in some cases lived and worked by, Machu Picchu, Bingham's expeditions made him a celebratory figure in the United States. His skill at managing complex expeditions, sponsors, the press, and local knowledge made him a pioneer of sorts in the field of exploration. Ricardo Salvatore has described Bingham's expeditions as "a moment when business and scholarship united in the construction of the U.S. informal empire."[30] The 1911 expedition featured seven members. As Bingham returned to Machu Picchu in 1912 and in 1914–15, the scope and scale of the expeditions grew as Kodak supplied cameras and the

Winchester Repeating Arms Company provided firearms. Influential U.S.-owned companies in Peru like W. R. Grace & Company and Cerro de Pasco Mining Corporation aided the expedition's activities. Gilbert Hovey Grosvenor, the editor of *National Geographic*, worked closely with Bingham to create interest through the magazine. *National Geographic's* April 1913 issue featuring Bingham's article on his exploits titled "In the Wonderland of Peru" broke the magazine's circulation records.[31] The early press on Machu Picchu also helped Bingham to present himself as a heroic figure who nearly singlehandedly uncovered a city lost for centuries. Despite his dependence on local knowledge and labor, initial publications often omitted the role of cusqueños in Bingham's expeditions.[32]

The fact that Machu Picchu entered the popular consciousness at the dawn of mass media aided its global rise to fame.[33] The *New York Times* captured public fascination with Machu Picchu, labeling it "the greatest archeological discovery of the age" in a June 15, 1913, article on Bingham's expeditions. "Just now, when we thought there was practically no portion of the earth's surface still unknown," observed the *Times*, "when the discovery of a single lake or mountain, or the charting of a remote strip of coast line was enough to give a man fame as an explorer, one member of the daredevils' explorer craft has 'struck it rich.'"[34] Peruvians also noted the new international attention on their country. News and photographs of Bingham's expeditions appeared in the Lima press during his work in Peru.[35] Javier Prado Ugarteche, a former prime minister and member of one of Peru's most prominent political families, thanked Bingham in an August 1913 letter, stating, "I owe you a thousand congratulations for your work, and thanks, as a Peruvian for your labor of propaganda in favor of my homeland."[36]

Bingham secured additional funding from Yale University and the National Geographic Society for another expedition to Machu Picchu in 1912 and a third trip in 1914 and 1915. However, as he returned to Cusco and Machu Picchu in search of greater fame and exploits, his ambition eventually collided with growing awareness of national heritage. Although Bingham's exploits have tended to overshadow earlier efforts, Peruvian public and private institutions boasted a long history of archeological activity and conservation. As early as January 1912, the first locally organized archeological expedition arrived at Machu Picchu under the guidance of José Gabriel Cosío.[37] Since independence Peru had passed legislation protecting pre-Hispanic sites and artifacts. However, at the start of the twentieth century Peru made more concerted legal reforms in regard to archeological protection that required state permission for excavations and the prohibition of the exportation of artifacts.[38] Prior to his 1911 and 1912 expeditions, Bingham received broad permission from the national government to excavate at archeological sites. Although policy often changed, Peru did place restrictions on Bingham's ability to export any artifacts and specified that the pieces from Machu Picchu were a loan to be eventually returned. However, Bingham arranged illegal and undocumented exports of various pre-Hispanic artifacts purchased from independent collectors and looters.[39]

During Bingham's third expedition his activities provoked serious conflicts with locals. Indigenistas and the Cusco press chafed at the fact that the Peruvian government had granted Bingham's expeditions, instead of locals, priority in excavation. Rumors also swirled over abuses against archeological sites and workers. The young indigenista Luis E. Valcárcel made a formal legal accusation against Bingham's failures to comply with preservation policy. Although Bingham escaped prosecution, the explorer was outraged that Peruvians dared to scrutinize him and found himself increasingly isolated as oversight of his expeditions became a local cause célèbre in Cusco. Now forced to strictly follow Peruvian law, the excavations were monitored by local archeologists including Cosío. Bingham, channeling feelings of Anglo-Saxon superiority common at the time, found these inspections bothersome and insulting. He abruptly stopped his work and left Peru in August 1915, but not before organizing several more illegal shipments of artifacts to the United States. Although few would have suspected it, Bingham would not return to Peru for another thirty-three years.[40]

Although spurned by Peru, Bingham did manage to publish a book on his expeditions titled *Inca Land*.[41] This volume gave broad political and geographical surveys of Peru as well as minutia of his expedition, but it contained surprisingly little information on Machu Picchu. Bingham justified the decision by describing *Inca Land* as a first volume to be followed by a second book that would focus on Machu Picchu. He wrote to the publishers on June 12, 1922, promising, "My next book, which I hope will be a companion volume to this, will deal very largely with the ruins of Machu Picchu and the things found there."[42] However, Bingham quickly became distracted by his growing political interests. After serving in the military during World War I, he returned to Connecticut to pursue a political career and eventually became a U.S. senator in 1925.[43] During his political campaigns, Bingham exploited his fame from the expeditions but held little nostalgia for Peru. He told the *Boston Daily Globe* in 1924: "[Peruvians] have no consuming curiosity about the past. Accordingly they were suspicious of our undertaking and their efforts, I assure you, were far from helpful."[44] Many cusqueños were

Hiram Bingham,
circa 1923

more than happy to forget Bingham. In 1926 UNSAAC rescinded an honorary degree it had granted him.[45] In a 1926 interview, Cosío stated: "I absolutely don't lament the departure of Bingham . . . The Yale commission never worked for Peru; its activities in our country were reduced to exporting in total secrecy."[46]

Of course, Machu Picchu never disappeared from the popular consciousness during the 1920s. Ironically, one of Bingham's most important scholarly legacies was that local opposition to his expeditions soon inspired renewed interest in Cusco's pre-Hispanic past.[47] Archeologists working and studying at UNSAAC continued to visit and analyze the site through the 1920s.[48] One local guidebook published in 1921 still recommended that travelers visit Machu Picchu, but advised that "if it is possible, a pair of peons should be sent a day ahead to cut the plant growth for a path."[49] General John

Pershing, famous for commanding U.S. expeditionary forces in Mexico and during World War I, visited the site with Giesecke in 1924. However, even Giesecke admitted later that until the completion of the Santa Ana Railroad in the late 1920s, visiting Machu Picchu was inconvenient and a rare occurrence.[50] When the British writer Anthony Dell traveled down the Sacred Valley in 1925, he declined to even visit the once-famous ruin. "The place is now overgrown with vegetation and is the haunt of poisonous snakes and spiders," commented Dell.[51] With the cultural and political ties that brought it to global prominence severed, Machu Picchu once again became a lost city in the popular consciousness.

From Andean Backwater to Andean Mecca

The decline of Machu Picchu's global appeal likely weighed little on the minds of cusqueños in the 1920s. However, local elites did express concern regarding the influence of travel accounts that described their city and region. Bingham's descriptions of Cusco followed a long tradition of travel writers who visited and recorded their experiences in Peru's Andes. Although these writers and their travel accounts often provided detailed descriptions of Cusco, the publications presented a problematic description of the Andes. Foreign, particularly U.S., visitors to the Andes often viewed the region through the perspective of the growing imperial reach of the United States. For them, Cusco and the Andes represented an exotic "other" America that both highlighted and justified the need for the modernizing promise of growing U.S. power.[52]

One of the first English-language books to describe Cusco in detail was authored by English geographer Clements Markham. Based on Markham's travels in Peru in 1852 and 1853, *Cuzco: A Journey to the Ancient Capital of Peru* provided readers with detailed description of the region's historical site and geography. However, Markham also colored his observations with laments over the state of the region. Markham declared: "Cuzco! once the scene of so much glory and magnificence, how art thou fallen! What suffering, misery, and degradation have thy unhappy children passed through since the days of prosperity!" Markham noted that Cusco's decline was reflected in the lives of its inhabitants: "thy sons, once the happy subjects of the Incas, are sunk into slavery. Mournfully do they tread, with bowed necks and downcast looks, those streets that once resounded with the proud steps of their unconquered generous ancestors."[53] Markham's description of Cusco as a decadent relic of its former Inca glory would set a common tone for future travel accounts of the city and its inhabitants.

Markham was followed by E. G. Squire, a U.S. commissioner who traveled extensively through Peru in 1863 and 1864. He published a book on his experiences in 1877 with the title *Peru: Incidents of Travel and Exploration in the Land of the Incas.*[54] While Markham's observations expressed sadness over the state of nineteenth-century Cusco, he did not blame its residents for its decline and even noted that the Indians were "a people of uncommon interest, and undoubtedly capable, as a race, of progressive improvement."[55] Squire was far more critical of cusqueños and commented "There is hardly anything that can be called society."[56] He counted only two forms of recreation in Cusco, "religious processions and cockfighting."[57] The author concluded by noting: "Of the filthiness of Cuzco every visitor must have sickening recollections. It offends the eye as well as the nose."[58]

Squire described the indigenous population of Ollantaytambo in the Sacred Valley as fundamentally incompatible with the modern world. He observed, "I must give them the credit of having followed my photographic boxes through the plaza with uncovered heads, kissing them devoutly, under the mistaken notion that they contained relics of the saints."[59] Squire regarded the non-Indian inhabitants of the city of Cusco as being equally ingenuous regarding their faith. Displaying the same feelings of Anglo-Saxon superiority that would influence Bingham, Squire attacked Cusco's public Catholic rituals as evidence of its decadence. Squire described a funeral procession he had witnessed, stating, "As they passed the various squalid homes in that quarter, the women rushed out with disheveled hair, and, huddling behind the bier, commenced the loudest and most extravagant wailings of which human organs are capable."[60] Thirty years later, another U.S. traveler, Harry Franck, also critiqued Catholicism in Cusco in his 1917 *Vagabonding Down the Andes*, opining that "the last foothold of Spanish power on the American continent bids fair to be the last of popery also."[61]

Another common theme in early travel narratives of Cusco was comparing the area's glorious Inca past with its apparent contemporary squalor. Writing on her trip to Cusco for *National Geographic* in 1908, Harriet Chalmers Adams praised the city as "America's ancient Mecca" while looking down upon it from the Inca fortress of Sacsayhuamán. However, she warned readers that the urban center "rivals Constantinople in unpleasant odors — in fact, I believe Cuzco holds the world's record."[62] Another travel writer, Annie Peck, offered readers an extensive description of the city's Incaic structures in her *South American Tour*, published in 1913. However, she juxtaposed the site against the current underdeveloped state of the city by commenting, "Yet how altered [it is] from the days of its glory!"[63] Recounting his 1909 visit to Cusco for North American readers, Bingham also compared Cusco's Inca structures of the past with its perceived present backwardness. "It is pathetic to see the filth and squalor that surround the walls of the magnificent old edifices," observed Bingham.[64]

Travel narratives of Cusco did note the city's progress. Even the often-critical Franck praised Cusco's natural beauty and noted the introduction of streetcars to the city.[65] However, authors often emphasized the challenges that faced the region as it modernized. Peck wrote of the recent arrival of the railroad to Cusco as one sign of progress for the city. However, she commented that "the hotels alas! leave much to be desired. Slow, indeed, are the people to realize the necessities which *must* be supplied if the town is to advance, to attract tourists and business men." According to Peck, only one of the city's lodging establishments, the Hotel Comercio, "may be endured for a night or two."[66] In her 1908 travel account, Marie Robinson Wright praised the city, noting that "Cuzco has made notable progress within the past few years and is constantly improving in social and economic development." However, Robinson Wright also noted that "the modern city must pay the penalty of past fame by a harder struggle for present recognition than new cities have to experience."[67] Robinson Wright argued that "the change from old to new conditions in Peru is a transition in which the Indian has had little share; not because he is prevented but because of his disinclination to learn new ways and his lack of capacity to receive and apply modern knowledge."[68]

In *Inca Land*, published in 1922, Bingham also offered praise for Cusco's modernization. "Telephones, electric lights, street cars, and the 'movies' have come to stay," noted Bingham. Yet, when describing Indians gathered at Cusco's market, Bingham painted the scene for his readers as "a never-ending source of entertainment to one who is fond of the picturesque and interested in strange mannerisms and customs."[69] Even if Cusco had slowly begun to modernize, according to international travelers its people and culture remained exotic and strange to the outsider. Bingham was not the only traveler to note how Cusco's indigenous population appeared to remain outside its modernization process. Franck described Indians in Cusco as "an enigma to the foreigner." He described Cusco's Indian population as "passively sullen, morose, and uncommunicative . . . [The Indian] lacks will-power, perseverance, confidence either in himself or others."[70] Visiting Machu Picchu, Franck often described the Inca as a "lost race" almost incomparable with their "ambitiousness descendants."[71]

Of more concern to cusqueño elites and intellectuals was how foreign travel narratives mirrored and legitimized existing Lima-based notions regarding Cusco's backwardness. Despite Cusco's ongoing modernization, most limeños regarded the region as part of Peru's *mancha india* that hindered the nation's progress. While limeño elites studied the history of the Inca, they saw few historical connections between the empire and the Andes of the nineteenth and early-twentieth centuries.[72] Many national leaders openly questioned if Cusco, or any of Peru's Andean regions, had a role in a country that increasingly concentrated its economic and political activity on the Pacific coast.[73] Commenting on the national elite's disinterest in Peru's Andes, Franck noted, "For one limeño who has visited Cuzco, the historical gem of the continent, a hundred have journeyed to Paris."[74] Peruvian-authored travel accounts of Cusco proved equally or perhaps more critical of the region's perceived backwardness. Hildebrando Fuentes, a former prefect for Cusco, published a guide of the region in 1905. Describing a typical Indian inhabitant of Cusco, Fuentes remarked, "In arts and professions he is an imitator, and has the ability to learn; but he does not invent: he does not have creative genius." Fuentes continued, stating that "I don't believe he is opposed to civilization—as one generally thinks—but yes, he is late to accommodate himself to it."[75]

Perhaps most concerning to cusqueños was the travel account written by the limeño intellectual José de la Riva-Agüero y Osma, who, unlike many of his peers, did elect to travel to Peru's interior in 1912. In the essays he composed as a result of his travels, known as the *Paisajes peruanos*, Riva-Agüero presented a consensus held by many limeño intellectuals. "The coast has represented innovation, swiftness, joy, and pleasure," noted Riva-Agüero; "the highlands, have symbolized an almost backward conservationism."[76] Unlike other observers, however, Riva-Agüero did envision a path for a modern nationalism in Peru that addressed the Indian question. He proposed a process of *mestizaje*, or racial mixing, in which indigenous populations would slowly merge with whites and other races in the production of a nationalism celebrating a mestizo Peru. Mestizo nationalism, embraced by the Mexican state, included Indians in modern nationalism. However, Riva-Agüero's position still assumed the inferiority of indigenous populations and implied that *mestizaje* would eventually replace Indian identity. Even more concerning to cusqueños, mestizaje nationalism ran contrary to their vision of indigenismo that celebrated the centrality of the Indian in Peru's national identity.[77]

As these debates swirled, Peruvian politics received a populist shock. Returning to the presidency by force in 1919, Augusto Leguía implemented the policies of his Patria Nueva (New Fatherland) government, which sought to wrest political and economic power from Peru's national and regional elites and place it under the control of a centralized authoritarian state. In addition to courting external investment and industrialization, Leguía hoped to bring economic modernization to Peru's Andean interior. In order to accomplish these goals, Leguía proposed an extensive road construction campaign.[78] However, even as Leguía's plans promised to bring increased travel to Cusco, the Lima-centric press continued to depict the Andes as antimodern. The cover of the February 1927 issue of the Lima travel magazine *Ciudad y Campo y Caminos* best depicted the imagined contrast between Peru's automobile-oriented modernization with the perceived backwardness of the Andes. The illustration showed a well-to-do family struggling to navigate their automobile among Indian peasants, llamas, and rural geography.[79] Even when reports emerged of new way to travel to Cusco, Lima's press portrayed modernization as opposed to the traditional character of the Andean city. Documenting infrastructure improvements taking place in July 1927, *Ciudad y Campo y Caminos* reminded readers that "Cuzco is a city that slowly advances with the progress of time."[80]

Cusqueños responded to these denunciations through a variety of political, artistic, and literary efforts that valorized their regional identity and folklore as compatible with the modern world.[81] As part of this effort, cusqueños embraced the discourse of tourism to refashion their region in the eyes of Lima and the world. Interestingly, the first call to use tourism as a force for modernization in Cusco originated from the Philadelphia-born Giesecke. In July 1920, Giesecke penned an article titled "Cuzco: Tourism Mecca of South America" for *Mercurio Peruano*, a journal influential among Lima's elite and intellectual circles.[82] The UNSAAC-managed *Revista Universitaria* republished the article in August 1921; in it Giesecke stated, "Without any doubt, during the centennial [of Peru's 1821 independence] the region that will offer the tourist more interest for its historical precedence is Cusco, seat of the old empire of the Incas; Rome of South America, or Mecca of tourism in all of America, as some justly call it."[83] Like the previous travel narratives, Giesecke's article highlighted the many historical sites Cusco offered a potential visitor. However, rather than emphasize the city's incompatibility with modern travel, Giesecke emphasized Cusco's refined amenities. His article assured readers that "streetcars and automobiles wait for the arrival of

CIUDAD Y CAMPO
y Caminos

LABORA POR EL PROGRESO MATERIAL DEL PERU

Cover of February 1927 *Ciudad y Campo y Caminos*. This publication represented the dominant thinking among most limeños who believed the nation's Andean regions were incompatible with modern travel. Hemeroteca de la Biblioteca Nacional del Perú.

the train" that could rapidly ferry visitors to one of the city's modern hotels. "For afternoon tea," Giesecke advised, "the traveler can go to the Maxim café on the ground floor of the Hotel Colón."[84] Giesecke highlighted how Cusco, far from being a dirty, outdated city, could accommodate a modern traveler. Suggesting that travelers visit Cusco during Peru's celebration of its independence centennial, he also emphasized its importance in the national narrative.

Giesecke's call to advocate for tourism provoked a burst of tour guide writing and promotion, much of it authored by the Generation of the Sierra. The work of these authors challenged the established view that tourist guidebooks were crassly consumerist, poor relatives to the more traditional genre of travel narratives. In fact, the work of Giesecke and his peers supports the argument that, while certainly consumerist, guidebooks served a critical role in creating and re-creating historical narratives, sites of importance, and identity.[85] In fact, the cusqueño-authored guidebooks were employed to present an effective counternarrative to the travel literature that had disparaged the Andes. The authors did not explicitly state who the intended recipients of such a message were, but one can assume they hoped to appeal to both a national and an international audience. By the 1920s, railways and connecting ferry service across Lake Titicaca provided relatively convenient international travel to Cusco from Bolivia and Argentina. The popularity of Cusco's folkloric groups in Buenos Aires during the 1920s evidenced the region's cultural appeal to potential Argentine travelers.[86] Still, it appears that the authors of the guidebooks hoped to use their descriptions to convince limeño readers of the cultural appeal of Cusco.

Cosío acknowledged the dual commercial and cultural role of the guidebooks when he published a tourist guide of Cusco in 1924. In his introduction, he informed the reader that his publication "is not a serious book of historical criticism nor erudition." Instead, "written to respond to an immediate need for the tourist, in the form of a simple, brief, and clear guide, it will fulfill its objective if the visitor to Cuzco can, with its direction and help, learn how much this millennial city possesses and guards that is important and worthy of admiration."[87] Cosío inserted photographic images taken from above Cusco to show the city's size and layout. Despite the modest tone of Cosío's publication, the guidebooks authored by cusqueños in the 1920s and 1930s made a serious effort to support the indigenista narrative, heralding Cusco's heritage and identity as central to modern Peruvian nationalism.

In order to refute the image of Cusco as backward, cusqueño guidebook authors stressed the city's ability to meet the demands of modern cultured travelers. In his 1921 article, Giesecke recommended that tourists visit UNSAAC, not only because it was one of South America's oldest universities, but also to observe one of Peru's first coeducational institutions and to visit its new archeological museum.[88] In 1924 Giesecke published *Guía del Cuzco: La Meca de la América del Sur, en la tierra de los Incas* (Cuzco Guide: The Mecca of South America in the Land of the Incas). This guide, published in Lima, repeated many of the earlier claims of his 1920 and 1921 articles and included photographs and more details for potential travelers. Giesecke repeated the theme that Cusco was an ideal location for a modern, cultured tourist and recommended that visitors purchase indigenista-authored studies on the region's society and history to become better acquainted. Giesecke suggested that tourists pick up copies of Clorinda Matto de Turner's publications, Cosí-o's study of the history of Cusco, issues of the *Revista Universitaria*, post-cards, and photographs.[89] In 1925 Giesecke, Valcárcel, and José Uriel García published another guide, titled *Guía histórico-artística del Cuzco* (Historic-Artistic Guide of Cusco), that also recommended that potential tourists visit Cusco's "important centers of instruction, including the university, two national institutes, and the seminary which dates to the sixteenth century."[90] The 1925 guide also recommended locales where visitors could find examples of local art, reminding readers that "Cuzco was a center of enormous and profound artistic production like no other city in Peru and even in South America."[91]

Unlike earlier travel narratives that emphasized the abandoned or decaying state of Cusco's archeological sites, cusqueño-authored guidebooks valorized Inca architecture, highlighting its appeal and arguing that its construction was comparable or even superior to that of other global cultural artifacts. The *Guía histórico-artística del Cuzco* recommended a visit to the town of Ollantaytambo, where "one can contemplate the stupendous ruins that still remain from the grand structures built over the summits of the surrounding hills."[92] The same guide highlighted Incaic walls along Calle Triunfo and Calle Belén in Cusco, stating, "They reveal the precision of the instruments used, as well as the great mathematical knowledge of their builders."[93] In 1927 Valcárcel published a tourism article in *Ciudad y Campo y Caminos* on touring Cusco's Inca heritage. Again, Valcárcel repeated local claims of the superiority and durability of Inca structures. "It appears that eternity will seal each wall that the Inka built for the perpetual memory of their race," boasted Valcárcel.[94] Focusing on architectural sites also permitted the authors of guidebooks to include many photographs of Cusco.

Cusqueños demonstrated a keen awareness of the importance of photography in early tourism promotion. John Urry has noted the strong connection between photography and modern tourism. Using photography, one can create a new narrative for tourism consumption. More important, easily reproduced photographs invite consumers to imagine themselves as travelers to faraway sites, aiding the identification of a location as uniquely touristic.[95] Bingham took thousands of photographs during his expeditions and skillfully employed them to publicize his work at Machu Picchu.[96] Regional indigenistas were drawn to photography as well since it provided controlled settings for them to present images that reinforced Cusco's modernity.[97] One of the most prolific photographers in Cusco, Martín Chambi, worked extensively with indigenistas and guidebook authors to visually capture the region's touristic qualities. Chambi promoted Cusco's tourist sites independently through his own studio productions and exhibitions. He also took multiple photos of Machu Picchu. James Scorer has argued that it was Chambi, not Bingham, who established the now-popular framing of Machu Picchu. Whereas earlier photos had largely been taken within or at an angle level with the archeological site, Chambi instead captured Machu Picchu from an elevated perspective. This angle, showing Machu Picchu's relationship to the surrounding landscape and Huayna Picchu rising in the background, established the iconic imagery of the site still recreated in tourist selfies today.[98] He also contributed to numerous projects promoting Cusco as well. One edited volume, *Cuzco histórico*, was published in Lima in 1934. Besides entries from prominent indigenistas, *Cuzco histórico* featured numerous photos by Chambi of the region. The book's authors explicitly thanked him for his contribution to *Cuzco histórico*, which many credited with building limeño interest in Cusco in the early 1930s.[99]

In addition to highlighting the architectural skill of the Inca, early guides established links between the pre-Hispanic and modern eras by emphasizing the academic study of archeology. In Giesecke's initial 1920 and 1921 articles, he reminded visitors of the archeological work conducted by Bingham's expeditions.[100] Cosío's 1924 guide invited readers to engage with sites of Cusco history as archeologists. For example, the guide instructed visitors how to walk around the city's Plaza de Armas to identify the foundations of the former Inca palaces and structures that lined the square.[101] Guiding visitors through the Santo Domingo church and Coricancha temple, García's publication invited its readers to study the site through detailed instructions: "Leaving the cloister, on the right hand side, one sees a beautiful Inca wall, well cared for and almost two meters in height."[102] A guide published by Valcárcel in 1934 also stressed ongoing archeological work in Cusco. Describing recent restoration efforts Valcárcel noted to visitors that "beneath the actual city, many ruins, remnants of buildings, dating from remote periods, remain to be discovered which today will be forever buried, unless another Mussolini can be found to lay bare these marvelous hidden treasures, as Italy's Mussolini did in Rome."[103] Valcárcel and his indigenista peers shared few sympathies with fascism. Instead, Valcárcel hoped to highlight how Cusco's archeological restoration work reflected modern global efforts to celebrate and study the past.

Local civic institutions also produced their own tourism promotion materials that, while not as academically-minded, echoed the narrative endorsed by the indigenistas. As early as 1921, the Society for Propaganda for

Martín Chambi photograph of Machu Picchu, 1925. This is one of many of the cusqueño photographer's images of Machu Picchu. Chambi's framing of the archeological site, with Huayna Picchu rising in the background, would be reproduced in tourist images throughout the twentieth century. Although one can see the areas cleared by Bingham's expeditions, it is worth noting the extensive vegetation that still covered Machu Picchu in the 1920s. Image used with permission of the Martín Chambi Archivo Fotográfico.

the South of Peru published its *Guía general del Sur del Perú* (General Guide of the South of Peru), which included a section on the tourist appeal of Cusco. While encouraging tourists to visit archeological and colonial-era sites, the guide also invited readers to use it to observe Cusco's "current life through its multiple sociological and commercial areas."[104] In 1937 the local government and chamber of commerce published an extensive tourist guide titled *Guía general del Cuzco* (General Guide of Cusco) that also emphasized Cusco's modernization and international appeal. Conscious of the city's reputation, the guide boasted that "the cleaning and canalization [new sewer system] of the city give it an appearance very different from the dirty and embarrassing image presented by the explorer Squire in 1863."[105] Along with travel and history descriptions, both guides emphasized local modernization and civic life. Hacendados, hoping to present themselves as the protagonists of Cusco's modernization, purchased numerous ads in the 1921 guide to highlight improvements made to their estates.[106] Manufacturers, merchants, and hotels in Cusco also placed advertisements that showcased Cusco's urban development.[107] Entries in the 1937 publication listed membership in the Rotary Club as well as its recent charity achievements.[108] The guide contained information regarding many modern professional and civic organizations, including the Medical Association of Cusco, the Association of Cusco Engineers, the Society of Cusco Artisans, and even the Sicuani Tennis Club.[109]

Locally produced tourist guides did more than defend Cusco from insults of backwardness. The guides also acted as tools for cusqueños to present their particular interpretation of indigenismo. Cusco was not the only center of indigenismo thought. During the 1920s, competing political actors in Peru claimed to be leaders of the indigenismo movement. The socialist thinker José Carlos Mariátegui, the populist Alianza Popular Revolucionaria Americana (American Popular Revolutionary Alliance, APRA), and even the Leguía government all aimed to place the Indian at the center of social reform and modernization, but differed greatly on how to achieve this goal.[110] While vying with different indigenista movements on a national level, cusqueños also had to confront local grassroots efforts. Despite the optimistic message of progress conveyed in the tour guides, in the 1920s and 1930s Cusco was fraught with violent social conflict over race. The arrival of the railroad, followed by Leguía's road construction, opened Cusco's agrarian zones to increased economic exploitation. Wealthy landowners bought or confiscated land from Indian communities that could not compete against the larger haciendas that stood to benefit from the new rail and road connections.[111] As a reaction, Indians joined with reformers of the Comité Pro-Derecho Indígena Tawantinsuyo (Tawantinsuyo Indigenous Rights Committee). Leguía had formed the Tawantinsuyo movement (named after the Quechua-language term for the Inca Empire) as part of his efforts to build a populist rural base for the Patria Nueva policies. Quickly, Indians and activists used the Tawantinsuyo organization to attack abusive rural elites and government authorities. Although the Tawantinsuyo revolts were originally considered a millenarian movement, scholars have reassessed the goals of the uprisings as a focused political effort by Indian communities to push for more inclusion in national and regional politics.[112] Violent agrarian revolts and land seizures by Indian communities rocked southern Peru from 1921 onward until the Leguía government outlawed the movement and jailed its leaders in 1927.[113]

Scholars of indigenismo have argued that Cusco's indigenistas failed to understand or support the political and social demands of rural Indians during the Tawantinsuyo revolts.[114] Instead, indigenistas, who often enjoyed the backing of Cusco's elites, celebrated Andean folklore and cultural movements while downplaying the social demands of the region's actual Indian population. By the late 1920s and early 1930s, indigenistas embraced the possibility of creating a "New Indian" through education and urbanization. Many scholars have identified this new focus as "neo-indigenismo."[115] Unlike Lima-based intellectuals, who often viewed race through physical characteristics, in Cusco race was defined in terms of cultural traits associated with modernization and urbanization. Being mestizo became increasingly defined by cultural acts such as speaking Spanish, abandoning indigenous styles of dress, and living in urban areas.[116] Travel guides sought to highlight the growth of culturally mestizo New Indians. As early as 1921, the *Guía del Sur del Perú* emphasized to readers that mestizos composed the city's largest ethnic group.[117] Introducing Cusco to visitors, the 1937 *Guía general* informed travelers that "eight to ten percent of the population has to be definitely white, natives, and foreigners; 60 percent is mestizo, creoles; and the rest, something more than thirty percent Indian."[118] The 1937 guide also predicted that "the urban population will be 40 percent literate and the rural population still remains almost entirely illiterate, something that does not prevent a current inclination towards education, even in the most impoverished *ayllus* (Indian communities)."[119] The progress perceived by the creation of New Indians through modernization, education, and mestizaje allowed the *Guía general* to conclude that "only [in] the dawn of the present century" has Cusco started to "reclaim its legitimate prestige and take its historic role as the nucleus and center of [Peruvian] nationality."[120] As cusqueños asserted their region's role as the true representation of Peruvian nationalism based on the New Indian, they sought out opportunities to highlight Cusco's national and international appeal. Fortunately for cusqueños, 1934 presented an important civic anniversary to underline their region's promise as a cultural and tourist center.

Cusco Quadricentennial and Tourism

By the 1930s, cusqueños had employed tourism to craft a narrative that highlighted the region's modernity and defined their vision of indigenismo.

Now cusqueños needed a platform to showcase their city's tourism potential. Tourism backers found the perfect opportunity in 1934 when Cusco planned to honor the 400th anniversary—the Quadricentennial—of the Spanish foundation of the city. Although the Quadricentennial did not match the scope of other regional civic celebrations held in Latin American history, it provided an important moment to assert Cusco's cultural and touristic importance on a national level.[121] The planning for the Quadricentennial took place amidst dramatic political changes in Peru that ultimately benefited the standing of Cusco's regional elites and indigenistas. Cusco's regional elite, battered by both agrarian revolts and opposition from the Leguía government in the 1920s, entered the next decade on more stable political ground.

The effects of the Great Depression severely weakened Leguía's control of Peru. In August 1930 Colonel Luis Miguel Sánchez Cerro led a successful coup deposing Leguía.[122] The anti-Leguía stance of Cusco's elites and intellectuals permitted many cusqueños and regional indigenistas to rise to prominence in the cultural and political bureaucracy of Lima after the fall of the Patria Nueva. For example, Cusco political leader David Samanez Ocampo headed an interim government following the coup. After several tumultuous years of changing heads of state, revolts, and assassinations, Peru's national constituent assembly appointed Óscar R. Benavides as president with the hopes that the army field marshal, who had previously occupied the presidency from 1914 to 1915, would provide steady, conservative leadership of the country. Benavides began to reestablish political ties between Lima and Cusco's regional elites that had been severed under Leguía. As a result, prominent Cusco political and cultural leaders enjoyed increased prominence in Lima during the 1930s.[123] Illustrating the national government's endorsement of the cultural campaigns led by Cusco's regional leaders, on January 23, 1933, it passed Law 7688 declaring Cusco the "Archeological Capital of South America."[124]

As political ties between Cusco and Lima were restored in the 1930s, memories of the indigenous agrarian uprisings were eclipsed by the cultural work of Cusco's indigenistas.[125] Cusqueños hoped to employ the Quadricentennial celebrations to help solidify these two positive trends. As part of these efforts, supporters of the proposed civic celebrations emphasized its potential to draw tourists to Cusco. The newspaper *El Comercio de Cusco* backed the efforts to secure funding in advance of the Quadricentennial, noting, "We would inaugurate numerous public works that would provide legendary and marvelous Cosko the characteristics of a civilized town, zealous of its monuments and capable of offering them for the veneration of international tourism."[126] Lobbied by cusqueño politician Víctor Guevara, on

September 13, 1933, President Benavides signed Law 7798 declaring that the Cusco Quadricentennial on March 23, 1934, was "to be celebrated as a national holiday." The law created the Comité Central del IV Centenario del Cuzco (Central Committee of the Fourth Centenary of Cuzco, or Quadricentennial Committee) and granted it a budget of 600,000 soles to prepare for the celebrations. The law also provided funds for restoration work and a new tourist lodge at Machu Picchu. Other benefits promised to Cusco for the 1934 event included a new Archeological Institute, civic improvements, and a new municipal hospital.[127]

From the outset, the goal of attracting international travel to Cusco remained a dominant theme in the planning of the Quadricentennial. Lima's *La Crónica* newspaper published a special section in its October 29, 1933, issue that urged the national government to "organize tourism propaganda and with that, allow the civilized world to know the excellencies of our land and the glorious achievements of our race" in preparations for the event.[128] A second entry in the newspaper, titled "The Future of Cuzco," highlighted the need for the Peruvian state to consider the region as a potential center for international travel. "Archeological Cuzco is truly a fortune in our hand, a beautiful and emerging good for which tourists pay and our country should be interested in selling," noted the article.[129] As the civic date approached, Peru's press closely followed the restoration of the city's archeological sites and Machu Picchu. *El Comercio de Lima* commented on the progress on March 9, 1934, by proudly noting that "surely the labors currently in progress will provide the best attractions for tourists."[130] The Lima-based Touring y Automovíl Club del Perú (Peruvian Touring and Automobile Club, TACP) also heavily promoted the celebrations and their possibilities for creating tourism in Cusco.[131]

As the national and local government prepared for the Quadricentennial, diverse groups used the language of tourism development to press for additional funds. For example, in 1933 the Cusco Provincial Council lobbied the central government for increased restoration funds for the Coricancha archeological complex "so that tourists can have free access to admire our glorious past, and so that the Patronato Arqueológico [Archeology Council] of this city may have immediate control over its most perfect historical site."[132] Local institutions were not the only ones who hoped to benefit from a potential tourism boost during the Quadricentennial. Several U.S. expatriates contacted the city government, inquiring about potential jobs promoting or organizing Quadricentennial activities.[133] Even a pastry chef named Moises

Ponce de León contacted the Quadricentennial Committee, offering his "knowledge in the areas of confection, fine pastry, and as chief of cuisine at your disposition" for the festivities.[134]

While some attempted to seek temporary opportunities during the Quadricentennial, other groups hoped to use the event to advocate for long-term change in Cusco. By March 1934, Giesecke joined with several prominent civic leaders of Cusco to form the Comité Central de Propaganda Turístico (Central Tourism Propaganda Committee, CCPT).[135] In coordination with the Quadricentennial Committee, the CCPT organized musical performances and exhibitions to show visitors Cusco culture and history and drafted reports on the need for lodging improvements.[136] On the eve of the Quadricentennial, the CCPT presented a report on ways "to convert Cuzco into a global tourism attraction." The CCPT's report argued that the national government needed to use the Quadricentennial to organize tourism development in Cusco. The report presented eleven recommendations to boost tourism that included the coordination of archeological preservation, the creation of a central tourism planning office, state funding for hotel construction, and increased publicity abroad promoting tourism in Peru.[137] An editorial in *El Comercio de Lima* appearing on April 4, 1934, endorsed the CCPT's report and recommended that the national government adopt all of the recommendations.[138]

While the CCPT advocated for long-term planning to develop tourism in Cusco, the Quadricentennial Committee had already taken steps to achieve such a goal. The committee contracted the architect Emiliano Harth-Terré to create a long-term urban plan for Cusco. In 1934 Harth-Terré completed Cusco's first urban planning guide, the Plano Regulador para la Ciudad del Cuzco (Regulatory Plan for the City of Cuzco). Endorsing the completed plan for the city, Valcárcel wrote, "The magnitude of the work of the Regulatory Plan for the City of Cuzco is the guide that the Municipal Council must follow when considering any urban modifications."[139] Although Harth-Terré's plan was only a general outline provided to regulate urban preservation and development in Cusco, many of the suggestions he proposed for the Quadricentennial in 1934 would continue to form the basis of cultural- and tourism-oriented planning for the remainder of the century. Harth-Terré's plan argued that technical oversight and careful planning would aid Cusco's development while preserving the city's architectural heritage to attract global interest. The plan proposed that Cusco be divided into distinct planning zones. The "archeological zone" outlined in the plan would encompass most of the city center, where "ruins and objects of architectural or artistic merit" would be administered by the Archeological Institute of Cusco.[140] Besides the historic center of the city, the 1934 plan advised the creation of commercial, industrial, and residential zones in Cusco. Harth-Terré's optimistic plan for Cusco even advised that future residential planning "should be created with discrete details in order to not discriminate against the aboriginal element, the under-salaried worker whose life is still primitive."[141] Unfortunately, the Quadricentennial Committee lacked funds to begin to implement the extensive 1934 proposal. Still, the reception of Harth-Terré's plan illustrated how tourism, once used to highlight Cusco's modernity to outsiders, had started to become an engine for modernization and planning itself.

However, as cusqueños prepared to showcase their city, fears lingered that arriving tourists would be disappointed with the actual state of Cusco's modernization, or lack thereof. Concerns emerged that tourists would find that Cusco's hotels and lodgings were not as modern as guides and promotions claimed. The Quadricentennial Commission created a specific subcommittee dedicated to preparing and inspecting lodgings with the hopes of maintaining high standards. This subcommittee worked in cooperation with a municipal hotel and lodging inspector to issue licenses and inspect businesses for safety and cleanliness.[142] Unfortunately for the Quadricentennial planners, Cusco still lacked many modern lodgings in 1934. A survey completed by the lodging commission found that Cusco had only ten locations qualified to house travelers. Of these locations only one, the Hotel Ferrocarril, qualified as a first-class hotel. Many of the city's other lodgings boasted less than spectacular facilities. The Hotel Colón, for example, had fifty-eight rooms but only four bathrooms. In fact, the lodging commission discovered from its survey that Cusco's hotels had only 128 rooms and twenty-seven bathrooms in total.[143] The lodging commission asked the Hotel Ferrocarril to double its beds in preparation for the Quadricentennial, but received a negative response.[144]

In reaction to the lack of sufficient resources and space in Cusco's established hotels, the Quadricentennial lodging commission began to solicit individual residents to provide temporary housing for expected visitors. At the start of 1934, Cusco residents living near the city center received form letters from the lodging commission that read: "We have the great satisfaction to approach you, relying on your true cusqueño spirit, and in honor of the quadricentennial of the Spanish foundation of our city, to ask you to provide lodging in the amount of—beds, for the visitors that you should be able to house after March of this year."[145] Allocating funds from the central government, the lodging commission organized a loan program to help support residents make preparations and any needed renovations for visitors.[146] City residents would use rents paid during the festivities to pay back the loans and earn a modest profit.[147] For example, one application estimated that the lodging loan would be repaid with 20 percent of the profits earned from guest stays during the festivities.[148]

Motivated by financial opportunity and civic obligation, residents responded to the call. Humberto Gil responded to the lodging commission in an enthusiastic letter, stating, "I wish to contribute to the celebrations of the upcoming Quadricentennial to be held in this historic city." Gil pledged that if the lodging commission allocated 5,000 soles for renovations to his property at 18 Calle Hatunrimiyoc, he would "set up lodging for visitors with breakfast and tea; and it will feature sufficient accommodations for the good service of the guests, with a capacity of 40 people."[149] Manuel Ávila applied for a loan of 3,000 soles to provide "a service of comfortable and very decent dining and housing."[150] Enrique Santos of 89 Calle Hatunrimiyoc wrote to the lodging commission promising housing for fifteen guests if he was provided with a loan of 1,500 soles.[151] Some homeowners received generous stipends to renovate in anticipation of guests. For example, Hermoza Santos received 10,000 soles from the lodging commission to renovate her house for Quadricentennial visitors.[152] However, not all residents responded positively to the offers of the lodging commission. Wenceslao Cano responded, "My house does not have the possibility of offering lodging, because it is small and only provides space for my family."[153] Despite the Quadricentennial Committee's efforts to improve lodging in Cusco, press reports indicated that the city still lacked adequate facilities to be considered a tourism center.[154]

Despite the lodging problems, the Quadricentennial celebrations commenced at noon on Thursday, March 22, when the city's churches rang their bells to mark the celebrations. In Lima, President Benavides saluted Cusco at a special Te Deum mass held at the Metropolitan Cathedral.[155] Cusco started the day with a twenty-one-gun salute, followed by inaugurations of public works, a military parade attended by Prefect Coronel Jorge Vargas, and a musical concert of folkloric songs at the municipal theater.[156] Despite indigenismo's urban and elite origins, Zoila S. Mendoza has noted that it also enjoyed popular support in Cuzco, especially in urban folkloric groups that hoped to use the cultural movement to assert their belonging in modern Peru.[157] This fact can certainly be seen in the broad local participation in the event. Every night between Mach 22 and March 25, a parade took place in the Plaza de Armas, often followed by a fireworks celebration. On Friday and Saturday nights, the municipality offered public screenings of films to city residents. The celebrations also featured traditional civic activities including a Te Deum mass in Cusco's cathedral, a reading of the Spanish act of foundation, and singing of the national and cusqueño anthems. Ceremonies marked the completion of historic restorations and new public works. Some of the most popular attractions included the inauguration of Cusco's new airport and the dedication of the recently restored Sacsayhuamán archeological complex. The Teatro Municipal held nightly concerts that featured local musical groups. The final concert, held on Sunday, March 25, featured the famous Centro Qosqo de Arte Nativo (Cusco Center of Native Art)—the region's most prominent folkloric music and cultural group.[158]

In addition to increasing national awareness, Quadricentennial spending helped inaugurate some of Cusco's first permanent tourism infrastructure. The opening of the new airport raised hopes for regularly scheduled flights between Cusco and Lima.[159] Even after the completion of the railroad, the journey to Lima required at least two full days of travel by train to the coast followed by another two days via ship to arrive at the national capital. When the first airplane touched down in Cuzco in 1925, the nearly monthlong civic celebration illustrated how important locals viewed the need to connect their region to the national and global community.[160] Quadricentennial spending helped open new facilities for the Instituto Arqueológico (Archeological Institute) which helped bolster cusqueños' plans to promote the region as a center for cultural and historical tourism.[161] After the civic festival in Cusco, inaugurations of restored archeological sites, including Machu Picchu, continued into July 1934.[162] Thanks to rehabilitation work at Machu Picchu, school field trips to the site began to become a common occurrence after 1934.[163] After years of neglect following Bingham's departure, Machu Picchu again waited for tourists.

Conclusion

It appeared that the Quadricentennial had achieved many of the goals of cusqueños who employed the promise of international tourism to reinvent their region in the eyes of the nation. The event even attracted international press. An article published in the March 24, 1934 issue of the *New York Times* marveled how "1,000 Indians had been at work restoring the ancient glories of the capital city of their forebears." The article also reported that "the government hopes to have Cuzco . . . recognized as the outstanding archeological city of South America."[164] Perhaps even more impressive was the recognition awarded by Lima's press. *El Comercio de Lima* lauded the celebrations in an editorial on March 23, 1934, that stated, "In this solemn tribute, the mind of the coast has merged with the mind of Cusco, and from this fusion of two spiritual worlds, surges the soul of Peru, synthesis of two fundamental psychologies that complement each other and strengthen in the common heritage of nationalism."[165] Once maligned, Cusco's culture was increasingly presented as a central component of Peru's national identity. Equally important, tourism lent the tools to Cusco's political and intellectual leaders to define and disseminate a specific regional vision of indigenismo over competing indigenista narratives. This indigenismo permitted cusqueños to assert a narrative that highlighted the compatibility of the region's indigenous culture with modernity. Additionally, the carefully packaged historical and folkloric narratives created for tourism also bolstered Cusco's indigenista efforts to distance their movement from more radical demands for social reform surging from the region's contemporary Indian communities.

However, as the Quadricentennial celebrated Cusco's achievements in the promotion of tourism, it also highlighted continuing challenges. *El Comercio de Lima* reported that "numerous tourists" had visited Cusco for the Quadricentennial. However, the paper could not produce statistics to support its claim.[166] The lack of reporting on specific visitor numbers suggests that the majority of visitors to events during the Quadricentennial arrived from Cusco or its nearby communities. In addition, the Quadricentennial Committee's last-minute scramble to compensate for Cusco's substandard lodging illustrated the many structural problems that challenged the region's plans to develop tourism. Finally, *El Comercio de Lima*, despite supporting the Quadricentennial, still displayed many of the paternalistic views cusqueños hoped would diminish with the recasting of Cusco as a modern destination. "*El Comercio* supports the development of tourism in Cuzco in 1934," stated the Lima newspaper's March 22, 1934, editorial reporting on the Quadricentennial celebrations; "what better honor can we offer to Cuzco than to incorporate into the present energy the four million pariahs that vegetate in the highlands of Peru?"[167] Despite the achievements in the decades leading to the Quadricentennial, perceptions of Cusco as an isolated and underdeveloped region persisted. However, as *El Comercio de Lima* dismissed the so-called pariahs of Peru's Andes, larger political shifts had begun to create national and hemispheric conditions to elevate tourism in Cusco as a national project. Soon, the transnational ties that helped elevate Cusco's regional identity in Peru would begin to raise the region's profile across the hemisphere.

CHAPTER TWO

Good Neighbors, Tourism, and Nationalism, 1930–1948

On a Sunday morning in October 1948, Hiram Bingham returned to Machu Picchu for the first time in over three decades. Accompanied by a group of dignitaries, he cut the ribbon to a new highway to Machu Picchu built with the hopes of receiving new waves of tourists and visitors. Speeches and press coverage of the visit celebrated Bingham as the heroic explorer who discovered Machu Picchu, thus bringing national and global attention to an important symbol of Peruvian identity.[1] Lost in the fanfare was the fact that such an event would have been impossible to imagine only thirty years earlier when Bingham left Peru under a cloud of criminal accusations and mistrust, and national leaders viewed Machu Picchu as an unimportant relic located in an economic and cultural backwater. Yet, in less than three decades Bingham and Machu Picchu had risen from pariahs to paragons in a national narrative that increasingly embraced Andean history and culture as representations of Peruvian nationalism.

The remarkable transformation of Machu Picchu and Bingham was no accident; rather, it was intertwined with the efforts to promote the Inca archeological site as a tourist destination during the Good Neighbor era. This was not the only case when tourism and touristic narratives were employed in the creation of national symbols.[2] As we have seen, in the 1920s and early 1930s, cusqueños had already adeptly used tourism to create and popularize a narrative that asserted their region's modernity and centrality to Peruvian nationalism. However, the emergence of Machu Picchu as a global symbol of Peru would ultimately depend on a transnational effort that linked U.S. goals to further hemispheric solidarity with activities of the Peruvian state, as well as local aims to promote the Cusco region. The rise of Machu Picchu during the Good Neighbor era points to the importance of understanding how tourism development in Latin America served the aims of U.S. foreign policy while creating a transnational space for local actors to assert their own cultural and political goals.

The 1930s and 1940s offered a unique moment when diplomatic, economic, and cultural actors outside of Peru, especially those associated with the Good Neighbor policy, worked with cusqueños to reinvent Machu Picchu as a national symbol and Hiram Bingham as a benevolent Pan-American figure who discovered the site. The Good Neighbor policy, a diplomatic commitment by U.S. president Franklin Roosevelt to nonintervention and hemispheric cooperation between Latin America and the United States, has long attracted the interest of historians. The Good Neighbor policy has also received renewed attention for its cultural activities and their influence in the United States and Latin America.[3] This new focus reflects a larger trend by scholars to draw attention to the role of cultural politics in U.S.-Latin American relations.[4] Less known is the fact that tourism also formed part of the cultural politics of the Good Neighbor policy.

During this era, tourism development emerged as a powerful cultural and political tool in U.S.-Latin American relations. In particular, Mexico adeptly coordinated its tourism policy to reflect the Good Neighbor policy initiatives.[5] However, compared to Mexico, the Peruvian state in the 1930s and 1940s lacked both the power and the willingness to initiate a national tourism development program. Instead, cusqueños and tourism backers relied on the diplomatic and cultural tools of the Good Neighbor policy to promote Cusco and Machu Picchu as travel destinations and, more importantly, as national symbols. The transnational links that disseminated and developed Cusco's folkloric and historic narratives for tourism consumption emerged as increasingly important tools in presenting the region as the representation of Peruvian national identity to a hemispheric audience. The elevation of Cusco and Machu Picchu as national symbols illustrates the influence of transnational contact zones in the formation of national identity in Latin America.[6] However, the influence of Good Neighbor era institutions in Cusco's tourism development did not signify the absence of the national state. We shall see how cusqueños employed their transnational links to influence and lobby the national state to adopt a larger role in the promotion of tourism and an embrace of indigenismo. As modernization and the economic crisis of the 1930s forced Peru's political leaders to confront populism through political and social reform, the transnational alliances built between Cusco and the United States would prove uniquely influential in guiding the state's early tourism and cultural policies.[7]

However, Cusco tourism's reliance on transnational forces posed risks, especially if hemispheric political conditions changed. Tourism promoters discovered this as they entered the Cold War era at the end of the 1940s when the cultural cooperation of the Good Neighbor policy receded in the face of a more aggressive U.S. foreign policy. A more important risk, however, was the legacy of the problematic narrative constructed to promote tourism at Machu Picchu. If tourism had the power to create new national narratives, it also held the power to distort existing ones. Dean MacCannell notably described tourism as the creation of a "staged authenticity" that strives to meet the tourist's expectations of how a site or event should appear rather than actually portraying reality itself.[8] The case of Machu Picchu illustrates how the staged authenticity created by tourism, in addition to serving the interests of travelers, also promoted much larger political aims and purposes. Cusco's regional elites, the Peruvian national state, and U.S. diplomats created narratives that bolstered their political goals, commodified Machu Picchu for tourist consumption, and silenced alternative or conflicting views. These actors employed tourism to promote an imagined, utopian Inca past that appealed to local and national elites as well as travelers and U.S. consumers. While this narrative did make Machu Picchu into an iconic national symbol of Peru, it continued to ignore the contemporary political demands of Cusco's exploited indigenous population. Meanwhile, Bingham was reinvented as a sympathetic Pan-American figure, while his dubious claims of discovery and his questionable conduct were altered to provide a positive narrative of U.S.-Peruvian cooperation and hemispheric solidarity.

Rediscovering Machu Picchu

Despite some early success, cusqueño efforts to promote the region as a travel destination remained limited. First, Cusqueños had to deal with competing, often more populist, indigenismo movements. Additionally, for most of the 1920s and the early 1930s, cusqueños met stiff resistance from the authoritarian Leguía government, which worked to downplay regionalism in favor of political and cultural centralization in Lima. However, by the early 1930s, political shifts in Peru created new opportunities for Cusco's regional efforts to promote their vision of indigenismo folklore and travel. The turbulent years at the start of the Great Depression in Peru were not kind to supporters of competing strains of indigenismo. José Carlos Mariátegui died in 1930, and the Leguía government fell from power that same year.[9] In 1931, the military leader who overthrew Leguía, Luis Miguel Sánchez Cerro, faced off against the American Popular Revolutionary Alliance (APRA), the populist party led by Victor Raúl Haya de la Torre, in national elections. Following Haya de la Torre's defeat, APRA militants led a failed uprising in 1932 based in the party's stronghold of Trujillo on Peru's north coast. Like Cusco, Trujillo boasted a dynamic regional economy, politically engaged intellectuals, and an extensive collection of pre-Columbian historical sites from the Chimú civilization. In fact, during the 1920s, Lima-based travel magazines consistently published articles highlighting Trujillo's Pacific coast and the impressive nearby archeological site of the Chimú city of Chan Chan—the largest pre-Columbian city in South America.[10] However, public perceptions changed dramatically when government troops executed thousands of APRA followers on the grounds of Chan Chan during the 1932 revolt. On April 30, 1933, an APRA militant assassinated Sánchez Cerro as revenge for the Trujillo massacre.[11] As a result, Chan Chan, now a symbol of APRA activism, received little attention from the national state during the 1930s.[12]

Cusco, where regional politics in the 1920s and 1930s was both anti-Leguía and anti-APRA, stood to benefit from the new national political landscape.[13] After the assassination of Sánchez Cerro, the constituent assembly governing Peru quickly appointed Óscar R. Benavides as president. As noted in chapter 1, the Benavides government aimed to restore the political alliances between Lima and Cusco's elites that had been severed during the Patria Nueva of Leguía.[14] Better political relations between Lima and Cusco also aided the careers of cusqueños who had led some of the first initiatives to promote cultural tourism in Cusco. The indigenista and early travel guide writer Luis E. Valcárcel became head of the National Archeology Museum in 1931. Albert Giesecke, the U.S.-born rector of UNSAAC, had moved to Lima in 1924 to work in various government and cultural posts in organizations that included the Ministry of Education and the Universidad Nacional Mayor de San Marcos before gaining a post at the U.S. embassy.[15] The national government's declaration that Cusco was the archeological capital of South America, as well as its support for the 1934 Quadricentennial, affirmed for cusqueños the importance of their city and region to national concepts of Peruvianness. By the early 1930s, *El Comercio del Cusco* proudly reprinted editorials published by newspapers throughout Peru declaring the city the "Rome of South America," the "Mecca of South America," and the "Living Museum of America."[16] Lima's *La Crónica* newspaper dedicated an entire section of its October 29, 1933, issue to Cusco that advocated for its importance as a national symbol of culture.[17]

La Crónica's coverage of the upcoming Quadricentennial also included an editorial that emphasized another growing consensus in Lima—Cusco's potential for tourism.[18] In 1932 the national government passed Law 7663, which, for the first time, provided funds for the promotion of international travel to Peru. The law's text stated that the funds were to be directed "especially to the city of Cusco and its magnificent Incaic monuments of its department."[19] The author of the law was a congressman from Cusco and a key supporter of tourism, Víctor J. Guevara.[20] Cusco's *Revista Universitaria* republished a speech given in the municipal palace by civic leader Miguel Angel Nieto on November 15, 1933, in preparation for the Quadricentennial. After recounting Cusco's long history from the time of the Incas to the fight for independence, Nieto concluded by reminding the audience of Cusco's increasing international appeal as a destination for enlightened scientists and well-to-do travelers. "It is also necessary to put in context the happy circumstance that this millennial city has been declared the Archeological Capital of the continent," Nieto noted. He concluded his speech by observing that "there should be no tourist that in his itinerary does not plan a visit to Cusco, just like a visit to Tibet or the Holy Land."[21]

Cusco officials offered optimistic predictions of tourism development based on continued infrastructure improvements in the region. By 1928 the newly completed Santa Ana Railroad provided a direct rail link between Aguas Calientes, at the base of Machu Picchu, and Cusco.[22] More importantly, persuaded by cusqueño congressman Guevara, the national government funded construction of an airport in Cusco. Opened in 1933 amid much fanfare, the airport was named in honor of Cusco native Alejandro Velasco Astete, who in 1925 became the first person to fly across the Andes.[23] Highway construction linking the region with Peru's coast continued through the 1930s.[24] The increased accessibility of Machu Picchu in the early 1930s permitted Cusco high schools and the Sociedad de Artesanos to organize field trips to the site.[25] As part of the Quadricentennial celebrations, the government funded the construction of a small lodge adjacent to Machu Picchu to permit small parties to stay overnight. Officials inaugurated the new lodge on July 31, 1934, by commissioning a special train to bring visitors to Machu Picchu.[26] The improvements at Machu Picchu even attracted the attention of the North American press, with the *New York Times* declaring the site "now accessible to visitors" in 1938.[27]

As transportation links improved to Machu Picchu, equally important cultural links between Cusco and the outside world also grew throughout the 1930s as the Andean region enjoyed renewed international attention. A year after his censure for ethics violations damaged his political career, then-U.S. senator Hiram Bingham rededicated his activities to archeology and published *Machu Picchu: A Citadel of the Incas* in 1930.[28] Since 1922 Bingham had promised Yale and the National Geographic Society that he would publish a follow-up volume to *Inca Land*, which did not dedicate substantial attention to Machu Picchu. In fact, Machu Picchu had faded from North American public awareness during the 1920s, so much so that the *New York Times* review of *Machu Picchu: A Citadel of the Incas* began by reminding readers, "Fifteen years ago, Machu Picchu, the white and beautiful citadel on a narrow ridge high above the rushing Urubamba River in Southern Peru, *was* well known by name and by picture to all Americans." The review, written by the archeologist and former Yale Expedition member Philip Ainsworth Means, described the new book rather positively but correctly criticized Bingham's conclusion that Machu Picchu was, in fact, Tampu Tocco, the origin of the Inca civilization. Means reminded readers that "the truth of the matter is, of course, that Machu Picchu is one of the frontier fortresses built by Inca Pachacutec (first half of the fifteenth century)." *Machu Picchu: A Citadel of the Inca* enjoyed only modest sales, perhaps because it sold for a rather expensive fifty dollars.[29] Bingham's publication did not prevent his electoral defeat in 1932, but it began a process that renewed public interest in the explorer and Machu Picchu.[30]

It is hard to estimate to what degree Bingham's publications stoked popular interest in Machu Picchu, but there is no doubt that, starting in the 1930s, a renewed U.S. interest in the exploration of South America began to blossom. Part of North American fascination with the Andes stemmed from the development of nascent programs of Latin American studies in various universities as well as the overall popularization of the fields of archeology and anthropology that, by the 1930s, had introduced scholars such as Franz Boas and Margaret Mead into the popular consciousness of the United States.[31] The *New York Times* noted the phenomenon, stating in 1931 that "South America is becoming a favorite haunt for explorers and adventurers . . . Men are cutting their way through the menacing forest of the Gran Chaco; they are delving into the ancient ruins of the Inca."[32] A similar article published in the *Washington Post* in 1934 announced to readers that "for travel off the beaten track South America holds a good place in the limelight," and described Machu Picchu as "the most amazing ruin in the world."[33] However, renewed interest did not always guarantee veracity. One article appearing in the *Boston Globe* on July 21, 1931, celebrated the twentieth anniversary of Bingham's discovery. The article played fast and loose with the legacy of Machu Picchu while repeating tired stereotypes of Latin American culture in general. The *Globe* proclaimed that Bingham's discovery of Machu Picchu was "nothing less than the find of the mother city from which the Incas of Peru spread their power," and that for centuries Spaniards and gold seekers had sought Machu Picchu, only to have their efforts thwarted when "wily Indians purposely misdirected the explorers to death and disaster." Bingham himself became a man of myth who "met an aged Indian whose fondness for 'fire water' was greater than his anxiety to continue the mystification of tribal secrecy," and surpassed the odds to find what the article questionably heralded as "the lost Inca city that cradled the potato."[34]

The increasing allure of Machu Picchu provided opportunities for amateur explorers, travel writers, and entrepreneurs who journeyed to the site in hopes of becoming another Bingham. Few if any of these future visitors achieved Bingham's success, but their dispatches to U.S. dailies often inspired additional—and almost always incorrect—publications on Machu Picchu. One amateur explorer, Richard Halliburton, traveled to Cusco in 1929 as part of a journey through South America. He arrived at Machu Picchu in search of the supposed one hundred Inca sun virgins who had fled to the site following Pizarro's invasion. In subsequent years, Halliburton explained to readers how he observed ninety-nine graves of his imagined Incan vestal virgins and concluded that the lack of the final grave was due to the fact that "no one came to bury the last to die." To conclude his research, Halliburton stayed the night at Machu Picchu in hopes of encountering ghosts of the sun virgins. Halliburton assured his readers, "There was no doubt—some young ghosts, some middle-aged ghosts, some very old ghosts, but all very virginal ghosts." Unfortunately for us, Halliburton never detailed exactly how he arrived at his findings.[35]

Peruvians themselves employed their intellectual connections with the international community to encourage and steer public interest toward Cusco and Machu Picchu. Giesecke, who aided Bingham's first expeditions and issued some of the first calls to develop tourism in Cusco in the 1920s, continued to play an influential role in promoting Machu Picchu. When the noted novelist Blair Niles arrived in Peru in 1935, Giesecke introduced her to archeologists and helped organize her visit to Cusco.[36] In 1937 Niles, who had previously gained fame among North American readers for her travel accounts of other Latin American nations, published *Peruvian Pageant*. The book, based on her travels and experiences in Peru, earned positive reviews from media outlets such as the *New York Times*.[37] Fictional literature and film also engaged North American readers with the Andes and Machu Picchu. Thornton Wilder's critically acclaimed *The Bridge of San Luis Rey* was published in 1928. The novel won the Pulitzer Prize and inspired more public interest in Peru.[38] Wilder's novel received two film adaptations: one silent picture released to relatively positive reviews in 1929, and a second "talkie" that debuted in 1944. The second film received a cool critical reception, but still managed to garner an Academy Award nomination for best original score.[39] Children's literature also invited readers to relive the imagined adventures of Bingham-inspired explorers. One book, titled *The Citadel of a Hundred Stairways*, featured an adventure between a young tourist from "Yankee-landia" and his cusqueño peer who discover treasure on "Machu Picchu Mountain." The novel, published in 1941, also featured engaging color illustrations for young U.S. readers.[40] In 1946 *The Quest for the Golden Condor* by Clayton Knight appeared on U.S. bookshelves. The book featured a Pan-American adventure that paired a U.S. child traveler with Peruvian peers on a treasure hunt that reached a plot climax at Machu Picchu. A book review in the *New York Times* praised the novel, especially the fact that "the final chapters are packed with excitement and lighted by the splendor of the high Andean scene."[41] Literary fascination with the Andes extended beyond the United States. The Belgian cartoonist Hergé set one of his Tintin adventure series, Prisoners of the Sun, in the Peruvian Andes in 1946.[42]

Pan-American Andes

However, in order to channel increasing global awareness of Cusco and Machu Picchu into larger tourist and cultural development, local elites would need a powerful ally. Cusqueños found that ally in the new Good Neighbor policy of the United States. Associated principally with the administration of Franklin Roosevelt, the noninterventionist and Pan-Americanist diplomatic shift of the United States toward Latin America began in the late 1920s. Realizing the animosity provoked by the United States' armed interventions in the Caribbean and Mexico, as well as the growing popularity of anti-imperialist rebels like Nicaragua's Augusto Sandino, U.S. State Department diplomats shifted their diplomacy toward a more consensus-driven policy with hemispheric neighbors during the Herbert Hoover administration.[43] Roosevelt placed additional emphasis on Hoover's policy, expanding its reach and labeling the new diplomatic shift the Good Neighbor policy, which pledged to honor Latin Americans' national sovereignty while building hemispheric cooperation. The need to secure good diplomatic standing with Latin America became ever more urgent as the 1930s drew to a close and the threat of global armed conflict loomed.[44] In August 1940, Roosevelt created the Office for Coordination of Commercial and Cultural Relations between the American Republics to direct U.S. cultural diplomacy efforts in the region. Nelson Rockefeller served as the head of the new office, renamed the Office of the Coordinator of Inter-American Affairs (CIAA) in July 1941.[45]

Before the creation of the CIAA, pro-U.S. interests in Peru expressed worries in regard to suspected Axis influence in the country in the late 1930s with some justification. Although Benavides held little sympathy for fascism, he did seek closer diplomatic and economic ties with Italy. Small but influential sectors of Peru's elite, most notably the intellectual and political leader José de la Riva-Agüero y Osma and the Miró Quesada family, which owned *El Comercio de Lima*, expressed sympathetic views of European fascism. As late as 1943, the U.S. embassy sent updates on the fascist sympathies of Riva-Agüero and the Miró Quesada family.[46] More populist fascist groups, many of them backers of the previous Sánchez Cerro government, also remained active into the late 1930s.[47] Additionally, Japan enjoyed extensive economic connections with Peru, consuming 59 percent of its cotton exports as late as 1941.[48] Even Nazis sought to portray themselves as "modern Incas" when they contacted the archeologist and anthropologist Ainsworth Means to publish a German edition of his research on pre-Hispanic Peru. Commenting to Giesecke, Means stated that he declined the German offer because he "refused to put in a lot of slop in praise of Nazis as 'modern Incas.'"[49]

U.S. diplomats and their Peruvian allies looked to create institutions to promote Pan-American cooperation. On June 2, 1938, Peru's minister of foreign relations, Carlos Concha, and U.S. Ambassador Lawrence A. Steinhardt announced the creation of the Instituto Cultural Peruano-Norteamericao (Peruvian–North American Cultural Institute, ICPNA). The stated goal of the new organization was to encourage cultural exchange between Peru and the United States.[50] Good Neighbor relations with Peru were also aided by the strong pro-U.S. political stance of President Manuel Prado. Succeeding Benavides as president of Peru in 1939, Prado promoted close political ties with the United States.[51] In May 1942, Prado became the first South American head of state to make an official visit to the United States. CIAA documents recorded that Prado's reception in Washington was the most significant visit by a foreign dignitary since King George VI's arrival in 1939.[52] In 1943 the United States returned the favor when Vice President Henry Wallace visited Peru in April of that year as part of a Latin American goodwill tour. After a large and enthusiastic reception in Lima, Wallace continued on to visit Machu Picchu. Speaking in Cusco, Wallace referred to Peru as "a country proud to be the cradle of the great Inca civilization."[53]

Cooperation between the CIAA, the Peruvian government, and the ICPNA quickly helped to increase cultural awareness of Peru abroad. More

importantly, the "Peru" presented in the Good Neighbor policy era emphasized Machu Picchu and other signs of Cusco's regional identity. When the
CIAA produced teaching aids about Latin America for U.S. schools in 1941,
the guides dedicated to Peru often highlighted the Andean culture of the
nation.[54] One lesson planner distributed by the CIAA, "People Who Live in
Thin Air: A Study of Life in the Andes Mountains of South America," outlined lesson plans for elementary school students focusing on the geography and culture of the region with a specific focus on the history of the
Inca.[55] In 1942 the CIAA worked with the U.S. Office of Education to develop
a nationwide exhibition "to aid schools, teacher training institutions, etc.,
which are interested in the inter-American field."[56] The project received
almost 1,000 requests, and by April 1942 had distributed 132 traveling
exhibits containing books, photos, and specimens from all areas of Latin
America. In regard to Peru, the exhibit emphasized its Andean culture. The
traveling exhibit contained copies of the books *Bridge of San Luis Rey* and *Old
Civilizations of Inca Land*. The inventory also included an example of an Incan "gourd bowl from Peru," a "woven Indian coca bag," a "pair of Alpaca
slippers from the Andes," and "1 knitted Andean Indian cap."[57]

CIAA efforts to increase U.S. awareness of Peru extended to radio. In 1942
the CIAA worked with Peru's Radio Nacional to coordinate an English-
language program broadcast on shortwave from Lima, *Peru Calls You*.[58]
These radio programs sponsored by the CIAA focused on Peru's Andean culture. When the radio series *Hello Americans* premiered in 1942 under the
direction of Orson Welles, the first episode focused on Peru and featured
the title "The Andes." It was broadcast on the CBS Radio Network on
November 22, 1942. *Variety* praised the radio special as "excellent entertainment and fair education."[59] However, when the Coordination Committee
for Peru proposed a radio special on Lima's historic Universidad Nacional
Mayor de San Marcos, the CIAA Central Office denied the request, labeling
the project "of little value."[60] The CIAA also collected rights to Peruvian
music for radio broadcast in the United States. Although many samples of
the music included coastal-originated Peruvian music such as the *vals criollo*
and *marinera*, the CIAA also included many folkloric songs to represent the
Andean highlands.[61] The CIAA even contacted the family of the Peruvian
composer Daniel Alomía Robles to acquire rights to broadcast his famous
Andean ballad "El Condor Pasa."[62]

In addition to radio programs, the CIAA collected and distributed films
to North American classrooms publicizing the Peruvian Andes. Films distributed by the CIAA included *Inca-Cuzco, Land of the Incas*; *Lure of the Andes*;

Peru, Indians of the Mountains; and *Peru, Land of the Incas*.[63] In July 1941, the CIAA signed an agreement with the newsreel company the March of Time to produce thirteen news shorts on Latin America, including one film on Peruvian archeological ruins.[64] Through 1942, the CIAA worked with the Hollywood-based Motion Picture Society for the Americas to continue production of Latin American–based film shorts. Films documenting Peru continued to emphasize the indigeneity and Andean nature of the nation. CIAA-sponsored film shorts on Peru from 1942 included features on Lake Titicaca, "Cuzko," and a MGM-produced short titled *Inca Treasure*.[65] Another CIAA-produced film by Howard Knapp, *Heart of the Inca Empire*, was released in 1943 and featured numerous color shots of Cusco and Machu Picchu.[66] With the assistance of the CIAA, in 1942 Disney completed the feature-length animated film *Saludos Amigos*, which included a segment on Peru that featured Donald Duck in Andean settings as he visited Lake Titicaca as an inquisitive—and comically dumbfounded—tourist.[67]

Good Neighbors Make Good Travelers

The visit of Donald Duck as a tourist reflected another trend of the Good Neighbor policy that appealed to the backers of Cusco tourism. As the activities of Good Neighbor cultural diplomacy drew global attention to the Andes, so did the promise of tourism development. International tourism in Peru remained limited through the 1930s, as most international visitors arrived in Lima as passengers on elite ocean steamer tours of South America.[68] Usually these visits lasted only a few days and rarely ventured beyond Lima. When *El Comercio de Lima* reported the arrival of an ocean liner in Lima's port city of Callao carrying 450 North American tourists in February 1938, it also noted that the group remained in Peru for only two days and limited their sightseeing to the Lima area before departing for Chile.[69] *El Comercio de Lima* observed that "currently, tourists stay a few short hours in the capital and many times travel on steamships that are subject to itineraries that impede them from staying more days," and argued that the Peruvian state needed to encourage investment so that "travelers visit our territory for longer periods that permit our national economy to make the most of their influence."[70] Tourism promoters pointed to the growth of aviation transport during the 1930s as one solution. Peru's commercial aviation did experience a period of rapid growth, from 145 total flights in 1928 to 34,571 flights in 1937.[71] Yet, observers noted that more reforms were necessary to develop tourism in Peru, especially beyond Lima.

One of the most influential voices calling for increased state investment in tourism was the Touring y Automovíl Club del Perú (Touring and Automobile Club of Peru, TACP). Originally formed as an advocacy group for increasing highway construction and investment, by the 1930s the TACP also began to lobby for attracting international travelers to Peru. The TACP president during the 1930s, Eduardo Dibos Dammert, enjoyed commercial and political connections in Peru and North America. He represented the U.S.-based Goodyear Tire Company in Peru and also served as mayor of Lima from 1938 to 1940. Under the leadership of Dibos Dammert, the TACP allied with cusqueño political leaders to promote the region as a center for international cultural tourism and used his organization's publications to encourage readers to visit Cusco.[72] In 1936 Dibos Dammert upgraded the TACP's news bulletin to a magazine named *Turismo*. A large photo of Machu Picchu graced the magazine's cover in its first year of publication.[73] The magazine also featured an article (published in English) about Cusco that stated, "To visit Peru and not include in your itinerary what is at once the center and circumference of Incaic and Spanish Colonial history is an unpardonable sin, a foolish lapse."[74] *Turismo* dedicated articles to many national topics, yet articles about tourism possibilities in Cusco often made regular appearances in the magazine's issues.[75] *Turismo* was not alone in pushing for greater national recognition of the tourism possibilities of Cusco and Machu Picchu. A 1938 editorial in *El Comercio de Lima* predicted that the treasures of Egypt were losing appeal, while Peru's archeological heritage "seduces even more."[76] Consensus in Peru had begun to emerge over the importance of Cusco as a tourism center.

Responding to increased calls for a coordinated travel policy from institutions like the TACP, Peru's Ministry of Foreign Relations commissioned Giesecke to visit the United States in 1936 to study possible strategies for tourism development.[77] Giesecke returned that year and gave the Ministry of Foreign Relations its desired report. Based on his findings, Giesecke recommended reforms that included increased state investment in publicity, hotel construction, and travel policy.[78] However, Giesecke's report focused on two overriding principles for tourism planning in Peru. First, Peru needed to craft a tourism policy to appeal to the United States. In his report, Giesecke noted, "It appears to me that the precise moment has arrived to attracted tourists from the United States of America, origin of more than three-quarters of global intercontinental tourism."[79] Second, Giesecke's report emphasized the importance of Cusco as a future tourism destination. He interviewed multiple tourism industry representatives in the United States. One interviewee

Cover of July 1936 *Turismo*. By the mid-1930s, tourism backers in both Cusco and Lima had begun to promote Machu Picchu as one of the country's key attractions, as evidenced by its appearance on the cover of Peru's most important travel periodical. Hemeroteca de la Biblioteca Nacional del Perú.

advised Giesecke that "Peru should procure accelerated services, by rail to Cuzco and direct service to [the Archeological] Capital of South America."[80] Serving in the TACP, Giesecke regularly repeated the conclusions of his 1936 report in the pages of *Turismo*.[81]

Soon, questions related to tourism policy became involved in larger debates regarding the role of the state in addressing the social consequences of modernization and industrialization. Confronted with populism from the left and right, the Benavides government expanded the role of the state to secure labor and social peace. While not as extensive as those undertaken by other Latin American governments, new housing, health, and welfare reforms begun under Benavides marked a dramatic expansion of the Peruvian state in the realm of social policy.[82] Tourism backers in Peru hoped that the push for social reform would also extend to travel. Their efforts reflected a larger global push in the 1930s and 1940s by capitalist, socialist, and fascist states to employ tourism to achieve social change and bolster nationalism.[83]

The June 1937 issue of *Turismo* featured extensive coverage of tourism policies in neighboring Chile, where state-run tourist lodges were already operating. *Turismo* published a photo of a new resort with the caption "Country estate, private property of a major landowner? No, it is the house for all the welfare beneficiaries; far from noise and urban centers, in complete nature, constructed through welfare reform to defend health, the precious capital of every worker."[84] The TACP would continue to publish editorials in *Turismo* to emphasize the social benefits of the creation of a new chain of state-run hotels as a central part of a national tourism policy.[85]

The TACP's efforts came to fruition on July 22, 1938, when Benavides proposed Law 8708 authorizing the construction of state-owned hotels. Law 8708, soon dubbed the Hotel Law, became finalized and enacted later that year, on November 2. The national government selected thirteen sites for new hotels and placed the small Machu Picchu lodge under the ownership of the new organization.[86] In many ways, the Hotel Law marked the first coordinated effort on the part of the Peruvian state to create a national tourism infrastructure. *Turismo* applauded the new law and predicted, "In the very near future the government will open the doors of Peru to a broad and beneficial current of contact with the rest of the world."[87] Reflecting the influence of cusqueños like Giesecke, the hotels were often touted for their potential international appeal. However, promotional publications did invoke nationalist language in praising the hotel constructions. "To know Peru is to admire it. Working to know Peru is to teach how to love it; it is to teach to have faith in her grandness; it is to undertake a task of true nationalism," concluded one report on the progress of the Hotel Law.[88]

National efforts to increase state investment in travel were encouraged by the United States, which also viewed tourism as an additional tool to support its economic and political goals in Latin America. Often identified with the Cold War era, the use of tourism to extend U.S. economic and political influence can be traced to the Good Neighbor policy.[89] The U.S.-influenced Pan American Union formed a Travel Division in 1935 to promote inter-American tourism. The division employed Peru's archeological sites, and Machu Picchu in particular, for tourism promotion. In its February 1938 *Bulletin*, the Pan American Union featured an article on Cusco by Means titled "Archeology as a Reason for 'Visiting the Americas.'"[90] Beginning in 1939, the Pan American Union held regular Inter-American Travel Conferences to promote hemispheric tourism, most of which were attended by representatives in the TACP.[91] The Pan American Union continually endorsed travel to Cusco as one of the more attractive and viable tourism possibilities in the hemisphere and even featured the city's Plaza de Armas on the cover of its July 1941 issue.[92] The U.S. government also used the State Department and the CIAA to explore the possibilities of transforming cultural cooperation into economic results through tourism.[93] One 1943 CIAA report on Peru predicted that "the tourist will play a large part in the financial future of the Republic [of Peru]."[94] As early as July 1943, the CIAA had contacted the Peruvian embassy's commercial councilor inquiring about the government-owned hotel chain and possibilities for U.S. investment.[95]

By 1945, director Rockefeller personally instructed the U.S. Good Neighbor agency (renamed the Office of Inter-American Affairs, OIAA) to focus on increasing tourism in all of Latin America.[96] By May 1945, the OIAA issued an internal planning report titled *Suggested Program for the Development of Inter-American Tourist Travel*. In the report, the OIAA encouraged continued hemispheric cooperation for the development of tourism, noting that "any project undertaken by the Office of Inter-American Affairs to promote travel of our citizens to other American Republics will, therefore, result in better economic and cultural relationships for us all."[97] Working with the publishing house Duell, Sloan and Pearce, the OIAA helped publish a travel guide of Latin America geared toward North American tourists. The guides recommended trips to Cusco, "the archeological capital of South America," and Machu Picchu, "one of the greatest archeological discoveries of recent times."[98] A Peruvian-produced English-language guidebook for Lima and Peru reflected the emphasis on tourist exchange as part of an overall hemispheric Pan-American policy. Featuring photos of Franklin Roosevelt and Peru's President Prado, the guide's introduction optimistically proclaimed: "We believe that a thorough understanding of each other is the firmest basis of mutual respect and friendship in the Americas. We extend then a cordial invitation to all American citizens to visit Peru."[99] For proponents of tourism development in Peru, the time to act had arrived.

Diplomats were not alone in anticipating a postwar tourism boom. An editorial in the November 1943 issue of *Turismo* commented on the upcoming efforts to hold a National Tourism Congress. It began, "Although it is true that the war has not yet concluded, already the victory of the righteous has appeared on the global horizon.," The editorial concluded that "Peru should, therefore, prepare with all foresight and organization its plans for tourism for the postwar"[100] The goal of postwar tourism preparation was best summarized in the January 1944 issue of *Turismo*. The magazine greeted the new year with an editorial titled "We Will Prepare for the Invasion." Using the well-known language of war preparation, the editorial rallied Peruvians in favor of a coordinated tourism policy to meet a welcomed invasion of tourists. "It will arrive principally from the North, blond, happy, and wealthy," predicted the opening line. "Uncle Sam, acting as commander in chief, will give the order to attack. They will arrive with the most powerful and famous weapon: money, money, money." The editorial predicted that "once again the Inca Empire will fall" and that "the flags of the tourists will fly above Macchupicchu next to ours. What a beautiful defeat!" The editorial's call to arms ended with the lines "We shall lose this war! We shall be patriots! That all shall come, nothing more. We will disarm ourselves so they do not fight the armies of malaria and filth. We shall not follow the orders of the high command of disorganization. General Tourism shall be the one who strategizes. Let it be him who receives our 'adversary.' That it be him who decides. Him who says to the invading army: You are at home in our house! Do you like it? On with the victory march."[101] For *Turismo* and the interests it represented, the planned second conquest of Peru would be welcome and, more importantly, profitable.

Tourism Triumphant

New state investment in tourism and its promise for Cusco enjoyed its debut in 1944 as the new state-built Hotel Cusco prepared for its opening. With ninety-three rooms, the planned Hotel Cusco would be the largest of the new venues.[102] Justifying the importance of constructing a new hotel in Cusco, promotional materials noted that the city "was declared the Archeological Capital of South America . . . and is on the road to quickly become one of the great tourist centers of the world."[103] The same publication detailed renovation plans for the Machu Picchu lodge, noting its proximity to "a spectacle that produces a profound impression on the spirit."[104] The intertwined relationship between Cusco folklore and tourism reached a new climax on June 24, 1944, when Cusco held its first celebration of Inti Raymi—a folkloric presentation re-creating the Incan winter solstice ceremony—in coordination with the Semana del Cusco (Cusco Week). The idea to celebrate a week of civic pride dedicated to Cusco originated among indigenistas looking to commemorate the importance of their region on June 24, the national Day of the Indian. President Prado himself embraced the initiative and arrived in the city for the celebrations.[105] The staging of the civic week, the Inti Raymi enactment, and the presence of Prado all helped legitimize the indigenista folkloric project as an element of both regional and national identity.[106] The Inti Raymi ceremony was performed at the Sacsayhuamán

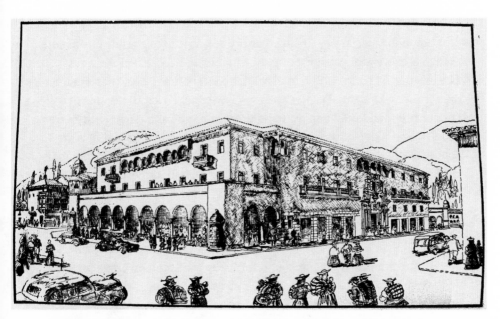

Hotel Cusco. The largest of Peru's new chain of state-owned hotels, the Hotel Cusco opened in 1944 to coincide with the folkloric celebration of Inti Raymi. For many it represented a new era in national investment in Cusco's tourism. Record Group 229, United States National Archives.

archeological complex overlooking Cusco's urban center in the presence of the president and "thousands" of observers, as reported by the local *El Sol* newspaper.[107] The ceremony evoked depictions of a utopian Incan past reinterpreted for the consumption of modern observers. Like many of the neo-indigenista cultural projects that preceded it, Inti Raymi heralded an imagined, glorious Inca past while simultaneously downplaying the political and racial divisions that marked the contemporary conditions of indigenous communities in Cusco.[108]

Inti Raymi and Cusco Week also shared previous indigenista obsessions with tourism development. As Cusco's Prefect Gutiérrez noted, the event would highlight "in the near future the development of not only internal, but international, tourism."[109] One of the most anticipated events during Prado's visit was the official opening of the new state-built Hotel Cusco. "This inauguration marks an important milestone in the work of the government towards the development of tourism," said Prado at the hotel's opening. The president praised the modern facilities of the hotel and predicted that "tourists will find in this hotel comforts that permit them to learn and study the most advanced culture of ancient America."[110] Lima's *La Crónica* applauded the new hotel, declaring, "In no other city besides Cuzco can one find a more reliable expression of what we can understand to be Peruvianness."[111] Cusqueños, of course, reveled in the national spotlight of the hotel inauguration and presidential visit. Cusco's *El Sol* reported that thousands of residents attended Prado's speech and greeted the head of state with "a true apotheosis of applause and enthusiasm." The assembled crowd became so enthusiastic that a large group of residents lifted Prado on their shoulders in "an improvised and popular civic act" and carried him back to the newly inaugurated hotel.[112]

The careful coordination between state policy and cultural tourism that debuted at the opening of the Hotel Cusco accelerated with the election of José Bustamante y Rivero as president in 1945. Bustamante's successful electoral platform called for populist reforms, expanded democratic inclusion of the previously banned APRA party, and a particular focus on state-led economic development to bring Peruvians out of poverty.[113] Much to the delight of travel interests and cusqueños, the new government promised increased state participation in tourism development. In November 1945, Bustamante formed a committee to organize a state tourism institution with the cooperation of the TACP leadership.[114] At the start of 1946, the national government budgeted three million soles for the promotion of tourism, an act applauded by *Turismo*.[115] In April 1946, the president submitted a proposal to Congress to create a government-administered tourism office. *Turismo* applauded the effort and called for quick approval in Congress for "the technical organization of tourism that promises to be one of the largest sources of wealth and grandeur."[116] On June 5, 1946, the Congress of Peru passed Law 10556, creating the Corporación Nacional del Turismo (National Tourism Corporation, CNT)—the nation's first state-supported institution tasked with developing a tourism industry.[117] The organization and institutional reach of the CNT reflected the wide range of coordination needed for tourism promotion in Peru. The legislation creating the CNT gave the new institution advisory duties to review projects with both the local Archeology Councils, Restoration Councils, and tourism-related projects created by the Ministry of Development. Additionally, the CNT assumed the administration of the state-owned hotels, the distribution of tourism propaganda, the opening of local tourist offices, and the management of a new tourism guide school.[118]

The first general director of the CNT was Benjamín Roca Muelle. Prior to his appointment, he served as finance minister in 1933–35 and 1937–38 under

Benavides. Roca Muelle also worked as general manager of the TACP between 1939 and 1941 as well as editor of *Turismo*. In both positions, Roca Muelle emerged as an enthusiastic advocate for greater government involvement in tourism investment, planning, and promotion. Giving an interview to *Turismo*, Roca Muelle discussed the great challenge facing him as he took the reins of the CNT. According to Roca Muelle, Peru's tourism development lagged behind that of most nations. Peru's highways and airports were deficient, the country had a dearth of quality hotels, national museums and archeological sites lacked coordination and funds, the country maintained arcane and cumbersome visa requirements, and tourism publicity abroad remained insufficient. Yet Roca Muelle remained optimistic. The fact that Peru had a centralized planning office for tourism with its own budget and staff marked significant progress. "In sum, tourism is an activity that spans an extraordinary field of action . . . It is a synthetic industry that, well used[,] can become a river of gold for Peru," observed the new director.[119]

In 1947 Roca Muelle and the CNT issued a dramatic call to highlight the importance that tourism would play in Peru's economic and social future. On June 7, Roca Muelle formally inaugurated Peru's first National Tourism Congress. President Bustamante attended the conference, providing a keynote lecture endorsing state-promoted tourism development.[120] *El Comercio de Lima* applauded the move, stating, "Tourism currently constitutes an activity that not only has industrial repercussions, but also efficiently contributes towards the better understanding between peoples since it permits individuals to become familiar with various aspects of a country."[121] Speaking on Radio Nacional, Minister of Development and chair of the conference Pedro Betin Mujíca noted that tourism growth promised gains for all Peruvians. "Tourists do not only come to visit our old cities and abundant archeological remains," asserted Betin Mujíca; "the tourist is a man accustomed to comfort and needs good hotels, efficient public services, and modern systems of transport . . . These services, logically, do not only benefit tourists, but all Peruvians."[122] *La Prensa* also agreed that the development of international tourism in Peru would result in better economic conditions for the nation. "One should understand," the newspaper noted in an editorial, "that the affluence of a considerable number of travelers would honor Peru abroad and would make it possible to achieve an exchange that would aid commercial and industrial development."[123] During the closing ceremony of the National Tourism Congress Roca Muelle announced an apparent new consensus regarding the importance of tourism for national development: "Do not forget it. The work of the CNT is the work of Peru."[124]

Although the CNT proposed to make tourism the "work of Peru," the organization's initial plans appeared to make the development more the work of Cusco. Reflecting the populist leanings of the Bustamante government, the CNT did enact reforms to bolster middle- and working-class tourism, including experiments in state-funded tourist packages.[125] Despite this, from the organization's start, CNT leadership reflected a preference for attracting international travel with a focus on Cusco. These measures departed from other efforts in Latin America where populist governments of the 1940s focused on serving their respective domestic tourism demands.[126] Reflecting the influence of Cusco's tourism backers, the CNT aggressively pushed to attract international travelers and stated in one of its first annual reports that "the conservation and restoration of historical and archeological monuments in the city of Cuzco, although outside the specific mission of the corporation, has deserved preferential attention."[127] In 1946 the CNT reported that it had even organized its own team to prepare a scholarly report for Cusco's local archeology council highlighting preservation priorities for sites in the region.[128] The policies that emerged from the first National Tourism Congress, held in 1947, only accelerated the CNT's focus on tourism. *El Comercio del Cusco*, reporting on the events of the conference, endorsed the importance of the work of the CNT and its 1947 meeting in a May 21 editorial. "The referenced congress presents the possibilities to obtain the spoils that Cusco deserves due to its singular touristic importance," argued the paper's editors.[129] *El Comercio de Cusco*'s interest in the conference proved deserved. Of the nineteen official recommendations agreed upon during the 1947 conference, five suggested a specific developmental focus on archeological zones, with an additional five mentioning the importance of developing tourism in Cusco. Specifically, the recommendations included the development of an urban plan for Cusco, declaring the city a national monument, as well as establishing a new regional archeological museum, an extensive restoration of local historic sites, and improved investment in folkloric studies.[130]

The new positions taken by the CNT proved especially helpful to ongoing local efforts to restore Cusco's archeological and historic sites. In May 1947, the CNT donated 100,000 soles toward restoration work dedicated to Cusco's Plaza de Armas as well as its churches and colonial paintings. That same year, the CNT funded a greatly expanded Inti Raymi festival.[131] Roca Muelle justified the CNT's expenses in Cusco, noting, "It is deserved considering the act from a touristic perspective."[132] The following year, the CNT joined the National Archeology Council to compose a report on restoration priorities for Cusco's archeological sites. *La Crónica* praised the efforts, noting, "This landscape of summits and ruins that dwell amongst the fair cusqueñas should painstakingly defend themselves for the nation and for tourism."[133] Machu Picchu emerged as one of the major beneficiaries of the funds from the CNT. A preservation team began work at the site in May 1948.[134] By that time the development goals of tourism had gained the support of all sectors of Cusco's society. Even the local Communist Party newspaper, *La Jornada*, called for increased state support for Cusco Week and Inti Raymi so that "we may concentrate in Cusco, and eventually everywhere in Peru, tourism visits from around the world."[135]

The "Discoverer of Machu Picchu" Returns

The CNT project at Machu Picchu accompanied a major promotional coup for Cusco. At the start of 1948, Cusco was selected as the site of the second Inter-American Indigenista Congress, which would gather political and cultural leaders from around the hemisphere to debate indigenous concerns. Regional and national officials expressed their pleasure that the conference was planned to coincide with Inti Raymi and Cusco Week on June 24, 1948. Promoters of the congress promised that the event would reaffirm Cusco as the archeological, folkloric, and touristic capital of South America.[136] Roca Muelle's CNT seized the opportunity for the proposed 1948 Indigenista Congress to accelerate tourism investment in Cusco. The CNT successfully secured funding for a new access road to Machu Picchu in preparation for the congress.[137] By the end of May 1948, as 140 workers labored to complete the road, the CNT proposed increasing the size of the tourist hotel at Machu Picchu as well as improving several roads that traveled through the Sacred Valley.[138] However, for the CNT and other tourism interests, the inauguration of the new highway provided an opportunity to promote Machu Picchu far beyond the audience of visiting indigenistas.

Roca Muelle and Giesecke viewed the opening of the highway as an optimal moment to seize the growing global interest in Machu Picchu. To do so, they turned to Hiram Bingham and, in the process, reinvented the explorer and his narrative. Giesecke and Roca Muelle initially proposed placing a plaque or pedestal to honor Bingham as part of the highway project. By March 1948, the CNT and Giesecke had persuaded the government to name the new access road to Machu Picchu in honor of Bingham and invite the explorer for the inauguration of the highway.[139] When Bingham departed Peru in 1915 accused of theft and malfeasance, the explorer and his hosts held few amicable feelings toward one another. Local distrust of Bingham proved warranted considering the fact that he had illegally exported artifacts from Peru over the course of his three exhibitions.[140] Besides his questionable activities, Bingham's earlier unapologetic support for U.S. power had framed his first publications through a distinct imperial gaze that now appeared opposed to the Good Neighbor discourse embraced in tourism promotion.[141]

However, it appeared that the passage of time as well as the promise of Pan-American interest in Machu Picchu had eroded the animosity between the two sides. As early as 1941, Bingham had contacted Giesecke expressing a desire to return to Peru.[142] Reaching out through mutual acquaintances, Giesecke contacted Bingham in May 1948 to inquire if the explorer was still interested in returning to Machu Picchu.[143] When Bingham confirmed that he could attend the inauguration of the new road, the CNT office in New York translated his speeches into Spanish prior to his departure.[144] To capitalize on the media attention surrounding Bingham's visit, *Turismo* magazine published a special English-language article for North American readers describing Cusco, "the millenary capital of the Inca Empire," as "the Peruvian city of major attraction to tourists."[145] Bingham's visit promised to be the dawn of a new era for both the CNT and Machu Picchu.

In addition to the transportation logistics, promoters of the Bingham visit faced an additional challenge; they had to rewrite the narrative of the "discovery" of Machu Picchu to reflect the Pan-American goodwill the visit sought to promote. Lauding Bingham as the discoverer of Machu Picchu obscured the narrative of actual events that took place three decades earlier and validated the erroneous scientific conclusions of Bingham himself. Initially, both Bingham and his hosts appeared happy to overlook the acrimonious end of his expeditions. When Bingham arrived in Lima accompanied by his second wife, Suzanne, on October 6, 1948, Giesecke reported that he "was received with real affection by the people."[146] Bingham returned the welcome with his own friendly thanks to Peru. Providing an interview with *El Comercio de Lima* upon arriving at the U.S. embassy, Bingham thanked his hosts and stated that he was looking forward to returning to Cusco after thirty-two years, concluding, "There is nothing comparable to Machu-Picchu."[147] Even Cusco's archeological scholars who had advocated for Bingham's prosecution in 1915 referred to him as a "romantic North American archeologist, enchanted by the past," in their 1948 academic bulletin.[148] It appeared that time, Pan-American sentiment, and the promise of tourism had erased former mistrust between Bingham and Peru.[149]

In Cusco, Bingham enjoyed both academic and civic support. He gave a lecture on the history of Machu Picchu at UNSAAC on October 14, 1948. In his lecture, Bingham reasserted his original theories regarding Machu Picchu. He argued that the city was both Tampu Tocco, the legendary origin of the Inca, and Vilcabamba, the last stronghold against the Spanish. Although both facts were seriously doubted by archeologists in Peru and the United States, no one offered public criticism of Bingham's theories.[150] Few moments emerged during the visit that countered the narrative praising Bingham as the "discoverer" of Machu Picchu. Surprisingly, Bingham himself was one of the few who acknowledged the help of cusqueños during his first encounter with Machu Picchu. Interviewed by *El Comercio de Lima*, Bingham acknowledged that Melchor Arteaga informed him of the ruin that lay atop his settlement.[151] An editorial published on October 17 in *El Comercio de Lima* also reminded readers that Bingham "was accompanied by two Peruvians, the guide Arteaga and a Sergeant of the National Army with the surname Carrasco."[152] In an interview with *Turismo* Bingham even acknowledged that the Richarte family was living at Machu Picchu and described how their young son guided him around the ruin during his first visit.[153]

The highway inauguration took placed on Sunday, October 17, 1948, and commenced with speeches delivered at the base of the mountain by José Cosío, Bingham, and Giesecke.[154] Cusco Department Prefect Tamayo then asked for Suzanne Bingham to lift the veil to reveal a plaque celebrating Bingham as the "discoverer of Machu Picchu." Suzanne broke a bottle of Champagne against the rocks near the plaque, and Hiram, reported as appearing "emotional," gave a short speech in Spanish thanking all those in attendance. *El Comercio de Cusco* reported on Bingham's presence in heroic terms. "The sunlight bore on him and revealed his white hair and handsome head," noted the local newspaper. *El Comercio del Cusco* recounted Bingham's speech, noting, "Bingham remembered his first ascension through these mountains, in the middle of a dense jungle, carried by the faith of a man of science; his emotion upon discovering the grandiose and full of majesty ruins."[155] Leaving Cusco denounced as a thief in 1915, Bingham had returned in 1948 as a benevolent Pan-American discoverer of Machu Picchu.

When the party ascended the highway to arrive at the entrance to the ruins, Hiram traveled by car and Suzanne by mule. *La Crónica* noted the significance of the two journeys: "He was the first passenger to travel the new highway by automobile and his spouse the last person to ascend the hill by the old path." At the entrance of the site, Suzanne inaugurated another plaque placed by the Rotary Club in honor of Hiram. After the ceremonies, the entire party, including U.S. Ambassador Harold H. Tittman, lunched in the tourist lodge as guests of the Rotary Club. *La Crónica* noted that, for the first time, guests who had had breakfast in Lima now could enjoy lunch at Machu Picchu.[156] *El Comercio de Lima* observed how "the stone city of Machu-picchu has suffered the first impact of civilization, but we speak of an impact that will not do damage, because [the ruin] finds itself destined to fulfill its archeological importance and its admirable beauty."[157] Bingham himself commended the work of the CNT and endorsed state promotion of tourism development in Cusco.[158] The CNT was equally grateful, as news of Bingham's visit gained the interest of U.S. publications, thus fulfilling a key goal of the visit.[159]

The 1948 return not only opened access to Machu Picchu but also rehabilitated Bingham's professional career and image. For this achievement, Bingham had to thank Peruvians, Good Neighbor diplomats, and tourism backers who, in the interest of promoting Machu Picchu, had rewritten the historical narrative. Bingham wrote to Giesecke following his 1948 visit: "Your thoughtfulness and your many kindnesses, so numerous that I cannot begin to enumerate them, have placed me under a heavy burden of obligations that will be very difficult to meet! I cannot remember a time when I owed so much in the way of honor, hospitality, and efficient help to one man!"[160] His 1948 trip inspired Bingham to revisit his exploits at Machu Picchu. Published in 1948, *Lost City of the Incas: The Story of Machu Picchu and Its Builders* would be Bingham's final publication.[161] Unlike Bingham's earlier publications that cast an imperial gaze on the Andes and its resources, his final book emphasized the Pan-American narratives crafted for his return to Cusco. Bingham informed readers of Machu Picchu's appeal as a tourist site, and also acknowledged help from cusqueños. He even thanked young Pablito Richarte for guiding him on his first visit to Machu Picchu.[162] Bingham's book drew mixed critical responses. The *New York Times* noted that "just as he himself had to clear away the tropical hardwood forest which had obliterated much of Machu Picchu, the reader has to hack through the underbrush of his awkward narrative and torturous exposition."[163] In another review, the archeologist Victor Von Hagen also pointed out that Bingham's theories regarding Machu Picchu were probably incorrect. However, Von Hagen still credited Bingham with drawing much-needed public interest to archeology and the Inca and kindly concluded that "the fabulous city of Machu Picchu, as revealed here, will forever stand as Dr. Hiram Bingham's archeological monument."[164]

Conclusion: Cracks in the Monument

Machu Picchu's emergence as "Bingham's archeological monument" by the late 1940s owed less to the activities of the explorer than to the shared interests of regional leaders, tourism promoters, and U.S. diplomats. Although each group had different motivations, all saw their goals fulfilled in the promotion of Machu Picchu and Bingham as symbols of an idealized past and the promise of an amicable Pan-American future. More importantly, these efforts elevated Machu Picchu and Cusco's regional folklore as national representations of Peru. The transnational networks of regional and hemispheric actors that aligned to promote tourism at Machu Picchu had defined Peru's national identity as a reflection of Cusco's regional history and culture. Thus, tourism had not only transcended but also redefined the relationship between regional and national identity in Latin America. In contrast to the experiences of many European countries that feared that postwar tourist visits would threaten their national identity, many in Peru viewed tourism as a key tool in reinforcing a new sense of Andean focused nationalism.[165]

Of course, the transformation of Machu Picchu into both a tourist destination and a national symbol created conflict as well as consensus. At times the promised Pan-American partnership of tourism failed to materialize. One U.S. embassy memo on tourists' activities from February 1, 1943, reported that "certain Peruvians of strong North American affiliation find it very hard to justify the virtues of the people of the United States . . . the spectacle of quantities of gringos huddled around the cocktail shaker like sheep, trying to find some sort of spiritual warmth, appears to them at variance with the American credo."[166] More importantly, the tourism-driven narrative crafted to publicize Machu Picchu overlooked the grassroots political and cultural demands of Cusco's indigenous communities that indigenistas had either altered or obscured. The same interests also silenced local connections to Machu Picchu while heralding Bingham and disseminating his erroneous claims about the site and his expeditions.

However, these efforts did not completely silence alternative narratives that used Machu Picchu as a potent symbol. Machu Picchu has always served as a symbol of alternate visions of the Andes and indigenous identities.[167] Pablo Neruda visited Machu Picchu in 1943 at the height of the site's Good

Neighbor reinvention.[168] Returning to Chile, Neruda reflected on his experience in the poem "Heights of Machu Picchu" to draw inspiration from the monument in a call for class unity of Latin America's oppressed. One stanza of the poem reads:

> Look at me from the depths of the earth,
> tiller of fields, weaver, reticent shepherd,
> groom of totemic guanacos,
> mason high on your treacherous scaffolding,
> iceman of Andean tears,
> jeweler with crushed fingers,
> farmer anxious among his seedlings,
> potter wasted among his clays—
> bring to the cup of this new life
> your ancient buried sorrows.[169]

Ernesto "Che" Guevara also drew a similar inspiration from Machu Picchu during two visits to the site, in 1952 and 1953. In his recollections, Guevara expressed his shock at the conditions of Peru's indigenous population and predicted that a violent revolution would take place.[170] However, Guevara did not fail to notice how "North American tourists, bound down by their practical world view, are able to place those members of the disintegrating tribes they may have seen in their travels among these once living walls, unaware of the moral distance separating them."[171] Neruda and Guevara drew revolutionary inspiration from Machu Picchu largely unaware of the fact that the site's narrative of a heroic indigenous past was developed to serve the interests of actors they largely opposed.[172] Still, their alternative narratives illustrate that even if tourism promotors had succeeded in exploiting Machu Picchu for their political and economic aims, they were unable to strictly control the narrative of its symbolism.

If Neruda and Guevara offered somewhat idealized views of Peru's indigenous culture due to their interactions at a Machu Picchu designed for foreign tourists, their suspicions of the United States proved accurate. Even at the height of Good Neighbor discourse, the United States remained wary of populism. When Neruda visited Machu Picchu in 1943, his activities were covered by a confidential informant who reported to the U.S. embassy in Lima. The informant reported to the embassy that Neruda was "especially critical of the work of the Coordinator's office," and expressed his concerns over the "Yankee profession of democracy and practice of Fascism."[173] Neruda's concerns would prove prescient. On October 3, 1948, a naval revolt planned in coordination with APRA militants erupted in Callao. Although Bustamante's government survived the uprising, the Indigenista Conference was delayed. Giesecke, Cusco officials, and Roca Muelle barely managed to avoid the cancellation of Bingham's visit. Shortly after the warm reception for Bingham, Bustamante's government fell to a military coup led by General Manuel Odría. The new Odría regime was backed by Peru's economic elite, who aimed to return Peru to an orthodox liberal economy and withdraw from the state-led development initiatives (like the CNT) endorsed by Bustamante. The Odría regime, quickly recognized by the United States, wasted little time in scaling back the work of the CNT as well as the indigenista and Cusco-backed cultural initiatives promoted by the Bustamante government.[174]

Rapidly, the successful transnational connections forged to promote tourism and cultural policy in Cusco became a liability. After the fall of Bustamante, the national state had little initiative to pursue development and cultural strategies that had largely bypassed it in favor of transnational institutions and links. By 1948 the United States had transitioned from the Good Neighbor era to an aggressive Cold War focus that viewed the nationalist and populist projects of Bustamante's government suspiciously. The Eisenhower administration, endorsing a mantra of "trade, not aid," withdrew political and economic support for state-driven tourism development in favor of private investment in developing markets.[175] Serious cracks had developed in the political, cultural, and economic foundations of tourism in Cusco and Machu Picchu. As Cusco entered the decade of the 1950s, it would once again have to rely on new transnational links to bolster Machu Picchu and the region's fledgling tourism economy.

CHAPTER THREE

Disaster Destinations, 1948–1960

On the afternoon of May 21, 1950, a major earthquake struck Cusco. The ground shook for only six or seven seconds, but the unusual strength of the earthquake inflicted tremendous damage on the city. The earthquake killed 67 people and severely injured 250.[1] Subsequent reports found that the tremor destroyed 3,000 homes in the city and displaced between 30,000 and 40,000 residents.[2] Damage to the city's cultural heritage also proved to be extensive. "Due to the blind forces of nature, Cuzco in one moment had lost its entire splendor. The Rome of the Americas was left in ruin and desolation," concluded one report of the damage.[3] The earthquake was the final, and most grave, of a series of crises that placed the development of tourism in Cusco in serious doubt by the start of the 1950s. Only ten days after Bingham opened the road to Machu Picchu in 1948, a military coup led by General Manuel Odría overthrew the government of President José Bustamante y Rivero. The new government eliminated most of the state-sponsored tourism development programs that had proved critical to Machu Picchu's rise. Additionally, the lack of a consistent preservation policy at Machu Picchu had allowed time and climate to wear down its structures to the point where some feared the ruin would disappear entirely. Many feared that the earthquake would strike a fatal blow against Cusco's nascent tourism industry. However, by the start of the 1960s, the promise of tourism development in Cusco appeared stronger than ever before. How did tourism in Cusco survive a disaster to achieve development with little support from the national state?

In the case of Cusco, the earthquake proved both a tragedy and an opportunity for the region's leaders. As we will see, Cusco residents and regional leaders skillfully channeled the financial and technical assistance made available through earthquake disaster recovery programs to spur local development—an example of what the historian Mark Carey has termed "disaster economics."[4] In particular, Cusco's leaders proved adept at employing the disaster economics of its earthquake recovery to sustain tourism during a time when the national state demonstrated little interest in its development. The changes that took place in Cusco following the 1950 earthquake reflect other moments from Latin American history when natural disasters created the conditions for social and political change.[5] What made

Cusco's case unique was the influence of tourism and transnational actors on the development of the region. Cusqueños once again built alliances with nonstate and transnational actors. These links included the national and international media, new transnational development and cultural organizations, and personal and political connections in Lima and abroad. Cusqueños would use nonstate actors to compensate for a lack of government support for tourism and cultural preservation or, whenever possible, use these networks to lobby the national state for resources to accomplish these aims. With surprising success, these transnational links permitted Cusco to shift from a destination of disaster into one of development.

The response to the crises affecting Cusco in the early 1950s not only highlighted the continued importance of transnational links in the development of tourism but also illustrated larger changes occurring in Peru. The consensus that Cusco and Machu Picchu needed to be saved from destruction highlighted their emergence as national symbols in Peru. Yet, debates on how to preserve and manage these cultural sites revealed continued tensions between Cusco and the national state. The earthquake response also highlighted how Cusco's regional leaders attempted to assert their influence in an era when political and economic power gravitated increasingly toward Lima. While the disaster economics of the earthquake recovery provided Cusco's leaders with an opportunity to undertake needed top-down reforms of their region's economy, this same modernization threatened to upend the social and political structures on which local elites relied for power. As a result, Cusco's leaders increasingly viewed tourism as a convenient solution that allowed them to undertake a limited modernization of their region that continued to emphasize a nostalgic vision of the past.

Political Shifts for Cusco Tourism

When Bustamante's government fell victim to Odría's military coup on October 29, 1948, it took with it one of the strongest supporters of tourism development in Cusco and Machu Picchu. The new military government forced Benjamín Roca Muelle to leave his post as the president of the CNT. Since the 1930s, Roca Muelle had used his various positions at the TACP, *Turismo* magazine, and the CNT to lobby for increased state participation in tourism development. By 1949 Ernesto Cánepa Sardón had replaced Roca Muelle as general director of the CNT.[6] After several expensive but marginally successful events, Odría appointed a special review commission of the CNT, which concluded its findings in March 1950. The predictable result was the termination of Peru's first attempt at using the resources of the state to encourage tourism development.[7] At a time when national states were undertaking a central role in planning and promoting tourism development in popular Latin American destinations like Cuba and Mexico, the Peruvian government began to draw back its investments in the tourist economy.[8]

The state's retreat from tourism development reflected larger shifts in the Peruvian political and economic landscapes. Although it achieved electoral success in 1945 by pledging populist and democratic policies, the Bustamante government depended on the support of an uneasy coalition between APRA and a diverse set of reformist parties. Political infighting quickly hamstrung most of the government's most ambitions reforms. As economic conditions worsened and inflation increased, many Peruvians viewed the experiment with state-led development under Bustamante as a failure. The United States also shifted its support away from populist political and economic projects in Latin America by the late 1940s. The CNT proved to be one of many state-sponsored industries that withered under the Odría regime's return to orthodox economic liberalism in the 1950s.[9] Echoing the policy of the new government, even *Turismo* was forced to conclude in its January–February 1951 editorial that "creating a costly and difficult-to-publicly fund entity with sights set on an eventual tourism increase was an adventure."[10] Other periodicals, such as *La Prensa*, argued that the CNT did not fail due to the flaws of state-led development, but instead from a lack of adequate government support and efficient administration.[11]

Although the causes of the CNT's demise were up for debate, Cusco's regional leaders understood that the resignation of Roca Muelle meant that they had lost a valuable ally in the national government. Roca Muelle believed that Cusco and Machu Picchu offered the most promising attractions for international tourists and used the power of his office at the CNT to direct a large amount of resources to the region. During its short existence, the CNT had overseen the construction Cusco's newest hotel, funded Machu Picchu's 1948 restoration, and planned Bingham's visit to the region.[12] This attention evaporated quickly after the departure of Roca Muelle and the demise of the CNT. Once full of articles lauding Cusco, after 1949 *Turismo* mainly focused on accomplishments of the new Odría regime or Lima society.[13] Eventually, responsibility for the promotion of tourism in Peru reverted to the private TACP, headquartered in Lima, and its local Cusco office. Although the TACP did continue to promote tourism in Cusco, it lacked the coordination and funding to fill the gap left by the dissolution of the CNT.[14]

The state's withdrawal from tourism represented larger policy shifts that disadvantaged Cusco. Economic policy under Odría was dominated by traditional elite families based on the Pacific coast who backed economic liberalism and free trade. While exports increased and foreign investment in Peru expanded, the economic and social inequality between the Andes and the coastal regions widened. Isolated from the lucrative export-oriented economic enclaves and with little support from the state, Cusco's regional elites proved largely unable or unwilling to invest in modernizing their haciendas. By the early 1950s Cusco's economy appeared to have entered a cycle of terminal decline. The region's stagnant economy could not absorb a growing population. As a result, nearly 800,000 people abandoned the regions of southern Peru that included Cusco between 1940 and 1961. Even as displaced cusqueños streamed into Lima's rapidly growing shantytowns in search of opportunities, the Odría government, loath to undertake measures such as agrarian reform or state-led economic development, took little action to address the crisis in Cusco and other Andean regions.[15]

In the wake of the CNT's termination, those working to draw attention to Machu Picchu returned to the strategies employed in the first decades of tourism promotion—efforts led largely through individual volunteers with international connections. The U.S.-born former rector of UNSAAC, Albert Giesecke, had led earlier efforts to promote Cusco and Machu Picchu as tourism destinations. Giesecke appeared happy to again volunteer to take a leading role in encouraging tourism development in Cusco in the 1950s. Speaking to Cusco's congressional delegation and the board of directors of the Club Cusco on March 18, 1954, Giesecke remarked on his activities to encourage tourism. "Even now, I continue daily providing facts and directions to visitors that want to visit Cuzco and Machu Picchu," he said. "[The region's] amazing monuments that are Cusco's pride should be preserved with veneration and admiration," counseled Giesecke, who concluded that it was a duty to "conserve and make them easily accessible to all who want to visit them."[16]

Giesecke's comments regarding his aid to travelers were not hyperbole. One U.S. traveler wrote to Giesecke in 1958 that "apparently all road[s] lead to Rome except in Peru where all Inca roads lead to you."[17] Using his contacts at the U.S. embassy in Lima, Giesecke often provided key travel information about Machu Picchu to airline companies and tourists. So notable were Giesecke's tourism contacts in Lima and Cusco that U.S. ambassadors across South America regularly referred any travel inquiries about Machu

Picchu to him.[18] Giesecke used his connections to coordinate a steady stream of visits from (primarily) North American politicians and celebrities. For example, Giesecke accompanied Joan Fontaine on her visit to Machu Picchu in 1951. Fontaine's visit to the ruin departed from the norm when she met and adopted a local girl named Martita Pareja whom she met at the Aguas Calientes train station. Giesecke even helped arrange the adoption and coordinate return visits that, as he had hoped, generated additional press for Machu Picchu.[19]

To compensate for the dissolution of the CNT, Giesecke also worked to publicize Machu Picchu in the national and international media. Similar to the strategies he employed in the 1930s and 1940s, Giesecke hoped to use any Pan-American sentiments and links that remained from the Good Neighbor era to maintain public awareness of Cusco and Machu Picchu in the United States. In 1951 Giesecke proposed the formation of a Machu Picchu Club to create an international group to coordinate preservation and publicity efforts for the site. He suggested that the influential North American journalist Julius Klien serve as the club's new president, with Bingham and *National Geographic* editor Gilbert Grosvenor serving as honorary chairs. Giesecke went so far as to propose that Fontaine's adopted daughter, Martita, serve as a "young officer" in the planned Los Angeles chapter of the club.[20] Giesecke worked to organize the booster club for Machu Picchu for several years. Many other prominent cusqueños, including José Gabriel Cosío, shared interest in the project. However, efforts to establish the Machu Picchu Club met a serious obstacle when Bingham declined to participate in the effort. Responding to Giesecke's request in 1955, Bingham, who would die a year later, replied that he was "too old and feeble to do much of anything," essentially stopping the formation of the proposed club.[21] Giesecke found more success in publicizing Machu Picchu in the media in 1952 when he produced a series of national radio programs, titled *The Mystery of Machu Picchu*, which earned praise from the TACP.[22]

Perhaps Giesecke's most substantial achievement in popularizing tourism development at Machu Picchu occurred in 1953 when he served as technical adviser to the filming of Paramount Studio's *The Secret of the Incas*. For a long time, numerous Peruvian business interests had hoped to attract major Hollywood studios to film in Peru. "North Americans and Europeans are going to visit Aztec ruins because they are familiar with Mexican cinema," observed *El Comercio de Lima* in 1950; "meanwhile Peru's Incaic civilization exists only in articles and books, advertising for people of high culture and limited numbers."[23] Upon learning of Paramount's desire to film a feature movie in the area, Cusco's *El Sol* newspaper proudly predicted that "this will save Peruvians—and particularly cusqueños—from the series of disinformation, disgraceful allusions, and bad jokes that we have seen in some pictures filmed abroad depicting Peru."[24] Produced by Mel Epstein, *The Secret of the Incas* was the first major Hollywood picture filmed in Peru. The plot of *The Secret of the Incas* reflected a typical Hollywood adventure film of the era. Charlton Heston starred as a treasure hunter named Harry Steele who arrives at Machu Picchu in search of a valuable Inca artifact, but not before meeting a beautiful European woman on the run and thwarting a rival treasure hunter. The famous Peruvian singer Yma Sumac also played a supporting role in the film.[25]

The film was far from perfect; the plot reflected the same touristic narrative created to promote Bingham by placing a North American protagonist at the center of a Peruvian archeological discovery. However, with Giesecke serving as technical adviser, *The Secret of the Incas* certainly took advantage of its on-location shooting to convey accurate and stunning images of Cusco and Machu Picchu. The film captured the local character of Cusco, right down to the pisco sour cocktails being sipped at the hotel bar. Over 400 locals participated as extras at the shoot at Machu Picchu, arriving dressed in traditional cusqueño style and often bringing their own llamas to the set to create an impressive atmosphere.[26] Many of the film's style and plot elements would later serve as a direct inspiration for Indiana Jones.[27] Reviewing *The Secret of the Incas*, the *New York Times* declared "the Peruvian highlands to be a natural for Technicolor and wide screen."[28] Another review praised its "authentic and truly colorful locales."[29] The film also was well received in Peru. César Miro, one of Peru's most famous writers, praised the film by stating, "*The Secret of the Inca* [sic] achieves the resurrection of Machu-Picchu and its fabulous scenery animates the forgotten city with new life."[30] In a 1955 letter to producer Epstein, Giesecke happily commented that the film "had turned out to be quite superior to what I anticipated."[31] Giesecke expressed happiness to his colleagues that, thanks to the film, Faucett Airlines had to schedule "five planes per week between Cuzco and Lima, and the seats have to be reserved weeks in advance."[32]

It is important to note that Giesecke was not a one-man tourism promotion machine. His efforts were matched and often exceeded by the Lima-based TACP and its local office in Cusco. Américo Luna, the owner of Inca Land Tours and the president of the TACP of Cusco, lobbied for better transportation funding from the central state.[33] The Cusco TACP office also published promotional guides, offered courses to certify tour guides, and held annual forums with local political leaders to promote tourism.[34] The national TACP also continued to lobby for better tourism coordination in Peru. In 1954 the TACP invited Laurence Tombs, the president of the American Association of Travel Agents, to Peru as part of a lobbying and fact-finding mission. As a guest of the club, Tombs announced to his hosts, "Peru is not one of the tourist destination countries in South America, it *is* the tourist destination country of South America."[35] However, in the 1950s the TACP and other tourism backers in Cusco would need more than kind words to overcome obstacles to development—especially in the wake of the destructive 1950 earthquake.

Seismic Shifts for Cusco Tourism

Although Cusco's fate appeared grim in the days after the disaster, regional leaders began to search for possibilities on how to use to the earthquake as a key opportunity for development and economic modernization. In the words of the historian José Tamayo, the 1950 earthquake, "closed the curtain on one era, and opened the road towards a different type of modernization."[36] Initially promising modernization based on industrialization and agricultural reform, regional leaders and tourism promoters worked to ensure that tourist development would also benefit through disaster recovery.

Odría took a keen interest in leading recovery efforts in the region. Although his government's policies largely spurned economic interventionism, Odría also understood the need to adopt certain populist actions to legitimize his rule.[37] Odría arrived in Cusco to assess the earthquake damage on May 23, 1950, and immediately declared his dedication to the city's reconstruction.[38] With the aid of Cusco's congressional delegation, Odría signed Law 11551 on December 31, 1950. The law created a new national 20 percent tax on tobacco to fund the earthquake recovery in Cusco.[39] Odría's quick response also illustrated the success of the previous decades of work by regional indigenistas in promoting Cusco as the folkloric heart of Peru. The Peruvian national press considered the reconstruction of Cusco a national duty. "We will reconstruct the archeological capital of America," promised *El Comercio de Lima* only three days after the earthquake.[40] *La Prensa*, based in Lima, granted an interview with the prominent cusqueño indigenista Luis E. Valcárcel, who stated that Cusco was the "base of cultural originality of America."[41] Emotional attachment to the cultural heritage of Cusco extended beyond Peru. Immediately after the earthquake, the government of Spain pledged funds to restore the city's cathedral.[42]

Most of the city's Inca structures withstood seismic activity and did not require extensive repairs—a fact that quickly emerged as a point of regional pride following the earthquake.[43] However, large swaths of the city center were heavily damaged. Additionally, the early phase of the earthquake recovery proved to be unorganized and unproductive. Engineers and locals conflicted over the locations of new roads, demolition of homes, and the schedule of repairs to critical infrastructure. Archeologists and preservationists led by Valcárcel objected that the recovery's early emphasis on clearing rubble and demolishing unstable buildings had inflicted damage on sensitive historical structures and neighborhoods in Cusco.[44] Some even proposed demolishing the old city center and replacing it with modernist style buildings. Others proposed reconstructing Cusco in a neocolonial style inspired by historical architecture, but made with modern materials and on a larger scale.[45] Valcárcel responded to such proposals by stating, "It's preferable that Cuzco remains destroyed than falsified," and organized a consensus on both the local and national levels that supported a restoration of Cusco that preserved the city's existing historic structures.[46] Valcárcel worked as the head of the first commission to oversee the restoration of the city, but found his task frustrated by a lack of funds and coordination.[47] However, Valcárcel, who had worked since the 1920s to popularize cusqueño folklore, pressed on. During his career as an anthropologist, archeologist, and journalist, he had established valuable contacts with other scholars in North America and Europe. Valcárcel, already comfortable working with transnational institutions, looked to international and nonstate actors to aid in the reconstruction of Cusco.[48] By the end of May 1950, Valcárcel had begun negotiating the possibility of the United Nations and UNESCO lending financial and technical support to the Cusco reconstruction.[49]

The United Nations mission, headed by Robert W. Hudgens, began working in Peru in February 1951. Hudgens boasted a long career specializing in rural development and centralized planning that dated back to 1934, when he coordinated New Deal era policies to promote growth in the U.S. South. Since 1948 Hudgens had worked as the executive director of former OIAA director Nelson Rockefeller's American International Association for Economic and Social Development. After months of research, Hudgens advised the Peruvian government that Cusco needed a centralized state authority to oversee the earthquake recovery. This was not the only example of the Peruvian state mirroring a global push for technocratic modernization. At the same time, in Peru's central highland region of Ancash, Cornell University inaugurated a project at the Vicos Hacienda to test new agricultural and community management practices, and the government-owned Santa Corporation inaugurated new development and hydroelectricity projects.[50] Following Hudgens's advice, the Odría government issued Supreme Decree 10 on January 10, 1952, creating the Junta de Reconstrucción y Fomento Industrial del Cuzco (Reconstruction and Industrial Development Board of Cuzco, or the Junta).[51] Initially, the Peruvian state and the United Nations missions envisioned the Junta as a state-owned corporation similar to the Tennessee Valley Authority. Although the Junta did provide funds for the restoration of historical structures in Cusco's city center, the original objectives of the institution focused on industrial development and agricultural modernization.[52]

However, in the months after the earthquake, a consensus began to form that the bureaucracy of the Junta could also help fill the gap left by the dissolution of the CNT in the promotion of tourism in Cusco. Only a few days after the earthquake struck Cusco, ex-CNT head Roca Muelle wrote a letter to his colleague and fellow travel promoter Giesecke regarding the possibilities of using the disaster economics of Cusco's earthquake recovery to support tourism development in the region. Referencing the earthquake recovery, Roca Muelle wrote that "God wants that this should be the cause to complete our dreams of making Cuzco a neatly protected treasure."[53] Early forums on the nature of the earthquake reconstruction organized by Valcárcel also emphasized the need to consider "tourism interests" in the reconstruction process.[54] Preliminary reports sent to the Junta emphasized the need for "the Junta to have great interest in the promotion of tourism and consider it part of its program."[55] However, the initial goals of the Junta still remained dedicated primarily to rural and industrial development.

Soon, locals and their political allies began to lobby for more post-earthquake investment in historical preservation and promotion of tourism. Valcárcel used his contacts with UNESCO to arrange for another United Nations–funded mission to aid Cusco's earthquake recovery. However, the second mission would focus primarily on restoration and preservation of historical sites. At the time of the earthquake, the leadership of UNESCO would prove to be especially keen on promoting American culture on an international scale. From 1948 to 1952 UNESCO was led by the Mexican diplomat Jaime Torres Bodet. Like Valcárcel, Torres Bodet was a prominent indigenista writer and scholar. During his leadership of UNESCO Torres Bodet sought to reassert global awareness of Latin American artistic achievement. When presented with Valcárcel's request for UNESCO to become involved in the protection of Cusco's cultural heritage, Torres Bodet did not hesitate to organize an investigation team chaired by the U.S. art historian of Latin America George A. Kubler.[56] The UNESCO Cusco Mission, often referred to as the Kubler Mission, surveyed the city in July and August 1951 and began to advise the Hudgens team on preservation needs during the earthquake recovery.[57] In 1952 the Junta created a restoration division that employed roughly one hundred laborers and artisans to begin restoration work in the city. Early preservation work focused on the historic churches in the center of Cusco and their collections of paintings, artifacts, and sculptures. The Junta's workers also completed restoration work on Inca walls, which were less damaged.[58]

Local support for the Junta's efforts to preserve Cusco's Inca and colonial structures revealed shifting attitudes toward how the region would employ tourism as an economic and cultural tool. In earlier decades, travel promotion strove to highlight Cusco's modernity. Now, tourism interests mirrored efforts in locations like Nantucket, Massachusetts, Santa Fe, New Mexico, and San Miguel de Allende, Mexico. Like Cusco, these cities had undergone periods of slow economic decline. However, their lack of modernization eventually permitted travel promoters to refashion these towns as timeless or nostalgic representations of a specific region. In order to accomplish this, these cities focused increasingly on historical preservation.[59] Cusco's regional leaders once used tourism as a tool to emphasize their region's process of modernization. However, as Cusco also became increasingly economically marginalized in Peru and the need for reform threatened traditional elites, regional leaders embraced a tourism that emphasized the region's nostalgic ties to the past.

The shift towards prioritizing preservation and tourism development can be seen in renewed calls to enact urban planning in Cusco. The Kubler Mission drew upon the earlier proposals outlined in Emilio Harth-Terré's urban plan drafted in preparation for the city's Quadricentennial celebrations in 1934.[60] Using the findings of the Kubler Mission, the Junta published an urban pilot plan for Cusco in February 1952. Like the Harth-Terré plan, the UNESCO-sponsored mission believed that the key to maintaining central Cusco's historic character while promoting tourism development lay in strict zoning of the city. The 1952 pilot plan proposed segmenting the city into several zones, each with its own purpose and character. The pilot plan designated Zone A the "historical archeological zone" and prohibited any form of new construction in the Incaic and colonial center of Cusco. Zone B—the modifiable urban zone—was reserved for more modern residential and industrial development. Plans for Zone C envisioned it as Cusco's new commercial heart adjacent to the historical center. The Junta even planned to regulate areas that had yet to see any sort of human settlement—the final Zone D outlined in the pilot plan. Reflecting its central goal, the report stated that any future development "should always be adapted to the guidelines of the pilot plan" and avoid any organic or spontaneous development.[61]

Zone A, the historical archeological zone, would receive the first priority of the Junta. The pilot plan emphasized that the center of Cusco would emerge as a "civic-cultural nucleus . . . congregated by public building and educational institutions such as museums, institutes of art, archeology, history, anthropology, etc."[62] The promotion of tourism emerged as one of the key justifications for this proposal. The pilot plan's introduction clearly stated, "The conservation of [historic Cusco] to its greatest authenticity and character," while unobjectionable in "recognition of its historic value, is also justified by the recognition of the economic factor of tourism."[63] Thus the pilot plan proposed altering the character of Cusco's historic center from a place of local commerce to a zone primarily dedicated to historical preservation and tourist activity. Although never strictly implemented, the recommendations reflected the shifting development priorities in Cusco following the earthquake.

The Ruins Are Going to Ruins!

Tensions between preservation and development also affected Machu Picchu. Although Machu Picchu avoided damage during the 1950 earthquake, the archeological site showed signs of significant ecological wear and abandonment. In prior decades, these problems had not caused much alarm outside of Cusco. However, as Machu Picchu emerged from the 1940s as an iconic symbol of Peru, the national press began to express concern over how to properly manage the site. Unfortunately, increased international interest in Machu Picchu did not translate into state support for preservation at the site. During its short existence the CNT had provided needed funds for the maintenance of Machu Picchu. However, after the dissolution of the state tourism organization, responsibility for funding restoration and preservation efforts for Machu Picchu fell back under the care of Cusco's Patronato Departamental de Arqueología (Departmental Archeology Council). Formed in 1929, the Archeology Council worked to protect and conserve pre-Hispanic monuments in Cusco. Generally, the Archeology Council depended on the volunteer work of professional and amateur regional archeologists.

Unfortunately, the budgetary limitations of the Archeology Council had become a source of surprise to visitors as well as a point of national embarrassment. The need for more preservation funds emerged as early as 1948. While reporting on Bingham's visit to Machu Picchu, *El Comercio de Cusco* reported that "all expressed an unpleasant surprise toward the state of conservation of the principal structures of the historic and millenarian city."[64] As a response to increased concerns regarding the state of Machu Picchu, the Archeology Council asked its engineer Manuel Briceño to assess the state of the ruins in 1952. Briceño found that the humid climate surrounding Machu Picchu had placed some structures at risk of collapse. Archeology Council president Luis Felipe Paredes also visited the site in December 1952 and confirmed Briceño's findings.[65]

Although Machu Picchu did need preservation work, by the middle of the 1950s Peru and Cusco had yet to develop any long-term plans to protect the site. Despite the fact that Machu Picchu had become a site of national importance, the state demonstrated little or no interest in protecting the ruin. On October 17, 1952, the national government announced the creation of the Office of Archeology and History as part of the Ministry of Education. The new office was created by the state in an effort to replace the locally controlled and often poorly organized departmental archeology councils. However, the office lacked the necessary funds and staff to complete its assigned task. In a 1953 report to his superiors in the Ministry of Education, Office of Archeology and History director Jorge Muelle reported that his institution's meager budget permitted the hiring of only twelve inspectors to monitor historical sites outside of Lima.[66] In fact, the majority of Muelle's reports to his superiors in the Ministry of Education were pleas for better funding and resources.[67]

Faced with uneven financial support from the national government's Office of Archeology and History, the Archeology Council of Cusco depended on independently raised funds to finance its operations in the 1950s. The largest portion of the Archeology Council's funds originated from entry ticket fees for Machu Picchu. Profits from admissions to Machu Picchu helped Cusco's Archeology Council remain solvent. However, the Archeology Council often failed to control the income from these sales. For example, in 1953 the Archeology Council received 24 million Peruvian soles from ticket sales at Machu Picchu. However, passenger statistics provided on visitors by the Santa Ana Railroad and the TACP indicated that the council should have received 50 million soles. In 1954 visitor statistics indicated that the Archeology Council should have received 30 million soles, when in fact the institution only recorded an income of 18 million.[68] The Archeology Council suspected that the tourist guides (who were responsible for collecting the tickets) were keeping most of the entry fees for themselves. The manager of the Machu Picchu Tourist Lodge admitted to witnessing such frauds in a 1952 letter to the Archeology Council president. In the letter, the manager confessed that most of the tourist guides "at times do not hand over to the treasury what they owe." Even worse, when employees of the Archeology Council confronted guides regarding the fraud, "sometimes the arguments have occurred in the presence of visitors, which does not fail to give them a bad impression."[69]

For the Archeology Council, lean budgets, small staffs, and patchwork preservation were not new problems. However, by the 1950s the national press began to report on Machu Picchu with greater interest. As Machu Picchu became more prominent in the eyes of Peruvians, so did the lack of preservation at the site. The caretakers of Machu Picchu soon discovered that the national press could serve as a powerful ally in their efforts to secure more funding. When the national Office of Archeology and History provided a meager budget for preservation work at Machu Picchu at the start of 1953, the national press advocated for more funds. Cusco Archeology Council member and UNSAAC professor Manuel Chávez Ballón appealed directly to the Lima newspaper *La Prensa* to lobby for more funds for Machu Picchu.[70] *La Prensa* followed its coverage with an editorial published on January 11 that stated, "Knowing that we are in imminent danger of losing our priceless cultural treasure, it is easy to explain the indignation that this has provoked in the public opinion."[71] The national press took great pride in its new role as an advocate for Machu Picchu. When the national Office of Archeology and History pledged to fund preservation work at Machu Picchu in September 1953, *El Comercio de Lima* characterized the government's response as "a result of the constant journalistic demands raised in defense of our archeological heritage." The article went on to declare that "if France marks its historical legacy with the Louvre, the Tuileries, and Notre Dame; and Italy does it with the Coliseum and the Appian Way; we have written the chapters of the greatness [of] our past in the impressive colossus of stone of Machu-Picchu."[72]

The comparison of Machu Picchu to some of Europe's most famous historic sites illustrated that Peru's leaders had joined many of their Latin American peers in adopting indigenous culture as a national symbol.[73] However, ongoing critiques over the maintenance of Machu Picchu reveal the continued cultural biases held against the Andes. Some Lima-based newspapers suggested that the conditions at Machu Picchu were the result of poor regional management on the part of Cusco. Rumors emerged in Peru that *Time* magazine had published an article entitled "Slipping City" in its January 5, 1953, issue that claimed that Machu Picchu was on the verge of falling into the Urubamba Valley and criticized Peru for not caring for its national heritage. Although no such article was actually printed, Lima's *El Comercio* reported that the rumored *Time* article was an embarrassment and urged Peruvian authorities to increase preservation efforts at Machu Picchu.[74] Cusco's *El Sol* newspaper took offense at the purported *Time* article and responded in a January 12, 1953, editorial, "The 'yanqui' magazine *Times* [sic] that has more than once treated Peru like a mooch, has clamored like one of the prophets who announced the destruction of Jerusalem." Even worse, *El Sol* claimed that many Lima periodicals had reprinted the nonexistent *Time* article to imply that cusqueños were at fault for the current conditions at Machu Picchu. "Just as it has not gone to ruin in two thousand years since its construction . . . Machu Picchu is not going to ruin now," declared *El Sol* in a defiant (but historically incorrect) editorial.[75]

Despite the intense criticism of the national and local press, neither Cusco's Archeology Council nor the national Office of Archeology and History managed to complete significant preservation work at Machu Picchu well into the mid-1950s. The funds promised by the national Office of Archeology and History for 1954 amounted to only 7,500 soles — insufficient to commence any major preservation efforts at the site.[76] In December 1954, *El Sol* reported that in Machu Picchu numerous walls and structures were supported only by makeshift tree branches.[77] By February 1955, the Archeology Council had collected enough funds to commission a new report on the status of Machu Picchu authored by the archeologist Lawrence Roys. The Roys report concluded that Machu Picchu was "in good condition," but warned that many of the ruin's individual structures and walls could collapse, and recommended restoration work before the next rainy season.[78] Despite these measures, *El Comercio de Lima* criticized that, at the start of February 1955, only three "peones" were working in Machu Picchu. "So this is [the] most captivating fortress in the world," sarcastically declared the headline of an article printed in the February 7, 1955, issue of *El Comercio de Lima* that displayed a photograph of a young peasant boy sitting next to a wall supported by a tree branch.[79] *La Prensa* described the situation in a more alarming tone when it published an article two days later declaring that "Machu Picchu runs the risk of disappearing."[80]

In March 1955, rumors continued to circulate that Machu Picchu's mortar house structure had indeed suffered a total structural collapse. Paredes, still acting as head of the Archeology Council, traveled to Machu Picchu on March 30, 1955, with a delegation of reporters to see if the rumors were true. The inspection team confirmed that a few rocks had fallen in the mortar house but that the damage was not grave. Even more, Paredes praised the work of the men the national press had declared "peones," stating that "we are working with the labor of skilled masons."[81] Paredes concluded that the principal problem confronting the restoration was not a lack of skilled labor but a dearth of funds from the state. He estimated that the most serious threat to Machu Picchu's structural integrity was the shifting foundation of the Main Temple area. If the foundation was permitted to deteriorate over time, a significant part of it, including the rare Intihuatana stone and religious area, could collapse into the valley below.[82] Paredes concluded in a report to the national Office of Archeology and History that "the impossibility of completing these works is due to the lack of necessary funds," and pleaded for more financial resources from the state.[83] Briceño estimated that to rehabilitate the site the Archeology Council needed 6 million soles and six years of labor.[84]

The deluge of negative press created an image of national crisis surrounding Machu Picchu. As early as February 1955, the Congress's Chamber of Deputies unanimously passed a resolution calling for the Ministry of Development and Public Works to "immediately initiate defensive projects for the millennial city of Machu Picchu."[85] That same month, the Asociación Nacional de Escritores y Artistas (National Association of Writers and Artists, ANEA) organized a national collection to save Machu Picchu.[86] In June 1955, the Lima-based magazine *Caretas* published a critical report on the lack of preservation work at Machu Picchu. Entitled "Machu Picchu: A Beggar," the article reported that Cusco's Archeology Council "lacked a budget that would purchase one sixth of a luxury brand car." The article concluded that "Machu Picchu's condition of being a beggar, no matter what painful or inexplicable reason why, must be attended to with all promptness . . . It would be a grave thing if the donation arrives late; it would mean that the clock of the Intihuatana has arrived at its final hour."[87]

The Junta appeared to be a natural source for preservation funding for Machu Picchu. However, by 1954 the Junta's spending on restoration efforts in Cusco had dropped dramatically, to 213,781 soles from the previous year's total of 4,574,442 soles. A major source of conflict arose over the fact that management of the Junta remained in Lima and thus did not share the same priorities as local political leaders over what aspects of the recovery should receive attention. As early as January 1952, the Cusco newspaper *El Sol* lamented the lack of progress on the reconstruction as a symptom of the larger problem of the Andes's political and economic isolation under the Odría government.[88] In an editorial published on January 10, *El Sol* blamed a lack of progress on the indifference of the Junta's leadership. *El Sol* argued that, instead, the earthquake reconstruction should be left in the hands of cusqueños. "There is nothing more natural than an owner who attends to the repair of his own house," observed *El Sol*.[89] In the view of the local press, Lima's indifference, not regional backwardness, was to blame for the abandonment of Cusco and Machu Picchu.

Despite these protests, the Junta made little progress in its preservation mission. Some of the Junta's problems stemmed from the national government's unsteady financial contributions. Restoration projects that were independently funded, such as the Spanish-funded restoration of the cathedral, progressed relatively quickly.[90] Junta-funded reconstruction projects, however, remained at a standstill. For example, although the Junta expected to receive 10 million soles for restoration from the central government in the 1953–54 budget, the fund received only 233,333 soles. Citing the paralyzed state of the rebuilding and restoration, *El Comercio de Cusco* lamented 1953 as a "lost year" for the city.[91] Unfortunately, continued financial problems meant that most restoration work remained uncompleted through 1954.[92] In December 1954, *El Sol* published an editorial observing that some of the city's most impressive historic structures had yet to be restored.[93] Other factors hindered the Junta's mission of reconstruction—especially local obstruction and abuse of funds. As early as 1951, Cusco's Chamber of Commerce reported, "Certain property owners believe that the Reconstruction Law is an easy path to obtain whatever loan they desire, [requiring] nothing more than presenting a loan solicitation."[94] In fact, reconstruction funds were largely diverted to roughly thirty well-connected property owners instead of to needed restoration work of living spaces in the city center—a pattern that worsened unequal housing conditions in Cusco.[95]

By 1954 Cusco's regional leaders had found allies in their fight to assert more local control over the earthquake reconstruction. By doing so, they spurred a larger discussion regarding the centralization of economic and political power in Lima. When asked about the lack of restoration progress in Cusco, the prominent Peruvian statesman and historian Raúl Porras Barrenechea responded, "I believe, like the cusqueños, that it is all due to the demanding tendencies of centralism, to the distain and ignorance that exists towards regional interests."[96] In April 1954 *Caretas* published an exposé titled "The Re-destruction of Cuzco" to bring national attention to the Junta's lack of progress. Like Porras Barrenechea, *Caretas* primarily faulted the Junta's isolation from Cusco, noting that the reconstruction was "working without order or coordination and with [the] evident fundamental error of putting aside the pilot plan and exporting its executive powers to Lima, far from the acts and facts." *Caretas* criticized the Junta, observing that "in almost four years since the earthquake, there certainly is not much that it has completed."[97] In 1955 national outrage over the lack of reconstruction continued to build. In January 1955, Aquiles Cacón Almanaza, a congressman from Cusco, denounced the rebuilding efforts in the Congress, stating that the city remained "a panorama of ruins" four years after the earthquake.[98] Outrage over the stalled rebuilding of Cusco grew, so that by December 1955, Odría sent a commission to investigate the lack of progress in the region.[99]

Not only did the paralyzed rebuilding of the city's historic center emerge as a national embarrassment, but the inactivity of the Junta threatened the development of Cusco's tourism economy. By 1955 tourism arrivals in Cusco had stagnated, indicating that the promised postwar boom in international arrivals had failed to take place, perhaps because tourists had chosen to visit other destinations in Latin America.[100] In fact, visits to Machu Picchu between 1953 and 1956 remained at a steady plateau of under 5,000 annual entries.[101] A simultaneous overall drop in international visitors to Peru in general suggested that the government ignored Machu Picchu in a way that put the national tourism economy at risk.[102] Poor infrastructure also hindered tourism development in the region. In 1951 Cusco's Chamber of Commerce reported that the Santa Ana Railroad, which carried tourists to Machu Picchu, "operates with material totally deficient in quality and quantity."[103] Deficits and bad equipment continued to plague the railroad into 1954.[104] Observers also criticized the condition of Cusco's airport, originally opened in 1933. One 1951 editorial in *El Comercio de Lima* noted that the current air travel infrastructure in Cusco "continues to display deficiencies, problems, and dangers."[105] Despite proposals to construct a new facility for air travel, plans remained undefined until the end of the decade.[106]

The stagnation of tourism in Cusco alarmed longtime promoters of the city, who urged quick action. During the stalled earthquake reconstruction, the TACP organized a forum to discuss tourism development and its challenges in Cusco in December 1954.[107] The 1954 tourism forum proposed that the national state invest to stimulate Cusco's stagnated and uncoordinated tourism development.[108] A year later, in a radio broadcast on *La Voz del Cuzco* (The Voice of Cuzco) on September 17, 1955, Giesecke emphasized the urgent need to develop tourism in the region. "More than anything else," said Giesecke, "I have to insist that tourism to Cuzco is the most streamlined and important gold mine that Peru has. Whatever effort and whatever cost that is completed in order to promote tourism will be paid back to the people and for the national economy in tangible and intangible benefits that are incalculable." Giesecke ended his broadcast with a challenge to national and regional leaders to work to develop tourism in Cusco and the Sacred Valley "with vigor, at whatever cost, and immediately. The time is now."[109]

From Disaster to Development?

The sense of national urgency to protect Machu Picchu permitted regional political leaders to push for substantive structural reforms in 1955 that would aid both preservation and tourism promotion. The Peruvian National Congress approved a series of laws to shore up restoration work in the city of Cusco and at Machu Picchu in 1955. The central piece of legislation, Law 12350, passed at the end of November 1955, replaced the former Junta with a newly organized Corporación de Reconstrucción y Fomento del Cuzco (Cuzco Reconstruction and Development Corporation, CRYF). The CRYF boasted several features that promised to address local critiques of the old Junta. First, unlike the Junta, the new CRYF remained headquartered in Cusco and was staffed by regional leaders. Second, the new legislation moved beyond the original rural and industrial development goals of the Junta to encourage the new corporation to invest in tourism. The new law specifically granted the CRYF the duty to "develop tourism in the Department of Cuzco." Finally, the CRYF enjoyed an independent budget, guaranteeing a reliable source of restoration and tourism promotion funds.[110] These reforms convinced cusqueños that the CRYF would serve local interests rather than those of the national state.

Elected president for a second time in 1956, Manuel Prado became a key supporter of the CRYF. Although Prado represented many of the same Lima elite interests that had backed Odría, the new government did not ignore Cusco. In his first government (1939–45), Prado pushed for many early tourism reform efforts, including the annual Inti Raymi folklore festival and the construction of the state-owned Hotel Cusco. Winning a majority in the Department of Cusco in the 1955 presidential election, Prado returned to the region in February 1956 to formally establish the CRYF.[111] Although the

CRYF-administered restoration efforts never achieved the levels established at the start of the decade, they marked a significant increase, with spending rising to 1,397,808 soles in 1956. The legislation creating the new CRYF included specific goals for tourism development that included the following:

1. Completion and progress on lodging, accommodation, and tourism attractions.
2. The establishment and maintenance of facilities for the development of tourism.
3. The organization of propaganda and information services in the country and abroad.
4. Opening new tourism centers.
5. Orientation of the tourism industry.
6. Studying and finding solutions for problems in the development of tourism.[112]

The new powers and funds granted to the CRYF appeared to produce results for the promotion of tourism.

Legislation creating the CRYF also provided for a new division to manage Machu Picchu preservation and development. The newly formed Supervigilancia de los Trabajos de Restauración de Machu Picchu (Machu Picchu Works and Restoration Supervision) replaced the Cusco Archeology Council as the primary organization responsible for maintaining the ruin. It named Cusco archeologist Luis A. Pardo as its director. The CRYF and the Supervision promised to bring much-needed funds—350,000 soles in the first year of its formation alone—and coordination to the incomplete restoration efforts at the archeological site.[113] However, the CRYF's new focus on tourism promotion and disaster recovery, along with its heavy-handed tactics, also brought new conflicts to Machu Picchu.

In his September–October 1956 report to the Ministry of Education, the regional inspector of archeology, Manuel Chávez Ballón, reported that the new restoration efforts at Machu Picchu "were continuing with some irregularities."[114] Chávez Ballón detailed the nature of these "irregularities" in his next report for November and December 1956. On August 13, 1956, the restoration workers went on strike for higher wages. Previously, the Archeology Council had sought out laborers from nearby haciendas who worked during times of low demand. For many local laborers, the Archeology Council provided convenient supplemental incomes between harvest seasons. However, the new Supervision of Machu Picchu demanded regular schedules and discipline from preservation workers—a substantial change from work conditions under the Archeology Council. According to Chávez Ballón, during the strike, the workers forbade tourists to enter Machu Picchu and in some cases threatened visitors to the site. As a result the CRYF relieved the long-serving engineer Manuel Briceño of his duties. The CRYF ended restoration work at the site, declaring that "it was necessary to do a better selection of working personnel."[115] Yet, Chávez Ballón's report for April and May 1957 documented that restorations of Machu Picchu remained unfinished due to problems with the workforce. Problems began when two managers, known only as the Salas brothers, entered into a dispute with a laborer called César Calderón. The fight provoked a larger conflict between the workers and managers that contributed to inconsistent work and poor-quality restorations. Once again, the CRYF had to temporarily stop restoration work.[116]

In addition to changing labor policy, replacing Briceño offered the CRYF a chance to adopt controversial new restoration techniques at Machu Picchu. Briceño and other employees of the Archeology Council used only traditional tools and materials in their preservation work. A new inspection completed by the CRYF on October 26, 1955, criticized the poor quality of the restoration work completed under Briceño's supervision. This was a surprising accusation against a person who in 1953 was described as "one of the few Peruvian technicians [who] specialized in the restoration of historical zones."[117] Critiquing Briceño, the CRYF hired a new team of engineers to supervise the restoration. However, the new team undertook the insertion of iron and cement to support Machu Picchu's foundations.[118] Prior to the CRYF administration, the general restoration policy at the ruin was one of preservation, not restoration. When the topic emerged in 1952, *El Sol* published an editorial defending the decision of the Archeology Council and Briceño to not alter Machu Picchu. "Engineer Briceño told us . . . he only attempts to 'defend,' not restore; and thus, we remain satisfied," stated *El Sol*.[119] However, with the end of Briceño's management, the CRYF was free to use controversial materials in the restoration of Machu Picchu.

Unlike in 1952, no regional or national opposition appeared against the new restoration methods employed by the CRYF at Machu Picchu. Reports on the progress of the Machu Picchu restoration reported, without any sense of irony, "They have employed the same methods of the Incas, with the advantage of using tools of steel, powder, wheelbarrows, and cement."[120] Chávez Ballón approved the new restoration techniques in his reports to the Ministry of Education.[121] In March 1957, *El Comercio de Lima* applauded the use of "modern techniques" in the restoration of Machu Picchu.[122] The prominent sociologist José María Arguedas, in a report published in *La Prensa*, also defended the use of modern materials. "The casual visitor, and even the educated visitor, but perhaps not an expert, will not be able to differentiate the original part of the ruin from the reconstructed," Arguedas wrote in a news article.[123] In fact, the only initial criticism that Chávez Ballón had of the restorations was that they lacked cameras and other equipment to document the work. "It would be laudable and correct to present an illustrated report of what they have completed, so that it can be viewed outside of Peru," wrote Chávez Ballón, "so that the world knows that Peruvians can complete restorations like in Mexico, Athens, and Egypt."[124]

Perhaps the most important factor that led the CRYF to adopt the controversial restoration methods stemmed from its mandate to develop the site as a tourism resource. The desire to remake Machu Picchu accessible to tourists began to consistently override conservation interests. Initial construction work in the mortar room structure completely rebuilt the room with modern techniques and materials. For example, the October–November 1956 report by the Supervision noted that the difference between the original Incaic and reconstructed portions of the mortar room was "quite visible." The Supervision justified the reconstruction by stating: "These rooms were only a pile of rocks, and now one can pass through them, granting the tourist more to see in Machupicchu."[125] By 1957, Chávez Ballón indicated some concern in regard to the restoration process. He argued that, unlike earlier restorations completed by Briceño, the CRYF work was completed without making any records and that "the interest of the archeologist has not been taken into account, but rather those of the tourist." Chávez Ballón concluded by sarcastically observing that "the archeologists of the future are not going to be able to explain why the Incas only used lime, cement, and iron at Machu Picchu," and nowhere else.[126] Despite this critique, the report continued to endorse tourism at Machu Picchu, including photos of the new restorations, and even superimposing an image of Bingham over the ruin in one of the illustrations.[127]

The CRYF's prioritization of tourism interests in the management of Machu Picchu extended beyond restoration methods. The new organization commenced plans for expanded lodging at the site. Since 1951 Giesecke and Cusco tourism interests had lobbied to improve lodging conditions in Cusco. A January 5, 1955, opinion piece in the newspaper *La Crónica* stated that the state-run lodge at Machu Picchu resembled "a slightly comfortable jail."[128] In 1951 Giesecke contacted the Chicago-based architectural firm of Schweikher & Elting, asking them to plan a modern hotel to be built at Machu Picchu. The firm proposed the construction of an ambi-

6.- LA RESTAURACION DE LAS ANDENERIAS DEL INTIHUATANA DE MACHUPICCHU

Uno de los trabajos más audaces desde el punto de vista de la
ingeniería, ha sido el realizado en la reconstrucción de las ande-
nerías del Intihuatana, para evitar de este modo el derrumbamiento
total de esta sección de Machupicchu hacia el río Urubamba, en la parte de San Miguel. Se han empleado los mismos métodos que emplearon
los Incas, con la ventaja de contar con herramientas de acero, pól-
vora, carretillas y cemento. El trabajo está casi finalizado, pero
ha surgido la crítica en el sentido de que toda la obra está en peligro de rodar hacia el río, 400 metros más abajo en línea perpendi-
cular, porque los andenes inferiores están sobre la base de tierra,
que en cualquier momento puede ceder ante la acción de las lluvias.
La verdad es, que humanamente, no ha podido realizarse mejor trabajo,
y que el peligro de un derrumbe total no existe, porque se han toma-
do todas las providencias técnicas posibles.

Foto 20

LAS ANDENERIAS DEL INTIHUATANA VISTAS DE ABAJO. Se comenzaron estos
trabajos sobre un precipicio de 400 metros, buscándo un punto de apoyo para el primer andén, sobre el cual se han elevado 11 andenes, a-
poyados en un 50 % en el andén inferior y otro 50% en el suelo exca-
vado. Los extremos de los andenes están apoyados en roca firme.

Report on 1950s reconstruction of Machu Picchu. Reports prepared
on the work of the CRYF in restoring Machu Picchu proudly displayed
before and after images to illustrate the major overhaul of the site.
The reports also documented the controversial use of modern
technology in the restoration of the site, which CRYF officials
believed would benefit tourism. Reproduced with permission of the
Colección Jorge Muelle, Archivo Histórico Riva-Agüero, Instituto
Riva-Agüero, Pontificia Universidad Católica del Perú.

tions seven-floor hotel built into the mountainside adjacent to the ruin. Their plans were thwarted by a lack of available funding. By law, the Junta could provide personal loans only to homeowners for restorations. The state-run hotel company, another likely source of financing, also suffered from lean budgets during Odría's government and declined to fund new hotel construction at Machu Picchu.[129]

However, with the formation of the CRYF, the central government greatly increased funding for hotel construction. With Giesecke's lobbying, the newly formed CRYF dedicated 600,000 soles—or 4 percent of its total budget—to hotel construction and restoration work at Machu Picchu.[130] Giesecke enthusiastically described Schweikher & Elting's plans to Bingham in 1955. According to Giesecke, the new seven-floor hotel would provide visitors with the most modern comforts available by allowing guests to "come out at the upper part of the ruins—with the wonderful panoramic view. Then the visitor would DESCEND most of the way to visit the different sectors of Machu Picchu."[131] Although Giesecke's enthusiasm for tunneling into the mountainside adjacent to Machu Picchu appeared at odds with his reputation as an early preservationist, his plans reflected the vision of Cusco's early tourism backers. For Giesecke and his peers, adjacent pre-Hispanic ruins and modern hotel construction appeared as complementary parts of the same goal of regional modernization.

The modernization efforts of the CRYF brought additional change to Machu Picchu that also threatened the ruin's historical setting. Although the Junta had begun plans to construct a new power station on the Urubamba River at Machu Picchu, the new leadership of the CRYF accelerated efforts to build a hydroelectric facility.[132] Beginning in 1958, the CRYF began construction on a new hydroelectric plant located adjacent to Machu Picchu. The natural curve of the Urubamba River around the Huayna Picchu peak and the plateau of the ruins created an optimal natural setting for electricity generation. Between 1958 and 1962, the CRYF funded the construction of a 120,000 kilowatt plant at the western base of Machu Picchu. In fact, the diversion tunnel for the generators runs for three kilometers directly underneath the historic structures of Machu Picchu.[133] Surprisingly, no protests emerged in regard to the new hydroelectric facility's threats to the historic site. Despite the fact that the new hydroelectric facility shared its name with the famous adjacent ruin, the original legislation and budgetary agreements between the national government and the CRYF for the Machu Picchu Hydroelectric Plant never took into account the potential effects the hydroelectric project could have on the existing historical surroundings.[134] Additionally, detailed construction reports and engineering surveys published during the construction project made no references to the Machu Picchu ruin.[135] Even *Caretas*, which had led a national campaign to protect Machu Picchu, enthusiastically supported the hydroelectric project.[136] Cusco's *El Sol* reproduced plans of the project showing its proximity to Machu Picchu and applauded the project when work commenced on the site in February 1959.[137]

Tourism promoters did not view the actions of the CRYF as excessive. In fact, at the end of the decade, many argued that the early achievements of the CRYF illustrated the need to involve the state in tourism planning and promotion. Pointing to the early success of the CRYF, the editorial page of *El Comercio del Cusco* advocated for a return of the defunct CNT to coordinate tourism as early as 1957.[138] During Cusco Week celebrations on June 25, 1959, Giesecke delivered a speech entitled "Cusco and International Tourism" at the Club Cusco. The speech, also broadcast over Peru's Radio America, emphasized the urgent need for state investment in tourism. Speaking to Cusco's political leaders, economic elite, and prominent intellectuals including Valcárcel, Giesecke argued that Peru enjoyed a small window of opportunity to exploit the growing international tourism market. In his speech, Giesecke warned that the increased reach of airplanes like the DC-9 and the Electra and new jet technology would soon allow travelers to bypass Peru in favor of other destinations. "For the new era of air travel, Cuzco has one chance to prepare itself if it wants to receive the benefits of increased tourism," stated Giesecke. "And I ask, where are the hotel facilities and ground transportation, well-trained guides and other essential aspects if 100 or even 200 air travel passengers arrive in Cusco daily?" He warned, "If we do not complete these projects immediately, Cuzco will lose the opportunity to attend to the notable increase of visitors. It would also probably lose sources for its economic life."[139]

Conclusion

On January 1, 1959, *El Comercio de Lima* published an article that praised "the journalistic campaign" in which it had played a central role "to avoid the massive destruction of America's principal archeological site—the fortress of Machu Picchu."[140] The next month, Prado and the first lady visited the newly restored archeological site to inaugurate the CRYF-funded expanded tourist lodge at Machu Picchu. Although the improvements stopped short of the bold plans proposed by Giesecke, *El Comercio del Cusco* proudly described the renovated hotel as "one more milestone for progress in Cuzco and an incentive for increased tourism."[141] The disaster economics of Cusco's earth-quake recovery and Machu Picchu's emergency restoration had permitted local leaders to channel financial and technical resources to replace leadership and planning roles originally fulfilled by the CNT. Not only did Cusco's elites manage to keep the promise of tourism alive in their region, but their efforts marked a rare victory against the centralization of political and economic power in Lima. Their efforts laid the foundation for the tourism boom of the 1960s. In fact, by July 1961 Cusco's tourism developments were sufficient enough that the region hosted a fiftieth anniversary celebration of Bingham's 1911 expedition. Once again, Giesecke used his informal contacts with Bingham's family, Yale University, *National Geographic Magazine*, and Peruvian political leaders to exploit the event for tourism propaganda.[142]

However, deeper conflicts developed alongside the apparent success of disaster economics in the 1950s that would continue to affect the Cusco region. In marketing their region's appeal to Lima and the international community, cusqueños discovered that their efforts could backfire. For example, Peru's national press suggested that the poor state of Cusco's archeological sites was a further indication of the region's backwardness. More critically, by categorizing the reconstruction of Cusco and Machu Picchu as disaster recovery and tourism development, institutions, especially the CRYF, downplayed concerns regarding preservation. Instead, Junta and later CRYF planners selected modern reconstruction techniques at Machu Picchu to increase the pace at which the repairs were completed. The same development-oriented motivations encouraged the CRYF to complete a major hydroelectric project in the ecologically and historically sensitive area surrounding Machu Picchu with little objection. When Kubler, the author of the UNESCO study for post-earthquake restorations, returned to Cusco in 1956, he expressed alarm at the methods of the CRYF. "An unparalleled opportunity for archeological work was lost," reported Kubler in his critique of the restoration techniques.[143]

Finally, the disaster recovery efforts aimed at tourism development succeeded at the cost of ignoring many of the original goals of the earthquake reconstruction. Although the Junta acknowledged the need to restore Cusco's cultural heritage, the original goal of the reconstruction centered on the need to reverse the region's decline through industrialization and agricultural reform. However, regional elites proved reluctant to reform the exploitative hacienda economy that formed the source of their social and economic power. Instead, Cusco's elites used reconstruction institutions to fund a tourism project amenable to their political and cultural goals. Even the nature of tourism in Cusco, focused on emphasizing a nostalgic narrative of the region's unchanging character rather than modernization, reflected elite fears of the threat of change. The Junta dedicated only 1 percent of its budget toward agrarian and industrial modernization, while the CRYF spent only 2 percent on those efforts.[144] As the TACP and tourism promoters like Giesecke pushed for new airports and luxury hotels, the majority of agrarian Cusco remained underdeveloped, isolated, and exploited.

On April 10, 1958, in the shadow of the colonial churches and structures under restoration, local laborers took to the streets in central Cusco as part of a general strike organized by the Communist-led Federación de Trabajadores del Cuzco (Cusco Workers Federation) to push for labor and agrarian reform. The strength and anger of the strikers, who even managed to temporarily detain an army general, shocked local and national observers.[145] However, this only served as a prelude to a much larger revolutionary agrarian movement in La Convención Valley northwest of Machu Picchu. Since the 1940s, La Convención had emerged as a production center of valuable cash crops of coca, coffee, cocoa, and sugar. Despite its role as one of Cusco's most productive agricultural zones, working conditions in La Convención remained so exploitative that the notable social historian Eric Hobsbawm described conditions there as "neo-feudalism." Tensions between workers and hacienda owners, simmering since the late 1950s, would explode in 1960 in an agrarian rebellion.[146]

Tourism in Cusco had survived a natural disaster in 1950 only to confront a much larger social disaster a decade later. With the advice of transnational experts and institutions, Peruvians created public corporations like the Junta and the CRYF in the belief that their technocratic reach could resolve Cusco's economic problems. These new institutions appealed to national leaders reluctant to abandon their liberal economic policies while also earning the support of Cusco's regional elites, who hoped to encourage growth while avoiding the thorny questions of social and agrarian reform. The same reluctance to undertake reform explains the increasing appeal of tourism, which also promised to provide economic benefits and modernization to Cusco without the risk of social change. However, the agrarian uprisings in the 1960s proved that tourism alone would be unable to address these challenges. Both national and local leaders recognized that substantial economic and social reform was unavoidable in Cusco. The next question facing cusqueños was the role tourism would play in a new era of reform.

CHAPTER FOUR

The Junta and the *Jipis*, 1960–1975

As head of Cusco's Archeology Council, Manuel Chávez Ballón should have enjoyed one of the most prized positions in Peru's archeological community: management of Machu Picchu. However, by the late 1960s and early 1970s, Chávez Ballón's reports contained more and more information regarding new and troublesome waves of international arrivals. The new visitors, according to Chávez Ballón, "are mostly called backpackers, 'qepiris,' and hippies, and do not want to pay for anything and create problems by wanting to violate policies."[1] Chávez Ballón complained that "tourists leave fruit peels, cans, paper, food scraps, plastics, etc." Even worse, "many times, unable to find a bathroom, they do their 'business' (*necesidades*) inside the ruins." When not leaving refuse, Chávez Ballón complained, visitors wanted to scale walls, damaging the ruins and causing personal injury. Problems of supervising backpackers increased in archeological sites near Machu Picchu, such as the Temple of the Moon and Winay Wayna, where the Archeology Council staff exercised less vigilance. In these sites, Chávez Ballón reported that "the backpackers sunbathe naked or attempt to explore difficult zones."[2] The lack of lodging facilities for backpackers also placed strains on Machu Picchu. Chávez Ballón estimated that, on any given night, twenty backpackers slept in unregulated tents around the ruin.[3] Since the 1920s, Cusco had worked to transform Machu Picchu into a global travel destination. Now, in the 1960s and 1970s, it appeared that cusqueños were becoming victims of their own success.

Promoted since the 1920s as a strategy to bolster local folklore and emphasize Cusco's place in a modern Peruvian nation, by the 1960s tourism had transformed into a promised source of regional economic development. In the wake of agrarian revolts and the collapse of the region's traditional agricultural economy and the elite-dominated political system it supported, local and national leaders scrambled to find new economic and political solutions for the mounting social crisis in Cusco. Although the question of agrarian reform would dominate these debates, many other leaders and institutions also looked to tourism as a potential solution for needed economic development in Cusco in the 1960s and 1970s.[4]

Beginning with the election of reformist Fernando Belaúnde Terry as president in 1963, the national state once again pledged resources and investment to use tourism as a source of economic development. These efforts accelerated after the 1968 military coup that brought General Juan Velasco Alvarado to power. Ruling with a mandate to undertake a revolution to fundamentally transform Peru's economy, politics, and society, the Velasco government enacted efforts to use tourism not only as a source of economic development but as a means of social transformation—especially in impoverished Cusco. No longer just a source of recreation and cultural promotion, tourism in Cusco would form a key part in the state's efforts to remake the region's economy and society. These reforms would also alter Cusco's relationship to the national state. Tourism policy, along with the far-reaching agrarian reform of 1969, would place the Peruvian state at the center of Cusco's development at the expense of the region's traditional political and economic elites.

Tourism not only helped define the national state's relationship to Cusco; it also illustrates the complex relationship between Velasco and global actors. Despite its nationalist rhetoric, in regard to tourism, the Velasco government worked closely with transnational institutions and capital to channel development to Cusco. No institution symbolized this cooperation better than the Plan Turístico y Cultural Perú-UNESCO (Peru-UNESCO Tourist and Cultural Plan, COPESCO), a joint operation between Peru and UNESCO. The COPESCO plan projected that, through an expansion of cultural tourism, the pressing needs of rural development and historical preservation could be resolved in Cusco. Of course, COPESCO was not the only transnational link that affected Cusco's cultural and economic trajectory in the 1960s and 1970s. Global technological and cultural shifts elevated interest in the Andes and Cusco to a level not seen since the era of the Good Neighbor policy. However, the same transnational links that brought promises of modernization, profit, and preservation also threatened to attract unwelcome visitors, investors, and sources of conflict, as evidenced by Chávez Ballón's increasingly frustrated attempts to manage Machu Picchu.

The futile efforts to rein in hippie backpackers at Machu Picchu were just one of the many unpredicted results of the tourism reform undertaken in the 1960s and 1970s. Aiming to use tourism to bring about orderly social change in Cusco, Velasco and his military allies found this easier said than done. Rather than become a point of consensus and reform, tourism policies became embroiled in new sources of conflict over development, preservation, and social change. Ultimately, the Velasco era oversaw a true tourism boom in Cusco that would fundamentally reshape the region, albeit in ways contrary to the initial goals of the government.

Preparing for Jet Set Tourism

When a Braniff International Airways Boeing 707 landed at Lima's Las Palmas Air Force Base in late February 1960, *Caretas* magazine announced the dawn of the "Jet Age" in Peru.[5] Pan American–Grace Airways (Panagra) introduced its jet service by May of that same year, and a few months later the Corporación Peruana de Aeropuertos y Aviación Comercial (Peruvian Corporation of Airports and Commercial Aviation, CORPAC) inaugurated Lima's new airport, Jorge Chávez International, which was designed specifically to receive jet aircraft.[6] The introduction of DC-6s on Panagra's routes between Lima and Miami in the 1950s had already improved international travel to Peru, but it still took nearly ten hours and two stops to complete the journey.[7] With the introduction of jet aircraft, Peru could now receive nonstop flights from the United States and Europe. Between 1963 and 1967, annual international tourist arrivals to Peru increased dramatically, from 62,000 to 108,000.[8] The entire South American continent saw similar results as total annual international tourist arrivals increased from 602,000 to 1,124,000—a trend chiefly attributed to the introduction of jets in the 1960s.[9]

The introduction of domestic jet service in 1968 between Lima and Cusco revolutionized the region's tourism development. Flying to 3,339-meter-high Cusco was a universally detested experience before the introduction of pressurized jet cabins. Travelers usually had to suck on air tubes or bottled oxygen while airborne, with numerous passengers simply passing out midway through the flight.[10] In July 1961, CORPAC announced plans to construct a new airport for Cusco in the Quispiquilla zone just a few kilometers to the southeast of the facility opened in 1933.[11] The new airport opened for service in 1965, and in 1968 Faucett Airlines debuted regular domestic jet service between Lima and Cusco, eliminating the need for uncomfortable flights with unpressurized cabins.[12] Jet travel connected Cusco to a global travel market at a propitious moment when rising wages and increased leisure time encouraged U.S. and Western European travelers to spend vacations abroad. Equally important, global institutions such as the United Nations and the World Tourism Organization pushed for investment and regulatory reform to help developing nations to take advantage of tourism.[13] Cusco's future as a tourism destination seemed bright.

However, concerns emerged in Peru whether the country had sufficient infrastructure to support increased international arrivals. A *Caretas* investigation into the state of tourism in Cusco in 1962 found that visitors to the city would leave with two general conclusions. "The first," stated the article, "of admiration before such wonder. The second, pity before the backwardness and abandonment" found in "a city of such renown."[14] By 1963 Benjamín Roca Muelle, former director of the defunct CNT from the 1940s, led a new campaign to advocate for the use of state resources to promote tourism in Peru.[15] As a response, in 1963 the Peruvian national government created a special tourism commission that recommended increased state investment in the tourist economy.[16]

The president who received the report, Fernando Belaúnde Terry, had a special interest in renewing state efforts to develop tourism, especially in Cusco. Elected in June 1963 after a short period of military rule, Belaúnde and his party, Acción Popular, campaigned on a platform of development that departed from the orthodox economic policies of the previous Odría and Prado governments.[17] The victorious Belaúnde campaign formed part of a larger hemispheric push toward reform. In the wake of the 1959 Cuban Revolution, a new generation of diplomats and centrist politicians believed that social reforms and inclusive economic development would be needed to stave off future social revolutions in Latin America. The United States also embraced these measures by formally announcing the Alliance for Progress to help support and finance reformist and democratic governments in Latin America.[18] Belaúnde's campaign promises of agrarian reform, state-led development, and political decentralization helped him win overwhelming support in Cusco.[19] Many cusqueños backed Belaúnde's government, hoping that his pro-development policies would also include state investment in the tourism economy. True to his promises, on March 6, 1964, Belaúnde approved Law 14947, creating the Corporación de Turismo del Perú (Peruvian Tourism Corporation, COTURPERU) to manage tourism funding and planning.[20]

Roca Muelle returned to head COTURPERU, an action he viewed as vindication of his original vision to use tourism as a force for national development. Speaking at the formal establishment of COTURPERU, Roca Muelle announced, "I am sure that this, together with the current agrarian reform law, will constitute two of the most important laws of the current regime to achieve the goals of economic development and social justice that constitute the most valuable objectives of the entire nation."[21] COTURPERU hired Checchi and Company of Washington, D.C., to draft a long-term tourism development plan for Peru. The plan, known as the Checchi Report, published in July 1965, outlined an aggressive strategy for state investment in hotel construction, tourism training, infrastructure improvements, cultural promotion, and advertising.[22] The report justified the enormous spending it proposed by arguing that tourism no longer served as a supplemental economic sector or cultural activity of the state. Peru had the possibility of attracting 268,900 international tourist visits and generating $70 million in direct annual tourism revenue by 1974. According to the report, spending by tourists would produce a total of $225 million in annual income for Peru by 1974, equivalent to 7 percent of the predicted national GDP.[23] For Peru, and Cusco in particular, tourism promised large economic gains.

COTURPERU, with the encouragement of the Checchi Report, directed a large portion of its energy toward the promotion of tourism in Cusco. The Checchi Report noted that "if Peru has a single attraction known throughout the world—it is Machu Picchu."[24] Cusqueños applauded the creation of COTURPERU. *El Comercio del Cusco* stated, "The creation of this organization . . . has particular importance for our department, because Cuzco, without a doubt, is the zone of the country where one finds the best archeological wealth and artistic treasures."[25] Immediately, COTURPERU began initiatives to study new hotel construction in Cusco, and it opened its first regional satellite office there on August 15, 1964.[26] COTURPERU allocated more than 5 million soles for various restoration and infrastructure projects in the region in its 1965 budget.[27] The efforts bore fruit, and between 1960 and 1970 annual tourism arrivals to Cusco doubled from 26,026 to 52,834. Equally important, the coveted international market composed a large part of the tourism increase in Cusco, rising from 40 percent to 63.6 percent of the overall tourist demographic.[28]

However, in order to capitalize on tourism and attract well-to-do travelers, the Checchi Report advised Peru to "improve its tourism 'product,'" or to make Peru a destination for elite, especially North American, travelers.[29] "Peru is competing for the U.S. market against places like England and France," noted the report, and, as a result, needed to remake its lodging and travel facilities appropriate to serve first-class visitors.[30] State-owned hotels and infrastructure needed to be renovated to receive modern jet travelers from abroad.[31] Tourism corridors, including Cusco's Sacred Valley, also required aesthetic improvements for travelers.[32] It appears that COTURPERU had already taken steps to attract elite travelers to Peru before the formal release of the Checchi Report. In 1964 COTURPERU invested in tourism promotion in Europe.[33] At the same time, the new agency pursued an aggressive propaganda campaign in the United States by buying advertising space in the *New York Times* and the *Miami Herald* and by funding an eighteen-meter-long billboard of Machu Picchu to be displayed in New York's Grand Central Terminal.[34]

North American consumers proved to be enthusiastic recipients of COTURPERU's efforts. Thanks to earlier Good Neighbor cultural diplomacy, Machu Picchu and Bingham already were familiar to North American travelers. In the jet age, these consumers (familiar with Frank Sinatra's hit song "Come Fly with Me," which invited listeners to "float down to Peru," where "in llama land there's a one man band and he'll toot his flute for you") gravitated toward the appeal of the Andes.[35] In February 1964, the *New York Times* travel section published glowing reviews of visits to the "magic land of the Incas" and Machu Picchu, "considered by many to be the most fascinating sight in the Western Hemisphere."[36] Museum exhibits also premiered in prominent tourist markets, appealing to potential cultured travelers by displaying artifacts of Peru's mythic and seemingly luxurious pre-Columbian past. Between 1960 and 1963, Miguel Mujica Gallo traveled the world exhibiting his *Gold of Peru* collection of pre-Hispanic artifacts.[37] In 1965 another prominent exhibit, titled *The Treasures of Peruvian Gold*, traveled to museums across the United States.[38] The *Washington Post* gave the exhibit's October 1965 opening at the National Gallery front-page treatment.[39] Peruvian ambassador Celso Pastor de la Torre accompanied the *Treasures of Peruvian Gold* exhibit to endorse it as a key tool for increasing cultural and touristic awareness of Peru in the United States.[40] These policies yielded results; by 1967 Peru was the fifth most visited country in South America. Although Argentina, Brazil, Chile, and Uruguay attracted more total tourists, in the competition for coveted North American travelers, Peru ranked first, with 40,000 arrivals.[41] By 1968, 40.5 percent of all international tourists in Peru, the largest demographic group, originated from the United States.[42]

The Peruvian media also embraced the concept of fashioning the country into a destination for the cultured international traveler. The November 1963 issue of *Caretas* sponsored a photo shoot of "Nordic vicunas" at Machu Picchu. The photos of European models, wearing modern fashions and posing among the stones of Machu Picchu, reinforced the touristic narrative that presented Cusco as an appealing international destination.[43] The following year, *Caretas* sponsored another photo shoot at Machu Picchu featuring young stewardesses representing airlines transporting Peru's new jet age tourists.[44] Cusco and Machu Picchu continued to serve as favorite fashion shoot locations for *Caretas* into the mid-1960s.[45] COTURPERU also sponsored its own fashion shoots with models posing in Cusco in 1965.[46]

Ironically, Machu Picchu's own singular fame resulting from tourism promotion threatened to overshadow archeological scholarship. For example, a 1960 travel column in the *Boston Globe* still erroneously described Machu Picchu as the resting place of Sun Virgins.[47] When the archeologist Gene Savoy revealed that he had found Vilcabamba, the true last capital of the Incas, outlets like the *New York Times* downplayed the significance of the discovery, offering limited press coverage.[48] Bingham's false assertion that Machu Picchu was the final capital of the Inca, repeated in the press and travel guides, proved difficult to dislodge from the popular imagination, which emphasized the archeological complex as the ultimate symbol of Peru's pre-Hispanic past. The *Boston Globe* perhaps stated popular disbelief of Savoy's discovery of Vilcabamba best by announcing that "Machu Picchu mightn't be Machu Picchu after all!"[49] As late as 1976, visitors could not access the Vilcabamba archeological complex, which, roughly one hundred kilometers northwest of Machu Picchu, remained isolated from the key tourism corridors selected for development.[50]

However, behind the glossy images of modern travel, multiple problems still afflicted Peru's tourism development. A travel article featured in August 1967 in the *Boston Globe* remarked that "in Peru the most exciting tourist attraction is nearly impossible to get to. Machu Picchu is a four day event from Lima and you have to fight for it all the way."[51] *El Comercio de Lima* also expressed its indignation over a perceived poor image of Peru received by tourists at Machu Picchu. "A semi-literate subject represents the fortress of Macchupicchu," complained the Lima newspaper, illustrating both the impoverished conditions of employees working at the site and continued limeño bias against the Andes.[52] Many of COTURPERU's failures to compete in the modern tourism economy were laid at the feet of its director, Roca Muelle.[53] In February 1966, Felipe Benavides, a former employee of COTURPERU, gave an interview to the newspaper *El Expreso* in which he argued that Roca Muelle managed the institution "as if it was private property." Benavides accused Roca Muelle of not keeping the executive board aware of new hotel construction contracts, failure to implement the recommendations of the Checchi Report, and personnel mismanagement. Most seriously, however, Benavides accused Roca Muelle of being out of touch with a new era of tourism. Benavides observed, "Yes, he was a pioneer . . . more than thirty years ago, when airplanes flew with wood propellers. He isn't familiar with the era of the jet."[54] Roca Muelle denied the allegations of mismanagement, but by 1967 he was replaced as head of COTURPERU.[55] Albert Giesecke died in 1968; another early tourism pioneer had gone.

However, the greatest threat to Cusco's pursuit of elite tourism was perhaps the precarious social conditions in the region during the 1960s. As early as 1958, workers and tenants in Cusco's La Convención Province began to strike for labor and land reform. By 1960 the La Convención strikes had expanded and occupied haciendas. Growing agrarian unrest in La Convención and other parts of Peru provided a key pretext for the military to oust Manuel Prado in the final weeks of his presidency in July 1962. The short-lived military junta immediately proposed agrarian reform measures for La Convención. The success of the La Convención uprising and the election of Belaúnde in 1963 emboldened campesinos in the traditional rural zones of Cusco's altiplano to seize the land of haciendas across the region.[56] Belaúnde supported agrarian reform. However, pressured by conservative parties in control of Congress, the president adopted a hard-line stance against the land seizures in Cusco. By February 1964, at least thirty-five campesinos had died in confrontations with the police. In March 1964, Belaúnde declared a state of siege in Cusco, suspending constitutional law. For the remainder of Belaúnde's administration, Cusco's rural communities remained locked in a tense social and political stalemate with the national government.[57] In Mesa Pelada, a zone near La Convención, guerrilla warfare groups inspired by the Cuban Revolution, Movimento de la Izquierda Revolucionaria (Left Revolutionary Movement, MIR) and Ejército de Liberación Nacional (National Liberation Army, ELN), engaged the military in a failed agrarian uprising in 1965. In addition to problems associated with social unrest, Belaúnde's agenda was frustrated by conservative opposition in Congress and a deteriorating economic environment, with 14 percent annual inflation and a painful devaluation of the sol in September 1967. When the politically sensitive topic of expropriating the U.S.-owned International Petroleum Company's holdings became mired in scandal in 1968, many observers predicted that military intervention was imminent.[58] The political and economic unrest in Belaúnde's government resulted in strikes, labor unrest, and budget cuts to preservation and tourism promotion institutions that all negatively affected tourism in Cusco.[59]

The ongoing social chaos did not go unnoticed by visitors. One *Boston Globe* columnist who visited Machu Picchu in 1960 praised the spectacular site, but also expressed his dismay at witnessing the stark poverty of Cusco. He characterized highland Peru as a mix of "beauty, squalor, and angry voices."[60] On July 4, 1965, Lima's Hotel Crillon, which catered to many international travelers, suffered a bomb attack by guerrillas likely seeking to protest U.S. influence in Peru.[61] The uncomfortable collision between elite international travel and Cusco's social tumult in 1965 was encapsulated on the front page of the October 19 issue of *El Comercio del Cusco*, which announced the arrival in Cusco of U.S. film stars including Gene Tierney and Barbara Bouchet, escorted by COTURPERU, alongside a headline on the ongoing MIR insurgency that read "Guerillas Captured!"[62] Although the Peruvian military suppressed the MIR uprising by the end of 1965, conditions had not improved by June 1968, when the front page of *El Comercio del Cusco* featured an article on hotel hygiene quality next to another announcing, "Hunger forces campesinos to sell their children."[63]

Tourism under the Revolutionary Armed Forces

As many predicted, on October 3, 1968, the military unseated Belaúnde in a bloodless coup led by army general Juan Velasco Alvarado. To the surprise of observers, the military officers dubbed their rule the Revolutionary Government of the Armed Forces of Peru and quickly redirected national politics to the left. Velasco and his supporters in the armed forces were alarmed by the growing popular radicalism that had emerged as Belaúnde proved unable to achieve reform due to the intransigence of Peru's traditional conservative elite. Once in power, Velasco claimed the mandate to undertake major top-down social reforms. Foreign-owned mining and oil interests were expropriated and nationalized, new development agencies to promote economic modernization appeared, and, in June 1969, the government implemented one of the largest agrarian reforms in Latin American history. Despite these measures, the military government remained wary of popular political mobilization. In fact, many have analyzed the Velasco government's actions as reactionary measures to prevent revolution from below by instituting controlled reform from above.[64] Historian Eric Hobsbawm dubbed the military's attempt to enact broad social reform while simultaneously spurning mass political mobilization a "peculiar revolution."[65]

Perhaps due to its ambivalence toward the political mobilization of everyday Peruvians, the military government demonstrated its leftist credentials through a raft of symbolic reforms. It declared Quechua a national language, opened up diplomatic and cultural exchanges with Cuba and socialist European states, and sponsored indigenous-focused art and folkloric projects. The military government produced posters and other visuals to communicate its populist development goals.[66] Machu Picchu also figured prominently in government cultural campaigns, often placed alongside images of industrious workers and rural development.[67]

Immediately the new government acted to consolidate tourism management under the rapidly growing state bureaucracy. As the military government reconfigured state institutions in late 1968, nearly all tourism matters were placed under the control of the Ministerio de Industria y Comercio (Ministry of Industry and Commerce).[68] In March 1969, the military government replaced COTURPERU with the Empresa Nacional del Turismo (National Tourism Company, ENTURPERU), a smaller institution tasked with managing the state hotels.[69] In December of that year, the state placed tourism development under the control of the newly created Dirección General del Turismo (General Office of Tourism, DGTUR) within the Ministry of Industry and Commerce.[70] National development plans placed tourism alongside agrarian reform, mining, and manufacturing as key economic goals for the military government. In addition to bureaucratic changes, the state increased its role in transportation. The Santa Ana Railroad became part of the state-owned Empresa Nacional de Ferrocarilles del Perú (National Railroad Company of Peru, ENAFER) in 1972 and the state-owned AeroPerú airline began service in 1973.[71]

However, the most ambitious proposal to develop tourism as part of the military government's reforms involved the cooperation of transnational institutions including UNESCO and the Inter-American Development Bank (IDB). As early as 1965, UNESCO and the Peruvian government began negotiations to involve the former in the restoration of Machu Picchu. In 1966 the head of UNESCO, René Vironi, arrived in Peru to formally begin working for the creation of a more comprehensive plan to promote cultural tourism with historical preservation. In the final months of Belaúnde's government, Peru and UNESCO announced the creation of the Plan Turístico y Cultural Perú-UNESCO (Peru-UNESCO Tourist and Cultural Plan, COPESCO).[72] The new military government continued COPESCO and, in April 1969, organized an executive committee headed by the minister of industry and commerce to assume and direct administrative control of the institution aided with advisers partially funded by UNESCO and the United Nations Development Programme.[73] Despite its nationalist rhetoric, the military government proved adept at securing international financing for COPESCO.[74] By 1972 COPESCO's total cost had reached $70,752,000, 60 percent provided by a loan from the IDB, the hemisphere's largest development finance lender, and 40 percent provided by the Peruvian state.[75]

COPESCO's area of influence extended 84,735 square kilometers, from Lake Titicaca in Puno Department to La Convención in Cusco.[76]

Unlike previous institutions that sought to develop tourism as a supplementary source of economic growth, COPESCO pledged to use tourist-oriented development to radically change the society of southern Peru. The military government envisioned COPESCO as an important institutional tool along with the agrarian reform in its goal to fundamentally reorder the colonial foundations of Cusco's regional economy. For Velasco and many of his closest allies in the military government, the uprising in La Convención and the experience of fighting the MIR and ELN in 1965 had served as a formative moment in their political evolution. During the counterinsurgency campaigns military leaders witnessed the stark underdevelopment of Cusco and the potential danger of ignoring the region's social and economic conditions.[77] In fact, the new minister of industry and commerce during the organization of COPESCO, Rear Admiral Jorge Dellepiane, emerged as one of the regime's more leftist leaders.[78] As a result, the new military government expanded the initiatives of COPESCO begun by Belaúnde. "In the Cusco-Puno zone, tourism is the sector that can channel investments for its own development and simultaneously provide an infrastructural base for the social-economic development of the zone," predicted one 1972 COPESCO assessment.[79] Tourism, like agrarian reform, would become an instrument of development and social change in Cusco.

In fact, COPESCO's planners correctly recognized that agrarian reform alone would not secure development for Cusco and neighboring Puno. It appears that COPESCO planners recognized what later scholars have argued the military government overlooked during the agrarian reform: the crisis in highland Peru derived not just from a concentration of territory in haciendas but, more important, from a general lack of arable land.[80] Even with the agrarian reform of 1969, 56 percent of Cusco's economically active rural population lacked steady employment.[81] To combat the region's underdevelopment, COPESCO planners envisioned an immediate injection of state spending in "fixed social capital" through the construction of roads, hotels, and tourism infrastructure. Such spending would encourage private investment in a service economy in the region.[82] COPESCO predicted that the combined public and private investment would quickly begin a "chain reaction of auto-generated profits and spending that will extend to all economic sectors." As a result, "tourism activity, not needing skilled labor, will become a generator of profits to absorb the workforce in a rapid, easy, and cheap process."[83] In the eyes of COPESCO, tourism would play a crucial role in absorbing rural labor into a modern service economy.

The COPESCO plan promoted tourism as a key force to achieve rural development in Cusco and neighboring Puno. From the start, the institution worked to assess and evaluate its effect on local employment and redistribution of tourism spending.[84] For Aguas Calientes, COPESCO recommended $217,000 in spending for a school, sanitary clinic, park, sewer system, and electrification.[85] COPESCO justified the spending by noting that a better-educated and healthier workforce would simultaneously improve tourism service and overall social conditions. Even the large upfront infrastructure spending of the COPESCO projects promised to "intensively absorb untrained labor," providing "cycles of general training that will quickly prepare personnel for services in hotels, vacation colonies, and youth lodges."[86] One of the project's most successful efforts was the pilot plan developed for the Sacred Valley village of Písac that emphasized restoring the town's archeological complex in coordination with rehabilitation of its small urban center.[87] Another COPESCO initiative sent young university students to hundreds of small towns in Cusco and Puno to assess the potential to use the sites for cultural tourism. Their reports, now buried in state archives, provided a fascinating snapshot of life in Peru's southern Andes. The town of Marangani received a positive assessment for tourism potential thanks to its well-preserved parish church and good road access.[88] Unfortunately for the small town of La Quebrada in the Lares district of Cusco, the report concluded that it "does not have any" tourism appeal and was simply a "typical agricultural settlement."[89] The project examined human capital as well as structures in assessing tourism potential. One report on the town of Kitapayara in La Convención Valley recommended future tourism potential due to the fact that the "native group is not well acculturated which permits [a visitor] to appreciate their old customs."[90]

COPESCO also provided much-needed preservation funds for Cusco. The military government dissolved or defunded institutions like the CRYF, COTURPERU, and the National Archeological Council that provided funds for Machu Picchu's preservation and operations, resulting in a dearth of needed funding. Between 1968 and October 1971, care of Machu Picchu reverted to the woefully underfunded Departmental Archeology Council.[91] "Only a profound care for Cuzco and archeology and a true spirit of sacrifice" sustained Machu Picchu's operations during the tumultuous years at the start of military rule, according to Archeology Council head Chávez Ballón.[92]

Working with the United Nations Development Programme, COPESCO created Project PER-39 as an extensive program to document and catalogue archeological sites over a two-year period.[93] Between 1973 and 1975, COPESCO worked in coordination with Project PER-39 to coordinate the restoration of twenty-seven different historical sites in and around Cusco. The funds also permitted a cataloging of all archeological sites in Cusco, as well as funding artisan workshops to repair artifacts in Cusco.[94] Project PER-39 included funding for photography and inspection of stonework in Machu Picchu in 1974.[95] That same year, the IDB awarded the Peruvian government a loan of $5,478,000 for historical preservation projects. With this start-up funding secured, the government formed a special unit to oversee a comprehensive maintenance and preservation program for Machu Picchu between 1975 and 1981.[96]

The announced spending received a warm reception in Cusco, where the regional-focused mission of COPESCO promised to avoid the past conflicts over the centralization of development. Cusqueños had already expressed concerns that the demands for elite-oriented hotels catering to international travelers exceeded the financial capabilities of local capital. Most new hotel construction in the 1960s was financed and owned by limeño economic interests. As early as 1967, *El Comercio del Cusco* criticized the increasing stratification of tourism development. The paper noted that the new tourism economy threatened to "place us in the role of the 'useful idiot' (*tonto útil*) in favor of outside companies and people."[97] Cusqueños welcomed state spending as an alternative to private, Lima-based capital interests. In August 1970, ENTURPERU announced plans to convert the San Francisco Monastery in Cusco's historic center into a modern 312-bed hotel.[98] The following year, ENTURPERU pledged a second luxury hotel in the city center at the former San Antonio Abad Monastery.[99] In February 1970, the government released plans to construct a new auto highway connecting Ollantaytambo directly to Machu Picchu to provide a second access route to the site running parallel to the Santa Ana rail line.[100] These new projects, which promised jobs and managerial positions for locals, enjoyed broad support in Cusco. When Velasco arrived in Cusco on September 27, 1971, to formally approve the highway project, *El Comercio del Cusco* applauded his initiatives, claiming that "they form a true rise in tourism promotion that Cusco needs and longs for."[101]

Despite the populist push of the Velasco government, it still viewed a tourism-based economy as best suited to serve elite travelers. COPESCO endorsed most of the conclusions of the Checci Report that recommended continued state investment be directed toward creating upscale hotels to market to elite international tourists primarily originating from the United States.[102] Both COPESCO and the Velasco government believed that elite tourism would provide the initial boost in economic growth Cusco needed for its travel economy to take off. The Velasco government did use tourism to support its leftist nationalist rhetoric. By 1972, Machu Picchu saw visits by dignitaries from the People's Republic of China and the Soviet Union.[103] However, the Velasco government used tourism as a tool to retain positive relations with the United States while it maintained a nonaligned Cold War position.[104] These efforts mirrored those of other nations, like Gaullist France, which also employed tourism to maintain Cold War economic and political links to the United States despite somewhat frosty diplomatic relations. In fact, after the 1970 election of the socialist government of Salvador Allende in Chile, the United States viewed Velasco as a moderate ally in South America. Tourism served as a source of positive commercial and diplomatic cooperation between the Velasco government and the United States. ENTURPERU signed lucrative hotel contracts with Holiday Inn, Marriott, and Braniff Airways. When Peru inaugurated its new nationalized airline, AeroPerú, the United States objected to granting it landing rights, only to quickly smooth over the dispute.[105] In fact, some of AeroPerú's first tourist advertising featured Machu Picchu prominently in an outreach to U.S. travelers. In 1974, at the height of the military government's populist and revolutionary message, the imagery of tourism remained associated with cultured, modern travelers from the global north.[106]

Hotel Machu Picchu

Of all of COPESCO's projects, none captured cusqueños' attention and hopes for tourism development in the region more than the proposal for a modern hotel adjacent to Machu Picchu. Unfortunately for the Velasco government, the project would come to represent the paradoxes of its tourism development plans in Cusco. For many years, individuals proposed constructing a modern hotel at Machu Picchu at the site of the lodge completed in 1933. Proposals to construct an ambitious hotel at the site appeared throughout the 1950s.[107] Backers of a hotel project initially hoped that the CRYF would construct a modern facility in preparation for the fiftieth anniversary celebrations of the Bingham expedition held in July 1961.[108] These hopes were never fulfilled, but, thanks to private investment, by 1966 Cusco boasted sixteen hotels with 1,058 beds.[109] Yet, these lodgings still proved insufficient—an important

The last Inca on Earth.
On a towering peak in the Andes the Incas built their final fortress then vanished from the earth forever.

AeroPeru

The world's newest...and perhaps oldest airline

AeroPerú poster. AeroPerú was the new nationalized airline inaugurated during General Juan Velasco Alvarado's military government. However, AeroPerú publicity in the United States did not highlight the leftist policies of the Velasco government, but instead promoted Machu Picchu and Peru as mystic and romantic sites. Author's personal collection.

local grievance against national tourism planning.[110] "Why do we do tourism promotion if when we receive a visitor we cannot offer him the indispensable: a bed?" asked *El Comercio del Cusco* in June 1967.[111] COPESCO planners estimated that, without immediate government investment in hotel construction, by 1975 Cusco could face a deficit of over 5,000 hotel beds. If hotel construction did not match growth, long-term tourism development in the region would suffer from missed opportunities and bad press.[112]

COPESCO proposed an ambitious policy to construct hotel facilities for modern elite travelers in Cusco. In addition to the proposed hotel at the San Antonio Abad Monastery, COPESCO proposed three additional new hotels featuring 200 beds each for the Cusco region: one at Machu Picchu, and two in the city of Cusco.[113] The plan also proposed a vacation colony for Urubamba

Cusco en el turismo mundial

January 1, 1974, edition of *El Comercio del Cusco*. The Velasco government and institutions such as COPESCO envisioned tourism as a key tool to bring revolutionary change in Cusco. However, images like this from Cusco's *El Comercio*, featuring jets, cameras, and binoculars, show that even at the height of these policies, tourism remained identified with elite travel. Hemeroteca de la Biblioteca Municipal del Cusco.

and a "youth lodge" for backpackers at Machu Picchu.[114] COPESCO backed the creation of a luxury hotel at Machu Picchu, justifying surveys stating that 77 percent of the coveted U.S. tourist market wanted to stay in first-class hotels.[115] Taking these recommendations into consideration, the national government issued Ministerial Resolution 192-72 on February 21, 1972, authorizing the Ministry of Industry and Commerce to allocate 31 million soles toward the project, and called for a commission of architects and planners to begin work on selecting proposals for the hotel.[116] By February 1972, the government completed formal estimates on construction costs and locations for the new hotel.[117] All proposals under consideration featured modernist designs and several floors of rooms. Most proposals also placed the new hotel adjacent to the archeological complex, often dug into the hillside.[118] On June 7, 1972, the Ministry of Industry and Commerce issued Ministerial Resolution 737-72, naming a planning commission to examine possible construction sites for new hotels in the Cusco region.[119]

So convinced were the military and COPESCO planners of the benefits of tourism development that they never predicted that proposals to construct a large hotel adjacent to Machu Picchu would cause an outcry. Employing

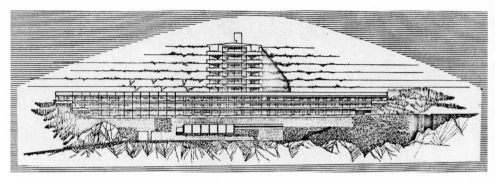

One of the proposed plans for the Hotel Machu Picchu. In this rendering of a
proposal for a modern hotel to be constructed adjacent to the Machu Picchu
archeological site, Inca terraces can be seen in the background. While the project
was popular among local leaders, it is easy to see why preservationists objected to it.
Biblioteca del Ministerio de Cultura del Perú.

Machu Picchu as a nationalist symbol, the military did not foresee the possible negative reaction produced by granting elite travelers prime access to
the site. More importantly, the Velasco government created and empowered
new bureaucratic institutions that proved ideally suited to fight *against* the
hotel project. In March 1971, the government created the Instituto Nacional
de Cultura (National Culture Institute, INC) to centralize national cultural
policy and historical preservation.[120] In November 1971, the INC assumed
control of all national historic and archeological sites, including Machu Picchu.[121] Following new policies, COPESCO sent the initial hotel plans to the
INC for review and received a response on October 12, 1971. The leadership
of the INC responded with a conditional "favorable opinion" but cautioned
that the National Archeological Council (now under the control of the INC)
needed to provide final approval for the hotel.[122] More ominously, the report warned that the hotel project could potentially conflict with several
national preservation laws, including the original archeological preservation
Law 6634 passed in 1929, the more recent Law Decree 14135 from 1962, which
declared Urubamba an "archeological province," and several international
planning and preservation policies that, by the 1960s, had emphasized keeping archeological sites and their surrounding environments unaltered.[123]
As a response, the national government sent an INC team to Machu Picchu
in early June 1972 and pledged to follow the recommendations of the
committee.[124]

Any hopes of quick approval for the hotel fell apart at a contentious forum
hosted on June 12, 1972, by the Ministry of Industry and Commerce. Five

panel members, all representing tourism interests, expressed approval of the project. However, the remaining fourteen members argued against constructing a new hotel on the current lodge site. The architect Santiago Agurto declared that a hotel on the site would be a "cultural injury." Luis Miró Quesada Garland, another architect who worked with the CRYF, seconded Agurto's objections regarding the project. A forestry engineer, Benjamín Almanza, voiced his objections by noting that a new hotel would threaten the biodiversity surrounding Machu Picchu. Luis E. Valcárcel also spoke against the project, and artist Fernando de Szyszlo warned that "it would be insensitive to only consider the tourist-commercial element" embodied by the hotel project. Others in attendance argued that the hotel project ran contrary to the aims of the Velasco government's revolutionary and nationalistic rhetoric. The architect Roberto Wakeham noted that constructing a hotel largely for wealthy foreign travelers did not conform to the current revolutionary goals of the military government. The sociologist Dr. Leopoldo Chiappo also argued that the plan of hotel construction needed to be reviewed "from the point of view of a revolutionary society that one wants to establish in the country."[125] International pressure also grew against the hotel project. Scholars meeting in Mexico City for a conference in August, including the prominent anthropologist John Murra and the archeologist María Rostworowski, signed a petition protesting the hotel project.[126] By August 1972, even U.S. dailies printed news articles regarding the uproar over the proposed hotel.[127]

The opposition to the hotel opened up long-festering wounds regarding Peru's endemic political and economic centralism. In Cusco, opposition to the hotel smacked of Lima-centric machinations against regional development. "Sabotage of an already-approved project?" questioned *El Comercio del Cusco* on June 12, 1972, following the first delays of approval for the hotel in preparation for the INC review.[128] For *El Comercio del Cusco*, the need to secure funding for the Machu Picchu project appeared increasingly urgent, as the government's proposals for hotels in the former San Francisco and San Antonio Abad monasteries had not progressed since 1970. An August 5, 1972, editorial in Cusco's *El Comercio* petitioned the government to proceed with hotel construction despite preservationist protests by appealing to the military's populist rhetoric, citing the "mindfulness that the people support said project."[129] Another editorial from August 22 sought to identify Lima's economic and political power as the key opponent. "The stubborn persistence of hidden but powerful economic forces encysted in Lima" was the true sources of opposition to the Machu Picchu hotel in the view of *El Comercio del Cusco*.[130] For cusqueños, COPESCO and the Machu Picchu hotel represented the region's best chance for economic autonomy, and well-financed investors in Lima wanted to scuttle the projects.

Seeking to reach a resolution, the national government called on the Ministry of Education to form a panel to evaluate the hotel project. The committee released its findings on August 14, 1972, recommending the implementation of a "protected zone" surrounding the archeological complex. "Machu Picchu is an extremely complex site, linked with the environment that surrounds it through a true harmonious relationship between architecture and the topography," argued the report's conclusion. The report proposed a protected zone of roughly 1,400 hectares.[131] By September 1972, the Ministry of Education had publicized its recommendations for the 1,400-hectare protected zone, thus arguing against the construction of a new hotel next to the ruin.[132] By early September 1972 rumors circulated that a compromise location near but not adjacent to Machu Picchu would be selected for the hotel project. Unofficial sources hinted that officials had selected a new location thirty kilometers from the ruin.[133]

Local interests, led by *El Comercio del Cusco*'s editorial board, reacted to rumors of the relocation as another threat from Lima-based economic interests, arguing that "enemies of Cusco do not relent."[134] Tensions mounted until the provincial mayor of Cusco called an open town meeting on October 10 to demand construction of the new Machu Picchu hotel on the current lodge site or an alternate location selected by COPESCO. Denouncing INC head Martha Hildebrandt, municipal leaders threatened a general strike if their demands were not met within fifteen days. Reporting on the meeting, *El Comercio del Cusco* proudly noted that "it had the virtue of certifying the unity of cusqueños when they see the goals of progress in danger for those who have a right to their land *(tiene derecho su tierra)*."[135] Although the calls for a general strike failed to materialize, two days later Cusco's leaders sent a formal petition addressed directly to Velasco to advocate for the hotel project.[136]

As cusqueños rallied to protect what they viewed as regional self-determination, in Lima INC director Hildebrandt viewed the mobilizations in Cusco as a shortsighted pursuit of development over the long-term needs of preservation. "Now," retorted Hildebrandt in an October 17 interview with Lima's *El Correo* newspaper, "we must defend Machu Picchu from cusqueños." The INC director continued her response, arguing, "It's incredible but odd that we, not the cuzqueños, are the ones concerned with Cuzco."[137] Hildebrandt's remarks did little to diminish cusqueños' suspicions of Lima's centralism and paternalism. In fact, Cusco's mayor demanded that Hildebrandt travel to Cusco to answer for her remarks, mocking her as one of "these *señores* that, at the eleventh hour, become *cusqueñistas* and look down from their balcony trying to devise tactics for the solutions that afflict Cusco."[138] *El Comercio del Cusco* criticized Hildebrandt and the INC as pawns used by monopolistic tourism interests in Lima that "will not have this valuable prey to suckle on" once the state-owned Machu Picchu hotel was completed.[139] Cusco's regional leadership continued to view the hotel project as a vital link in Cusco's revolutionary and populist development. To bolster this view, in early October labor unions representing the region's brewers, bank workers, hotel employees, drivers, industrial workers, and even employees of the Coca-Cola bottling plant formally petitioned the national government to back the hotel in the name of workers' rights.[140] As a final justification, *El Comercio del Cusco* reminded hotel opponents that cusqueños backed the recommendations of the Plan COPESCO, which had been "developed by national and foreign experts of the highest level" and therefore conformed to preservation standards.[141]

It is important to note that not all cusqueños supported the hotel project. In fact, prominent Cusco-based archeologists who had worked extensively at Machu Picchu, including Manuel Chávez Ballón, publicly supported Hildebrandt's efforts to stop the hotel.[142] Hildebrandt also wisely appealed to the nationalist rhetoric of the revolutionary government in her recommendations against the hotel project. In her October 1972 official report to the council of ministers, Hildebrandt noted: "Monuments of our old culture represent cash capital (*capital contante y sonante*). *It is necessary put the ruins to work*, it is true, but not in a hurried search of the ephemeral dollar, but in the employ of affirming our national identity." The report went on to detail that "Peru has many ruins, large ruins, magnificent ruins. But amongst all of them only Machu Picchu has reached the dimension of a symbol. Machu Picchu is Peru, just like Túpac Amaru." Employing the symbol of Túpac Amaru II, the cusqueño and anticolonial rebel who had become a key symbol of the military government's propaganda, Hildebrandt equated preservationist policies with the nationalist goals of the military leaders. Hildebrandt ended the report by noting that "conservation of cultural patrimony and tourism development has led to the creation of seemingly equitable, but false expression: *cultural tourism*."[143] The conclusion appeared to refute one of the central goals promoted by COPESCO—the compatibility of development with preservation in Cusco.

By the end of October 1972 the national government reached a compromise regarding the Machu Picchu hotel. Issuing Decree Law 19597, the government declared that the new hotel for Machu Picchu was an "urgent necessity," but that the project would not be built in the immediate environs of the ruin.[144] A new commission arrived at the site in November and recommended the lower zone of the Mandor Hacienda, located along the Urubamba River at the base of the ruin, as the best alternative option for the hotel.[145] Less than a week later, the provincial mayor of Cusco promised that the new Machu Picchu hotel would open by July 1975.[146] Yet, by February 1973, the minister of industry and commerce still predicted that it would be "four or five weeks" until authorities finalized the exact location for the new hotel. As usual, *El Comercio del Cusco* blamed "large economic interests sealed off in Lima" for delays with the hotel.[147] However, Cusco's suspicions of a Lima-based conspiracy against the hotel were likely overblown. For example, Lima's *El Comercio* editorial board continued to support efforts to construct the Machu Picchu hotel.[148] As cusqueños would discover, the government's own deteriorating economic and political conditions, not Lima's economic interests, would emerge as tourism development's greatest threat.

End of the Vacation

By February 1973, the military's "revolution" had developed serious problems. The agrarian reform and expropriations of foreign economic assets had exceeded expected expenses and had failed to deliver promised revenue. Meanwhile, Velasco's deteriorating health and growing opposition to the regime eroded the government's political standing.[149] On June 1, 1973, *El Comercio del Cusco* reported delays in the construction of a proposed modern state hotel near Cusco's city center originally proposed along with the Machu Picchu facility. The editorial board of Cusco's *El Comercio* refused to believe that the government would delay "the construction of a great hotel complex in our city, serving as a source of work and unforeseen progress for this part of the country."[150] As had been the case with the Machu Picchu project, *El Comercio del Cusco* speculated that "economic forces, once disguised as 'machupicchólogos,' or 'lovers of the land'" that derailed the Machu Picchu project lay behind the Cusco hotel proposal.[151]

In September 1973, the national government announced over 1 billion soles in tourism infrastructure investment in Cusco, yet work on nearly all large tourism projects, including the hotel and the highway to Machu Picchu, failed to commence.[152] With the hotel project suspended, local interests lobbied the government to at least complete the highway to Machu

Picchu. Seeking to conform to the military's populist goals, locals argued that the limited transportation options had driven ticket costs so high that working-class Peruvians could not access the ruin. "Open the doors of Cusco's own house to all non-privileged Peruvians," pleaded *El Comercio del Cusco* in an October 11, 1973, editorial.[153] If appeal to the government's populist rhetoric failed, the local press exploited the military's nationalist sentiment. For Peru's Independence Day in 1974, *El Comercio del Cusco* announced a campaign to push for the highway construction dubbed "Machupijchu, Symbol of Peruvianness."[154]

Despite local lobbying, the national government made no progress on the hotel or highway projects. Relations reached a nadir in November 1973 when locals attacked and burned the Cusco headquarters of the Sistema Nacional de Mobilización Social, (National Social Mobilization System, SINAMOS), the chief administrative organization of the military government.[155] As late as 1974, the government continued to promise to complete COPESCO projects.[156] In 1975 COPESCO presented plans that called for an eleven-story hotel to be built into an Incaic terrace at Huayrac Tambo that lay just outside the newly declared protected zone.[157] The project again sparked the protest of preservationist institutions in Project PER-39 and the INC.[158] However, budgetary pressures proved more effective than preservation concerns in preventing the project from going forward. In August 1975, General Morales Bermúdez ousted the ill and politically weak Velasco. The internal coup represented a rightward shift for national politics and development. Immediately, the government looked to cut spending and rein in the growing national debt.[159] Despite the government's pledges to continue tourism investment, by 1976 austerity measures forced even a modest restoration of the 1933 Machu Picchu lodge to be scaled back.[160]

The simultaneous goals of development, preservation, and social justice at the heart of the military's tourism plans provoked conflicts beyond the controversial Machu Picchu hotel project. Even the military's vaunted agrarian reform brought different government institutions into conflict over Machu Picchu. Four haciendas surrounded Machu Picchu prior to the 1969 agrarian reform.[161] After the agrarian reform promised to redistribute ownership of the haciendas, officials in the cultural preservation bureaucracy raised objections over the potential consequences these changes posed to Machu Picchu. Concerns grew after a serious incident occurred in September 1971 when Carlos Zavaleta, owner of the adjacent Hacienda Mandor, burned undergrowth to clear a zone for sheep grazing. The dry conditions permitted the fire to burn out of control and threaten Machu Picchu. Two weeks later, another set blaze ascended Huayna Picchu and "entered the ruins, burning the plaza of the sacred rock and the eastern slope of the Intihuatana hill." After this incident, archeology head Chávez Ballón concluded that "this should serve as a motive to resolve once and for all the need for Machupicchu to be considered as a national park." Chávez Ballón recommended that legislation be proposed creating a national park extending from kilometer 86 to kilometer 122 of the Urubamba River, urging the state to use the ongoing agrarian reform to expropriate lands not for campesinos, but for the new reserve.[162]

For preservationists and officials in the INC, their goal to secure territory for conservation around Machu Picchu placed them in conflict with one of the central reforms of the Velasco government, which had placed emphasis on the redistribution of land. In a 1975 report prepared for the INC, preservationists presented several potential negative scenarios that the agrarian reform posed for Machu Picchu. Included in the report's predictions were "total acquisition of lands into a cooperative, social company, or whatever it may be called," a "future avalanche of people," and "indiscriminate exploitation of forests." The report recommended that INC leadership work to acquire as much surrounding land as possible to prevent it from being redistributed to campesinos.[163] An additional report on the need to create a national park surrounding Machu Picchu appeared in March 1977 in cooperation with Agrarian Zone 11 officials. Once again, the report stressed the need to take urgent measures, citing recent incursions into the Sacsayhuamán archeological complex and efforts to create a new agrarian cooperative along kilometers 108 and 109 of the Urubamba River adjacent to Machu Picchu.[164]

Conflicts between tourism development and land redistribution also emerged among local communities in Cusco. The government faced difficulty justifying the reservation of prime tracts to serve foreign elite tourists while continuing its rhetoric of populist land reform. In October 1973, campesinos invaded the territory reserved for one of Cusco's proposed tourism hotels. Despite the government's rhetoric, police were sent to dislodge the campesinos who had seized the hotel property.[165] In other instances, campesinos themselves rejected the goals of the agrarian reform. The military government's land reforms emphasized the formation of worker cooperatives on the expropriated land of haciendas. However, campesinos residing near major tourist attractions showed little interest in forming agricultural cooperatives. Campesinos residing in Aguas Calientes who received the land of the former Hacienda Mandor began negotiations to resell parcels to private hotel developers in the early 1980s.[166]

Jipi Tourism

Since the 1920s, cusqueños had employed tourism to illustrate how their region's indigenous character appealed to global elite travelers. They did not suspect that this same indigeneity would, by the end of the 1960s, prove equally appealing to the emerging global countercultural movement that rejected the modernity cusqueños hoped to deliver to their region. Throughout the 1960s, most tourism planning was based on attracting elite and upper-middle-class travelers. For example, the Checchi Report recommended that "'rock and roll' music should not be played in the lobbies of the hotels."[167] These assumptions continued in COPESCO planning documents that estimated that the average traveler to Peru in 1971 would be "a business man or professional between thirty-five and forty, with a high degree of education and cultural level. It is almost guaranteed this man will travel with his family."[168] As late as June 1972, Lima's *La Prensa* called for increased luxury hotel construction based on the observation that "an important percentage of tourists are people of advanced age, for whom comfortable accommodations prove essential. Very few are those who are willing to undertake adventures or stoically support difficult situations."[169] The Velasco government did promote efforts for "popular tourism" in Cusco.[170] However, the initiative was directed more toward middle-class nationals instead of international backpackers. In fact, domestic tourism to Cusco spiked in the first years of the Velasco government, most likely due to the expansion of state bureaucracies and industries that swelled urban and middle-class incomes.[171]

However, by July 1972, hippie (often written as *jipi* in Spanish) travel to Peru had become prevalent enough that *El Comercio de Lima* dedicated a special Sunday supplement to investigating the new wave of "travelers with long hair, worn-out *bluejeans*, or dressed in colorful clothing." *El Comercio de Lima* continued to describe Peru's new visitors, observing: "They are people who want to see things deeper, that look to introduce themselves in the most tantalizingly distant from the West, that want to live like the Indians of Mexico, understand the misery of India, investigate socialism in Chile, or experiment Malaysian hospitality." *El Comercio de Lima* noted that hippie arrivals to Peru were indeed part of a global phenomenon. "Our country's embassy in France is literally assaulted with requests for information or for visas from young students who want to 'share in the life of the Quechua Indian,'" remarked the article. The article also correctly correlated the rise of hippie tourism with a global rejection of modernity in the late 1960s and early 1970s. "Young people raised in an enormously technological society want to remember what pure air is, and their search for early ways of life is a return to roots lost over various centuries," noted the article, which concluded that the most common destination of Peru's new hippie tourists was hardly surprising: "In the age of Aquarius, Machu Picchu is one of the most sacred places of the world."[172]

For many countercultural travelers of the late 1960s and early 1970s, Peru and the Andes did indeed serve as icons for the mystic. One U.S. backpacker who arrived in Cusco with her husband in the 1970s recalled how visiting Peru was an opportunity for "going back to Earth."[173] Transnational economic and cultural links also helped reintroduce the Andes into the counterculture's subconscious. Che Guevara, increasingly viewed as a romantic figure following his 1967 death, had celebrated Machu Picchu in his popular memoirs of his journeys across South America in the 1950s.[174] In 1970, Simon & Garfunkel released their Grammy-winning album *Bridge over Troubled Water*. The album featured a renewed version of Peruvian composer Daniel Alomía Robles's "El Condor Pasa." Recorded using Andean instruments, Simon & Garfunkel's "El Condor Pasa (If I Could)" increased global awareness of Cusco's folkloric music.[175] Dennis Hopper, a countercultural star following the success of *Easy Rider* released in 1969, arrived in Cusco in 1970 to star and direct his own film, *The Last Movie*. Beset by production problems, the film was released in 1971 to limited audiences.[176] Despite this, the cultural appeal of the Andes continued to grow. Even global fashion trends celebrated the Andes. Alpaca coats and skirts increased in popularity in the United States during the late 1960s and early 1970s, while the New York Jets star quarterback Joe Namath appeared in magazines displaying his llama hair carpet-covered Manhattan bachelor pad.[177]

Peruvians themselves helped reimagine the image of Peru and Cusco as antidotes to the modern world. When a young German filmmaker named Werner Herzog arrived in Peru in 1971 to film a television special and ran low on funds, José Koechlin, a future hotel entrepreneur, stepped in to provide financing with the hopes that filming at Machu Picchu would promote the site and encourage travel to Peru. The final version of Herzog's project, *Aguirre, the Wrath of God*, quickly developed a following in art houses across Europe and the United States.[178] For countercultural travelers, regional political changes, particularly the Mexican state's crackdown on hippies in 1968, most likely played an important role in elevating Peru as an appealing destination.[179] Although the military government viewed youth counterculture suspiciously, it never unleashed the kind of state violence experienced in other Latin American countries during the 1970s. This, combined with the regime's leftist political stance, made it an attractive destination in an era when countercultural travelers had to avoid other Latin American countries.[180]

Locals recognized the potential benefits of serving backpackers and independent travelers. By 1973 *El Comercio del Cusco*, in cooperation with local tourism promoters, began to publish an English-language "Tourist Supplement" that contained tips for all visitors, but offered content geared especially toward backpackers and independent travelers. Articles featured basic instructions for sending and receiving packages and listed the ingredients of common local dishes. Other entries contained lessons on Peruvian culture and history.[181] Some editions of the "Tourist Supplement" even outlined the goals of COPESCO. In one article, titled "Tourism Can Mean Social Progress," from the September 7, 1973, issue, international readers learned about how COPESCO and the state were "taking a closer look at the advantage of promoting social help projects with income from tourism."[182] "Tourist Supplement" articles also recommended backpacking trips to less-visited archeological sites.[183]

For many locals, however, hippie tourism brought more imagined threats than profits. In Cusco, where tourism and international travelers were previously associated with civility and modernity, the arrival of hippies proved especially shocking. Cusqueños had a low opinion of hippies before their arrival to the region in large numbers. As early as 1969 *El Comercio del Cusco* warned local parents to look out for "the appearance of Cusqueño hippies, which constitute grotesque caricatures of their overseas peers."[184] By the early 1970s, however, the wave of countercultural travelers in Cusco was difficult to ignore. During the peak tourist season of June 1971 local relations with hippie travelers appeared to reach a breaking point when numerous hippies arrived at a municipally organized pop festival. According to Cusco's *El Sol*, they "set up their tents, sleeping bags, and began to drink. Some observed drug use." Witnesses reported that "they began singing totally obscene songs . . . [to] the admiration, stupor, and indignation of those present."[185] One can imagine the shock of many of *El Comercio del Cusco*'s readers when they saw the June 1, 1971, headline announcing that hippies had turned Machu Picchu into a "nudist paradise."[186]

The arrival of hippies in Cusco forced many to rethink the cultural assumptions they held in regard to tourism and "modern" foreign travelers. Suddenly, tourists from the global north and Lima now appeared as representatives of the same backwardness once assigned to Cusco. Now the developed world appeared as a cultural threat. A report appeared in *El Comercio del Cusco* warning that "'hippismo,' born in the West of North America, equal to *rocanrolerismo* and other forms of juvenile misconduct, has extended through America, threatening to destroy the most vital elements of the nation."[187] Another article in *El Sol* argued that "hippismo" was born "in October 1968 in the barricades of Paris."[188] However, the little evidence available suggests that the majority of hippies arriving in Cusco were actually nationals or from other Latin American countries. Following a mass arrest of 300 hippies after they crashed the June 1971 concert, *El Sol* reported that most of those detained were from Lima and that the police were "calling their parents."[189] Despite their Peruvian nationality, Cusco's mayor lamented the presence of hippies as a foreign force, arguing that they consumed the region's goods while "not producing anything, not bringing us anything positive."[190] It appeared that many cusqueños had lost faith in tourism as a positive cultural, political, and economic force.

By the end of 1973, the local press expressed concern that, rather than being a curious destination for the counterculture, Cusco had become a center of hippie life. "Cusco is converting into an operations center of international 'hippismo,'" complained *El Comercio del Cusco*.[191] In fact, the local press reported that Cusco's Plaza de Armas had been transformed into a makeshift "Hippie Market" where backpackers sold their own artisan goods and travel material, to the chagrin of local merchants.[192] Relations between locals and hippies reached a low point in June 1974 during Operation Clean, a student civic campaign to pick up litter in Cusco. Participants began hanging makeshift signs in Cusco's Plaza de Armas stating, "Cusco: Clean of Hippies," to much applause and approval from locals.[193]

Local media quickly associated rumors of increased drug use with the arrival of hippies in Cusco. In early September 1972, police arrested two hippies—one Peruvian and one Uruguayan—on charges of marijuana possession. *El Comercio del Cusco* published photos of the Uruguayan suspect demonstrating for police how he prepared his marijuana before, in the reporter's words, "flying." The article concluded by reminding readers of the "grave danger" drugs posed to the community.[194] Local concerns over the relationship between hippie backpackers and drug consumption increased in June 1973 when authorities discovered marijuana in backpacking lodges in the vicinity of Machu Picchu.[195] Later that month, police arrested another suspect on charges of possession of marijuana inside Machu Picchu.[196] Drugs proved to be just one of the moral dangers of hippie tourism, according to many observers. In April 1973, Lima's *La Prensa* newspaper reported that

Hallan marihuana en poder de hippie

September 5, 1972, edition of *El Comercio del Cusco*.
The photos show a detained *jipi* demonstrating his
use of marijuana to the local police and press. The
drug use and the hippie's indigenous-inspired
clothing shocked cusqueños, who had previously
associated tourism with culture and modernity.
While the newspaper editors hoped that such
images would discourage similar behavior by local
youth, young cusqueños likely drew different
conclusions. Hemeroteca de la Biblioteca Municipal
del Cusco.

backpacking shelters around Machu Picchu "were converted into 'refuges' for groups of hippies that stayed there weeks and had all kinds of orgies."[197]

While the regional press scorned the influence of hippies, it appears that the younger generations of Cusco welcomed the arrival of the countercul-ture in their still-conservative and somewhat provincial city. For university students and other middle-class youth in Cusco, the "Global Sixties" that had swept Latin America finally arrived during the tourism boom of the early 1970s.[198] Roger Valencia, who attended UNSAAC in the early 1970s, remem-bered skipping class with many of his peers to attend a countercultural gathering organized by foreign hippies. "That was our first contact with this international movement," he recalled. Predictably, the hippies' camp was raided, with students arrested and "parents called." Yet, these actions, along with constant negative articles in the regional press, did not dampen local students' enthusiasm.[199] Another Cusco resident who witnessed the arrival of the countercultural activities recalled, "At the end of the day, the kids of the newspaper owners were out with the hippies," despite their parents' own stern editorials in the regional press.[200]

As bars opened to serve tourists, local youth took advantage of these new social settings to meet their peers visiting from Lima and abroad. Yet, as Cusco's young generation took part in the global counterculture, interactions with tourists also provoked new debates on their own connections to the indigenous culture so appealing to the new tourism boom. As reflected in locally produced guidebooks from the 1920s and 1930s, race in Cusco remained a largely cultural construction that labeled residents who lived in an urban setting and spoke Spanish as mestizos rather than indigenous.[201] However, in an era when indigenous culture had become increasingly attractive to visitors—and potential dates—young students who identified as mestizos rethought their identity. Carlos Milla, who grew up in Cusco in the 1970s, remembers that some tourist-friendly locales would often feature a regular patron who would prominently display his indigenous heritage as almost an "attraction of the bar." However, when asked, "Are you an Inca?" by a group of visiting female tourists, Milla and his friends didn't know how to respond. They eventually adopted the label "brichero," a modification of the English term "bridge man" (although others claimed the term originated from the Cusco slang for woman, *hembrichi*). Urban youths could thus engage with tourists by drawing upon their university education and knowledge of English, while also acting as key interlocutors with cusqueño indigenous culture and history. This identification allowed them to refashion their claimed mestizaje while also emphasizing their indigenous heritage, which now appealed to visitors.[202]

The increased cultural interactions offered through tourism did not reach all of Cusco's youth in an equal manner. Young females remained largely excluded from the new public spheres opening up around the tourism trade. As economic and social change swept Cusco in the middle of the twentieth century, existing concerns regarding preserving traditional female gender roles and women's "virtue" became even more heightened. Concerns regarding female interactions with male counterparts in markets and urban settings quickly extended to tourism venues.[203] Milla remembered that "some bold women met their 'gringo.'" However, parents and even young males strongly discouraged women from visiting bars. This informal prohibition even discouraged young women from visiting bars in groups or accompanied by a man. "We didn't bring women we knew to bars," said Milla.[204] María Cristina Calvo Jara, who attended UNSAAC in the early 1990s, recounted that, even a generation after Milla's experience, "women had to go with escorts like brothers, if at all," if they wanted to go to a bar or other establishment frequented by tourists.[205] If Cusco's parents were willing to bend the rules in regard to their son's interactions with counterculture through tourism, they drew the line when it came to the conduct of their daughters.

Conclusion: The Legacy of "Developmental Tourism"

How do we assess the legacy of tourism development during the Velasco era, and, more importantly, what can it tell us about larger questions regarding the decision to rely on tourism-centered development as an answer to Cusco's social and economic crises of the 1960s? As Abraham Lowenthal has noted, although the military government did not achieve many of its original goals, the broad consequences of its programs makes it difficult to judge the regime a failure.[206] By this standard, tourism policy was quite successful. COPESCO oversaw $93 million in investments in Cusco and Puno, and tourism arrivals increased steadily throughout the 1970s—an achievement not matched in other economic sectors during the tenure of the military government.[207] In addition, COPESCO completed important infrastructure projects, including 322 new kilometers of highway improvements and electrification projects that benefited residents living in rural towns along tourist routes, especially in the Sacred Valley.[208]

Yet, the state-led tourism development model also had flaws. First, the goals of cultural tourism pursued in Cusco were inherently contradictory; these included modern projects to endorse preservation, developing elite hotels to redistribute wealth, and a highly technocratic organization to produce populist change. As a result, a policy endorsed to create social and political unity in Cusco became a point of conflict. The Peruvian scholar Julio Cotler has noted, "Contrary to its hopes, however, the GRFA [the military government] became tangled up in the hostile actions its policies unleashed."[209] It appears that tourism policy in Cusco suffered the same fate as the military saw its own bureaucratic institutions and rhetoric employed against each other in increasingly bitter fights regarding regionalism, preservation, and land redistribution. Even the unpredicted arrival of hippie travelers caused many to question the value of tourism. Second, tourism plans, like many of the military's economic policies, ultimately failed to redistribute wealth.[210] COPESCO's strategy to absorb Cusco's underemployed rural workforce in tourism proved ambiguous and overly optimistic.[211] Even at the height of COPESCO's hiring in 1974, the local press reported thousands of laborers unsuccessfully seeking employment with the institution.[212]

COPESCO's plans to use tourism spending as a trickle-down or multiplying factor also largely failed. By 1981 jobs and investment provided by tourism employed only 3 percent of Cusco's regional workforce.[213]

The failure to redistribute wealth points to the final problematic legacy of tourism development in Cusco under the military. Tourism failed to bring promised development and arguably deepened Cusco's political and economic dependence on Lima. Historians of Cusco have noted the paradoxical effect of Velasco's reforms, which, instead of achieving their goal of empowering the local economy, ultimately contributed to increased regional reliance on the central government's spending and patronage.[214] The highly technocratic and centralized nature of tourism development under the military continued this pattern. Although COPESCO did create jobs, most positions ultimately provided little training or capital for workers to actually use as small entrepreneurs in the tourism economy. Materials, plans, and investments for COPESCO projects originated from outside Cusco.[215] Finally, by focusing on attracting elite international travelers to Cusco, COPESCO ensured that tourism development would require capital investment and technical training beyond the ability of local economic actors. After 1972 domestic travel to Cusco leveled, while the elite-oriented international tourism dominated by Lima and international capital increased.

An IDB report assessing COPESCO warned that its policies led to the creation of a "dual economy" of separate agrarian and tourism interests.[216] In 1975 an INC report alerted the government that its strategies had led to "consolidation of groups of power, in sectors dedicated to commerce, industry, and tourism."[217] The INC concluded, "This reflects a clear loss of initiative on the local level, as well as the entrepreneurial sector, leadership, and social conditions."[218] The opening of Cusco's Libertador Marriott in 1976 signaled a clear shift away from the public sector and locally controlled tourism development envisioned by the military government and COPESCO.[219]

Although observers correctly noted the negative effects of the centralized policies of the military government, it was incorrect to diagnose a lack of local initiative. The military government, by wiping out the political base of Cusco's traditional elite, had unwittingly created a vacuum for new tourism actors. Ironically, the hippies and countercultural travelers so scorned by elder cusqueños would soon emerge as the leaders of new initiatives to remake tourism in Cusco. Eventually, their grassroots networks, constructed working with younger cusqueños equally interested in engaging with new global visions of the Andes, would become critical by the 1980s as the Peruvian state entered an era of political and economic instability.

CHAPTER FIVE

Between Maoists and Millionaires, 1975–1996

In September 1992, cusqueño tour guide Roger Valencia led a small group of Australian tourists down the Inca Trail hiking path toward Machu Picchu. Considering the political and economic conditions in Cusco and Peru, Valencia was fortunate to lead even a small group of international travelers. For many, 1992 marked the nadir of tourism in Cusco as a stream of bad news regarding a cholera outbreak, President Alberto Fujimori's self-coup in April, and the growing power of violent insurgent groups such as Shining Path virtually shut down international travel to Peru. As the hikers progressed toward Machu Picchu, Valencia's shortwave radio picked up a news flash from Lima that promised to change his and many other cusqueños' fortunes. The broadcast announced the arrest of Abimael Guzmán, the leader of Shining Path, who had commanded the Maoist insurgency's efforts to overthrow the Peruvian state since 1980. The following morning, Valencia arrived in Machu Picchu, where every guide and porter was celebrating and hugging each other as they shared the news. Valencia would go on to head a successful tourism agency in Cusco, and in 2018 became Peru's Minister of Foreign Commerce and Tourism.[1]

Valencia's story illustrates the tremendous challenges that Cusco's tourism economy faced in the 1980s and early 1990s. However, the story also reveals the many important changes that occurred during the crisis years of tourism in Cusco. As the Peruvian state's plans to lead tourism development collapsed and the country descended into internal war, a new travel economy began to emerge on the grassroots level. Backpackers, adventure travelers, and students arrived in Cusco despite, and in some cases because of, the perceived danger in the 1980s. To cater to these new arrivals, former hippie expats and local entrepreneurs refashioned Cusco's tourism market to include adventure, cultural, and environmental tourism. Such groups not only helped tourism survive but also expanded and diversified Cusco's travel economy. Unlike earlier efforts that promoted Cusco and Machu Picchu as appealing modern destinations, the new wave of tourism activity built off of the countercultural appeal of the Andes and the Inca as timeless, natural, and even mystic symbols. When tourism recovered after 1992, the new activities pioneered by the grassroots actors of the 1980s emerged as the dominant model for travel to Cusco.

More importantly, in the 1990s these new fields of travel became increasingly lucrative activities that drew not only larger numbers of tourists but new levels of investment and spending. The origin of Cusco's contemporary tourism boom appears to be a classical case study in Schumpeterian creative destruction; economic actors responded to crisis by developing a more dynamic and robust tourism economy.[2] However, it is important to note that Cusco's shift to a tourism economy guided by a free market was deeply influenced by the actions of the Peruvian state. At first, the Peruvian state encouraged private investment in tourism as part of a piecemeal effort to reduce government spending in the midst of debt crises in the late 1970s and the 1980s. Then the government of Alberto Fujimori (1990–2000) enacted wide-ranging neoliberal financial reforms in its efforts to remake not only the Peruvian national economy, but the political structures and institutions upon which it rested.[3] The state's reforms encouraged the influx of new private investments that built off of earlier grassroots reforms while it also modified Cusco's travel economy to meet the demands of a new wave of global tourism.

As in previous eras of Cusco's tourism development, transnational links also proved to be critical in defining the boom of travel to Machu Picchu. New waves of noncusqueño and non-Peruvian travelers redefined tourism in the region. More importantly, new transnational networks of capital would transform the tourism market in Cusco by injecting unprecedented levels of investment and capital into the region's travel economy. However, cusqueños also discovered the risks of outside and transnational influence. As investment and tourists poured into Cusco, locals found that their efforts had led to the creation of, in the words of Hal Rothman, "devil's bargains" with nonregional interests.[4] Although the symbolism of Machu Picchu emphasized its rustic nature, the tourism that emerged in 1990s Cusco became more lucrative than ever before. Increasingly, the demands of Cusco's growing luxury-oriented tourism exceeded the capacity of local actors and investors. Thanks to the new boom in tourism, Machu Picchu had emerged as the most famous global symbol of Peru. Yet, as Cusco's cultural heritage was spread across a globalized world, local actors increasingly felt excluded from the same lucrative tourism economy that had spread the region's fame. As tourism took off in 1990s Cusco, many locals and the original adventure travel pioneers began to question the benefits of the new regional economy, which increasingly became dominated by noncusqueño interests.

Austerity Politics and Tourism

After the fall of Velasco and his allies in 1975, the succeeding military regime led by General Francisco Morales Bermúdez began to dismantle the state-led economic model constructed by his predecessor. The deteriorating economic situation and mounting national debt forced Morales Bermúdez to cut state spending and subsidies to address a balance of payments crisis. Although wide-ranging austerity imposed by the regime staved off default, the measures worsened economic conditions in Peru.[5] Facing bleak economic fortunes and political instability, the Peruvian military looked to relinquish control over the state and agreed to convene a constitutional convention in 1978 and hold national elections in 1980. Running on a centrist platform, Fernando Belaúnde returned to the presidency in 1980. The victory of Belaúnde ensured that the departure from state-led development begun under Morales Bermúdez would continue during the return to civilian government.[6]

The Peruvian state's return to economic orthodoxy affected tourism policy. The Morales Bermúdez government took measures to encourage private enterprise in tourism. In October 1977, the government implemented a general tourism reform that provided financial incentives for private investment. The reform also created the Fondo de Promocion Turística (Tourism Promotion Fund, FOPTUR), a new agency managed by representatives of both state and private interests to promote tourism in Peru.[7] FOPTUR was originally funded by the state, but in 1980 the Morales Bermúdez government shifted the source of its budget to rely on taxes on tourist businesses and hotels.[8] The Belaúnde government continued FOPTUR's structure and funding model and also retained a Vice Ministry of Tourism in the new Ministry of Industry, Commerce, Tourism, and Integration (MICTI).[9] While planning reports cited the achievements of Velasco-era policies in developing tourism, new assessments, including one planning document from 1982, criticized strategies like the Plan COPESCO for "not yet achieving a significant participation of the private sector in this field."[10] Following this thinking, the state began to withdraw from the direct management of many tourism development projects.

Despite these challenges, international arrivals to Cusco continued to rise through the late 1970s. By 1979 Cusco boasted forty-eight hotels with a total of 2,909 beds.[11] In 1980 Cusco achieved a record of 223,479 tourist arrivals, of which 146,025 were international travelers.[12] Much of this growth stemmed from earlier state investments in tourism. Due to Plan COPESCO's funding agreements, its projects continued to be fully financed until the expiration of the Inter-American Development Bank loan in 1980. COPESCO continued to complete infrastructure projects in Cusco, including backpacking lodges, information centers, and highway paving in the 1980s.[13] COPESCO's "Phase II," proposed in 1980, envisioned a bold set of infrastructure development projects.[14] However, the Peruvian state, already facing a sovereign debt crisis, showed little interest in applying for more foreign loans. Instead, funding for COPESCO's second phase originated entirely from the Peruvian state. The total spending for the second phase reached $34,329,700, a significant sum, but approximately a third of the original COPESCO plan's budget.[15]

While overall funding for tourism development decreased, the Peruvian state still sought to pursue several infrastructure projects originally proposed by COPESCO. MICTI planners debated introducing a COPESCO proposal to introduce passenger helicopter flights between Cusco and Machu Picchu before dropping the project in the early 1980s.[16] The construction of a cable-car system at Machu Picchu received more serious consideration. As early as 1975, the military government had approved the cable-car proposal and sent out bids to international engineering firms. Distracted by political and economic crises, it eventually dropped the project.[17] In 1982 the possibility of completing the cable-car project emerged again when MICTI signed agreements to proceed with construction with Swiss- and Lima-based contractors. However, the project never progressed beyond 1982 due to a lack of funds.[18]

The proposed Chinchero International Airport project received the most interest at both the local and national levels. Some perceived that Cusco's Velasco Astete Airport in the city's Quispiquilla zone was incapable of handling increased demand. The crash of a LANSA airlines flight into the hills surrounding Cusco following its takeoff from Velasco Astete in 1970 killed 101 people and raised concerns regarding the airport's location.[19] In 1978 COPESCO selected a plateau of land in Chinchero, located twenty-four kilometers northwest of the city of Cusco, as the preferred site for the new airport. In May 1980, the military government issued Decree Law 23028 declaring the new airport a priority for the state.[20] COPESCO continued plans to construct the proposed Chinchero Airport, and MICTI approved a contract with construction firms in 1982 to proceed with formal plans to commence construction.[21] COPESCO estimated that the new facility could open as early as July 1985.[22] By 1986, however, the Chinchero Airport had not passed beyond planning documents despite lobbying by local officials and the press.[23] As late as 1987, locals still hoped that the government would finally act on constructing an international airport that, in the words of *El Co-*

mercio del Cusco, would serve as "one of the best contributions for the promotion of receptive tourism."[24] However, by 1989 limited state funds permitted only modest security upgrades at the existing airport.[25] Looking back in 1993, *El Comercio del Cusco* expressed its outrage over the fact that the Chinchero Airport remained only a project on paper.[26]

The fate of the Chinchero Airport reflected the challenges that faced Cusco in the 1980s as the Peruvian state under Belaúnde sought to cut spending in the face of a mounting economic crisis. In 1980, 54.63 percent of tourism investment in Cusco was provided by public funding. By 1983, that level had plummeted to 4.57 percent.[27] FOPTUR did not escape the austerity measures enforced by the Belaúnde government, and it lost one-quarter of its income due to government cuts in 1983.[28] By 1985 COPESCO planners admitted that their goals had changed to small-scale projects because "the state was not able to provide necessary budgets as in the initial period [of COPESCO] and until 1979."[29] The withdrawal of the state not only affected funding but removed a key coordinating institution for long-term tourism planning. Even representatives of the private sector Cámara Nacional del Turismo (National Tourism Chamber, CANATUR) lamented the withdrawal of state planning and investment in tourism. In a 1985 report, CANATUR argued that the lack of state involvement left private tourism interests uncoordinated and limited.[30] "The absence of technical support has characterized the taking of many operative, normative, and investment decisions with results not favorable for the development of the [tourism] sector," concluded one review of state policy completed by MICTI in 1986.[31]

With unreliable state support, tourism infrastructure in Cusco fell into disrepair. An article published in 1982 in *Perspectiva* magazine highlighted the conditions in Aguas Calientes, once seen as the primary beneficiary of the Plan COPESCO. The district mayor, José Nouchi Portillo, lobbied the INC to share some of its ticket revenues so that the town could enjoy basic services. The mayor noted: "As anyone can see, in this town, the people live in inhumane conditions. Essential public services like water, sewer, and power are only enjoyed by a minority."[32] Deferred maintenance and poor management by the state-owned rail company, ENAFER, took a toll on the operations on the Santa Ana Railroad that led to Machu Picchu. A train derailment on the switchbacks leading from Cusco on June 25, 1985, left seventeen passengers dead.[33] Another derailment that occurred on April 3, 1986, injured eleven tourists.[34] MICTI's 1987 annual assessment described Cusco's roads as being "in a terrible state" and its airport as outdated and too small. The report also documented that the Santa Ana Railroad "finds itself in a bad state of conservation and operation, operating with the use of old cars without bathrooms and/or in terrible condition." The buses that transported tourists between Aguas Calientes and Machu Picchu, operated by the state-owned ENTURPERU, were described as "a risk for tourists."[35] By 1989, an English-language backpacking guidebook also warned of bad travel infrastructure and noted that "the operations of the railroad company have become highly erratic and capricious lately, partly due to a chronic shortage of spare parts, locomotives, etc."[36]

In the wake of national austerity, local governments struggled to meet tourism and preservation needs. Local efforts received a boost with the election of Socialist Party candidate Daniel Estrada Pérez as mayor in 1983.[37] Estrada promised a series of populist reforms for the city that also touched on tourism development. While campaigning, Estrada made headlines when he promised to "lie down in front of a plane [or hijack it, according to some sources] if the central government did not support the municipality economically."[38] Even before Estrada became mayor, local organizations had found independent sources of funding. In 1978 the INC, Cusco municipality, and the Archdiocese of Cusco had signed an agreement to form the Boleto Turístico (Tourism Ticket), which charged a flat ten dollar fee to access all of the major tourist sites in the city. The three institutions then shared the funds from the Boleto Turístico to fund preservation.[39] Following through on his promise, Estrada introduced the Tasa Municipal de Embarque (Municipal Boarding Fee) and began charging nonresidential aviation arrivals two dollars. The municipal fee worked in tandem with the Boleto Turístico to contribute to the maintenance of historical sites and tourist infrastructure.[40]

The national state did not ignore the growing problems with tourism. Lobbied by the cusqueño congressman Guillermo Bellido Yabar, the national state began to research reforms to revitalize tourism levels with a special focus on Cusco. As early as February 1981, a bicameral congressional commission visited Cusco as part of its mandate to address tourism needs.[41] Having limited spending capabilities, the state attempted to attract private investment in tourism by offering tax breaks and other market-based incentives. In December 1984, the government passed the Ley General del Turismo (General Tourism Law, Number 24027). The law created the Consejo Nacional del Turismo (National Tourism Council) to coordinate policy and propaganda between state and private interests. It cut electricity rates for new hotels, lowered tax rates, and reduced tariffs for importing foreign-made products and construction materials for use in tourism. "If we attract big hotel chains, they alone will pull tourism traffic," said Bellido, who favored the state's efforts to attract foreign private investment in tourism.[42]

Despite proposals for reform, tourism in Peru continued to suffer. In 1984 a dispute over landing and air transit rights between the United States and Peru resulted in the suspension of many routes between the two countries during the height of the traditional tourist season.[43] Only at the end of 1986 did the two nations agree to reestablish regular commercial service. Unfortunately, the lack of direct routes between Peru and the world's largest tourism market had already produced dramatic declines in travel to Cusco.[44] In 1985 cusqueños had lost faith in the promises of Belaúnde and his Acción Popular party as they prepared for new national elections. Campaigning for president, APRA candidate Alan García made a symbolic visit to Machu Picchu to express his concern with the southern sierra and associate himself with nationalist symbols.[45] García's promises to pursue a heterodox economic development strategy using a combination of state and private funds won the cusqueño vote in 1985 in his victorious presidential campaign. However, after a short economic recovery, García's government descended into economic chaos. By 1989 annual inflation in Peru reached 2,776 percent, throwing any investments or planning for tourism into disarray.[46]

Tourism and Terror

Political and economic instability in the 1980s led to widespread and often violent general strikes. In Cusco, regional work stoppages often interfered with tourism, especially during the high season between May and August. In 1981 general strikes by state and industrial laborers, including the railroad employees, disrupted travel to most of Cusco's tourist sites, including Machu Picchu, at the height of the tourism season, the month of June.[47] In 1988 a strike by the historically militant teachers union nearly forced the cancellation of that year's Inti Raymi festival.[48] In addition to labor unrest, the local press argued, the worsening economy led to an increase in criminal activities that often took advantage of tourists. One editorial appearing *El Comercio del Cusco* on June 4, 1981, lamented that "the tourist that visits Cusco is threatened with assaults, robberies, and abuses, cases that are common and daily."[49] One particularly audacious assault involved the use of fake police uniforms to rob an entire bus of French tourists traveling through the Sacred Valley on June 3, 1984.[50] *El Comercio del Cusco* worried about the effect of such notable attacks on visiting tourists. "Above all else, it is another hard and grave strike against the industry of tourism . . . it will force the tourist to think twice before coming to Cusco," observed one editorial published a few days after the robbery.[51] In preparation for the traditional tourist draw of Inti Raymi in 1985, police in Cusco declared a state of emergency, permitting them to detain without charges any suspects believed to be a threat to tourism. The focus of these crackdowns often reflected ongoing local suspicions and biases. Most of the suspects sought by the police were, as described by *El Comercio del Cusco*, "youths with hippie appearances" and "a majority of elements of 'morenos' [having dark skin] that have begun to rob without fear."[52] In addition to fears about violent crime, guidebooks aimed at foreign travelers warned of a high risk of pickpocketing and purse snatching, especially on the train journey to Machu Picchu.[53]

Concerns about labor unrest and crime paled in comparison to threat that Peru's internal war posed to tourism in Cusco. Formally named the Partido Comunista del Perú—Sendero Luminoso (Peruvian Communist Party—Shining Path), the Maoist Shining Path emerged in the neighboring region of Ayacucho in the 1970s under the leadership of Abimael Guzmán. In 1980 Shining Path formally declared its intent to violently overthrow the Peruvian state. With brutal tactics and coercion, Shining Path expanded in Ayacucho and then throughout many other zones of Peru. It is worth noting that Shining Path was not the only insurgent group during this era. The Movimiento Revolucionario Túpac Amaru (Túpac Amaru Revolutionary Movement, MRTA) also declared an armed fight against the Peruvian state. The Peruvian state called first on the police to suppress the spreading radicalism, and later handed counterinsurgency policy to the military. Increasingly, the armed forces adopted dirty war tactics to confront the insurgencies, killing many innocent civilians in the process. The resulting conflict between the insurgents and the state resulted in nearly 70,000 deaths, the majority being Peruvians of indigenous descent and residents of the Andean highlands.[54] Based on its long history of leftist political mobilization, Cusco would appear to be fertile ground for Shining Path. Yet, as in other regions with a history of rural political activism, the ultraorthodox politics of Shining Path did not initially appeal to locals. Although the internal war affected Cusco, the region largely escaped the worst violence, which devastated many neighboring regions in southern Peru, among them Ayacucho, Puno, and Apurímac.[55]

However, Cusco was far from immune to Shining Path attacks.[56] By the final months of 1980, Shining Path militants occupied land in Cusco's Urubamba Province and had attempted to plant explosives near City Hall and to attack the electric supply.[57] Some of Shining Path's first propaganda actions in urban Cusco involved attacks on tourism symbols.[58] On the night of January 11, 1981, cusqueños discovered Shining Path images and slogans painted on the Sacsayhuamán archeological complex and the famous Inca stone of the twelve angles.[59] The editors of *El Comercio de Cusco* expressed their bewilderment at the actions of "a splinter group called Shining Path," wondering why they were "producing such strange things" around Cusco.[60] By the end of January, locals began to take Shining Path more seriously. The propaganda actions were quickly followed by a dynamite explosion on Calle Zarzuela and attacks against the Banco International and the local army barracks. More serious attacks destroyed the Banco de Crédito and a local office of the Ministry of Education.[61] Within a month, locals already noted that Shining Path attacks had provoked a reduction in the amount of visitors, particularly international tourists, arriving in the region.[62] Cusco's hotels agreed to lower their rates that month in hopes of attracting tourists, but these measures accomplished little, as Shining Path attacks continued.[63] On September 11, 1981, Shining Path executed a dynamite attack on the Coca-Cola bottling plant in Cusco.[64] The next day, Shining Path attacked the Hotel Savoy. The attack on the hotel did not result in deaths, but *El Comercio del Cusco* reported "a great alarm amongst the guests and workers," and the attack likely struck another blow against tourism promotion.[65] By 1983 Shining Path had dynamited electrical transmission lines between Cusco and the Machu Picchu hydro plant, causing blackouts in the city. These tactics mimicked the ongoing attacks against Lima's power supply that repeatedly plunged the capital into darkness.[66] Like many Peruvians, as attacks increased with each year, cusqueños felt under siege from economic chaos and political violence. "It gives the impression that Cusco is an unprotected city (*ciudad deguarnecida*)," lamented *El Comercio del Cusco* in a June 14, 1983, editorial.[67]

Shortly after García ordered the Peruvian military to suppress prison riots led by the Shining Path in June 1986, the Maoists responded with a high-profile attack on Cusco's tourism economy. At 8:23 A.M. on June 25, a bomb exploded on the tourist train to Machu Picchu while it prepared to depart San Pedro Station near Cusco's city center.[68] The bomb, left in a red backpack on the storage rack above row thirteen in car 1523, killed seven tourists and injured an additional thirty-eight. Among the dead were a family of German tourists, a Brazilian, and one traveler from the United States. Journalists reported a chaotic response to the bombing. Police "acted with confusion," and most victims had to find taxis to bring them to Cusco's regional hospital, where "confusion reigned and post-operative attention was embarrassingly

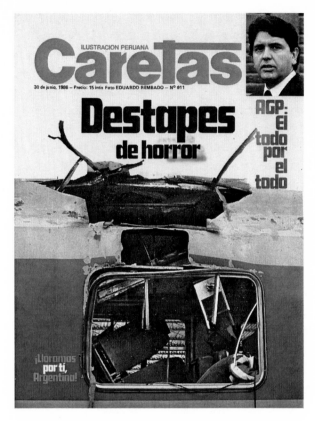

1986 *Caretas* coverage of tourist bombing. The photo shows the aftermath of a 1986 bombing of the tourist train to Machu Picchu that killed seven people. Although Cusco was spared the worst violence of Peru's internal conflict in the 1980s and 1990s, its tourist sites and symbols were attractive targets for Shining Path. Image reproduced with permission of Editora Novolexis.

'off-hand.'" One tourist from the United States noted, "I have been in South Africa, Lebanon, and Cambodia, and never have I seen similar chaos." One tourist who was also a member of the Red Cross had to go to a local television station to plead for medical specialists to be sent from Lima to care for the injured.[69] Initially rumors appeared that MRTA had organized the attack, but no group took responsibility for the bombing. In 1987 investigators announced that Shining Path had executed the bombing.[70]

El Comercio del Cusco immediately recognized how, in addition to the loss of life, the bombing damaged the region's image in Peru and abroad. "Now, the consequences of the most condemnable act of terrorism against Cusco is traveling around the world with its resulting charge of negative propaganda that will not cease to inflict serious setbacks not only for this part of the country, but for all of Peru," lamented the newspaper.[71] Travel articles referenced the train bombing in warning to tourists thinking of vacationing in Cusco. "Travel in the Peruvian Andes has become more risky lately with the increase of terrorism by the rebel group Shining Path," warned an October 1986 travel article in the *New York Times*.[72] Fears of terrorism attacks on tourists were common throughout the 1980s. On the eve of the 1987 Inti Raymi festival, police announced that they had prevented a terrorist attack on the ceremony.[73] Between 1986 and 1988, Shining Path increased its presence in Cusco, particularly in the southern areas of the region bordering Puno; it also continued attacks against police, civic institutions, and the UNSAAC campus.[74] Besides Shining Path, other groups also engaged in violent attacks in Cusco, including anti–Shining Path paramilitaries who took responsibility for a series of bombings in 1987.[75]

In 1987 Cusco received the death knell of international tourism; the U.S. State Department issued a travel warning that advised against trips to Peru.[76] Although Shining Path activity in the Cusco countryside began to decline after 1988, tourism arrivals continued to plummet as international news regarding Peru's instability continued to grow.[77] Hoping to dispel notions of their region as dangerous, authorities in Cusco, led by its mayor, Carlos Chacón, arranged the establishment of a sister city relationship with Jersey City, New Jersey, in 1988. The mayor of Jersey City, Anthony Cucci, his wife Anna, and several other civic representatives arrived in Cusco, but instead of providing an opportunity for positive media coverage, the visit ended in tragedy. Delegations representing both cities traveled to Machu Picchu on December 1, 1988. A ten-inch rod stuck into the tracks forced their railcar to derail and plunge down a cliff. The sabotage severely injured Mayors Cucci and Chacón and killed their spouses.[78] Peruvian authorities blamed leftist guerillas, but others suspected that the sabotage also had origins in an ongoing general strike.[79] Some even suspected that disgruntled ENAFER employees had committed the sabotage.[80] *El Comercio del Cusco* condemned the attack as a "tragic act." The paper's editorial lamented, "In the world we are living in, no one can take life for granted."[81] Cusco's tourism fortunes worsened in 1989. Security threats forced police to issue a "red alert" for Cusco during the traditional height of the tourist season in June. That same month, the INC closed the Inca Trail, declaring it unsafe for transit due to security threats.[82] Despite such measures, *El Comercio de Cusco* stated that the city "is converting into an open field and easy access for the proliferation of crime." The paper noted the particularly bad effect the growth of crime and disorder in the city had on tourism, "because it gives Cusco the worst image abroad, and for that reason the industry without chimneys has decreased so much."[83]

The election of Alberto Fujimori as president in 1990 did little to bring security to Cusco or to aid the tourism economy. In fact, acts of violence continued, and tourism entered a nosedive. Only several days after Fujimori's electoral victory in June, a car bomb exploded on Cusco's Avenida El Sol, killing one person.[84] Local officials attempted to encourage tourism and even organized a "Concert for Peace" featuring the National Symphony that took place at Machu Picchu on June 22, 1990.[85] Yet, worse news arrived as a cholera epidemic broke out in Peru at the start of 1991.[86] By February 1991, FOPTUR admitted that tourism had entered into a critical state in Peru. The combined news of political violence, a cholera epidemic, and states of emergency made the country a pariah in the eyes of potential travelers. According to observers, cholera had a larger negative impact on tourism than news regarding terrorism. "Until 1991, nothing had succeeded in stopping the flow of visitors to our country like the news of the epidemic of *vibrum cholerae*," observed *Caretas* in September 1991. The president of CANATUR estimated that cholera had reduced the tourism revenues by $300 million.[87] *Caretas* summed up the state of tourism in Peru during the era with a headline published in November 1991, stating "Goodbye Peru" alongside an image of foreigners lining up to depart the country on an airplane.[88] As late as February 1993, the U.S. government continued to warn tourists against hiking on the Inca Trail due to security concerns.[89]

Cusco's economy suffered disproportionately during the lowest days of tourism. *El Comercio del Cusco* claimed that, by 1991, "three plagues" — insecurity, cholera, and lack of investment — afflicted the region. "The famous 'industry without chimneys,' as tourism is known, is in virtual collapse," announced the local paper in June 1991.[90] *Caretas* published an article on the lack of tourism in Cusco headlined "Last Call" that showed photos of empty restaurants and hotels. The article estimated that Cusco, with facilities to serve roughly 2,000 tourists daily, hardly received 200 visits per day by August 1991.[91] Between 1989 and 1991, the estimated economic loss of tourism revenue in the Inka Region alone was $60 million.[92] The Cámara Hotelera del Cusco (Hotel Chamber of Cusco) reported that by April 11, 1991, 38 of Cusco's 114 hotels had closed their doors due to a lack of business. Souvenir shops on Calle San Augustín had reported a total combined income of $250 during the first three months of 1991 — a dramatically low figure considering that in previous years each business estimated that it earned $600 daily under normal conditions.[93] By July 1991, in the middle of Cusco's traditional high tourist season, eighty hotels had closed their doors.[94] International tourist arrivals to the region became so scarce that on April 2, 1992, when ninety-eight tourists arrived in Cusco from Miami, the news made the front page of *El Comercio del Cusco*.[95] Only three days later, Fujimori would take dictatorial power of Peru in a self-coup on the pretext of providing national security. Despite this, violence against tourists in Cusco and attacks by Shining Path on police stations remained a nearly daily problem after the coup.[96]

Grassroots Growth

For many observers, the 1980s marked a decade of lost opportunities. However, as the region's tourism economy entered a tailspin, state preservation reforms and grassroots economic activity quietly laid the foundation for new growth. The bitter fights over hotel proposals and agrarian reform around Machu Picchu during the Velasco government eventually revealed a silver lining. The preservation conflicts highlighted a flaw in Peru's preservation policies, which protected historical structures but nothing else. In 1977 the INC began to draft plans to create a national park surrounding Machu Picchu.[97] On January 1, 1981, the government issued Supreme Decree 001-81-AA creating the Machu Picchu Historical Sanctuary. Containing 32,592 hectares extending from the peak of Salkantay Mountain in the south to the base of Willka Wiqi (also known as Nevado Verónica) in the north, the new historical sanctuary contained thirty-one archeological sites.[98]

Progress continued on the protection of Machu Picchu as a natural as well as an archeological site. In 1983 the Belaúnde government's Foreign Ministry coordinated with UNESCO to have both Machu Picchu and Cusco declared World Heritage sites.[99] Management of Machu Picchu fell under the responsibility of two institutions: the INC, which controlled the archeological sites, and the Instituto Nacional de Recursos Naturales (National Institute of Natural Resources, INRENA), a division of the Ministry of Agriculture that was responsible for environmental management. Although both institutions suffered under economic strain during the years of state austerity, for the first time the national state took over the long-term management of Machu Picchu. With the expiration of the COPESCO and PER-39–funded preservation efforts at Machu Picchu in 1982, the INC conducted restoration work at the site.[100] The INC funded restoration projects at Machu Picchu in 1984, 1986, and 1987.[101] Few opposed increased state investment and management at Machu Picchu. However, the process created tensions with residents of Aguas Calientes. As noted earlier, during the agrarian reform the INC and preservationists expressed wariness towards settlement surrounding Machu Picchu. When the Machu Picchu Historical Sanctuary was created, the state sought little input from residents of Aguas Calientes. Campesinos who had received parcels through the agrarian reform now located within the new sanctuary suddenly found their activities restricted by the INC and INRENA; others who lacked property titles were thrown into legal limbo. As Pellegrino Luciano's ethnographic work has shown, locals viewed the creation of the sanctuary as part of a larger trend of preservationists ignoring the social needs of Aguas Calientes.[102]

Another key preservation policy that would benefit the development of adventure tourism was the creation of the Inca Trail. Bingham's first expeditions cleared parts of the Inca road network leading to Machu Picchu that would become the Inca Trail. Later archeological expeditions undertaken by Paul Fejos and Victor von Hagen in the 1940s and 1950s brought further attention to the Inca road network of the Sacred Valley. However, the beginnings of the Inca Trail as a backpacker route stem from local efforts that commenced in the late 1960s. UNSAAC professor Victor Ángeles Vargas, with the help of the archeologist Manuel Chávez Ballón, led restoration and hiking trips down the route that would become the contemporary Inca Trail.[103] Maintenance on the Inca Trail continued in the next decade thanks to cooperation between preservation institutions and backpackers. In 1972 Cusco's Archeology Council conducted an annual clearing of the Inca Trail in the weeks before Inti Raymi in preparation for visitors.[104] The following year, César Morales Arno coordinated an expedition on the Inca Trail organized by the Ministry of Education as well as the New Zealand tour company Venturetreks.[105] Despite reduced budgets, the INC and MICTI coordinated to maintain the Inca Trail through the 1980s.[106]

The continued demand for backpacking expeditions and Inca Trail trips derived largely from the countercultural travelers once scorned by locals. Suspicions about travelers labeled hippies persisted. In June 1980, *El Comercio del Cusco* reported that the Hotel Bolívar on Calle Tecsecocha had become "a nest of hippies."[107] By 1981 *El Comercio del Cusco* even suggested that the police conduct sting operations to round up hippies who had overstayed their tourist visas and deport them from the city.[108] However, local opposition overlooked the dynamic changes that many expatriate and former countercultural travelers had begun to introduce into the local tourism economy. The story of Wendy Weeks and her husband, Robert Randall, is indicative of many expatriate experiences. Both arrived to Cusco in 1975 as backpackers, settled in the area, opened their own lodge in the Sacred Valley village of Ollantaytambo, and began to cater to fellow adventure travelers by the late 1970s, charging between one and five dollars per night. While operating the lodge, Weeks, Randall, and their expatriate colleagues organized hiking trips in the surrounding zones. "We uncovered what eventually were going to become very popular Inca roads," recalled Weeks. The informal hiking reaped immediate benefits in the 1980s when well-financed adventure travelers began to arrive in search of hiking. "The '80s were boom years; boom," remembered Weeks. "It wasn't a hassle and you didn't need a lot of money to make it work."[109]

The growth of backpacking also encouraged Peruvians to participate in the new adventure tourism economy. UNSAAC students, particularly those who spoke English, were recruited to aid backpacking expeditions in the Sacred Valley. For many UNSAAC students, these early jobs provided background and training that they used to establish their own agencies catering to adventure tourists.[110] Alberto Ferreyros arrived in Cusco in 1973 to open a local print shop. When two tourists fresh from hiking the Inca Trail arrived at his shop to print a guide for other hikers, Ferreyros became interested in the tourism potential of trekking. He met with Chávez Ballón to learn more about the road networks around Machu Picchu and, in 1974, hiked the Inca Trail. The following year, he founded Exploreandes as one of the first adventure tourism companies operating in Peru. Ferreyros's company began to offer regularly scheduled trips on the Inca Trail and quickly expanded to other trekking routes in the Cusco region and other areas of Peru through the 1980s.[111] In 1984 backpacking excursions to Machu Picchu provided the subject for articles in the *New York Times* travel section.[112] Besides hiking, other sectors of adventure tourism began to open up in Peru. By 1986 at least twelve companies, most based in Cusco, catered to "hundreds" of annual tourists interested in rafting adventures.[113] Despite the increasing Shining Path attacks, adventure tourism continued to expand in Peru through the late 1980s.[114]

The emergence of adventure travel in Cusco changed the tourism market in the region, which now catered to a new demographic of tourists. In some ways, the image of countercultural travelers, once scorned in the 1960s and 1970s, became a sign of Cusco's growing—but perhaps kitschy—cosmopolitanism.[115] Nightclubs and bars in the city center appeared to cater to university-age travelers originating from Lima or from abroad. Establishments with names like Banana Club, Kamaikazee, and Kings Cross appeared in the Cusco's city center to serve travelers. Lonely Planet's 1987 *Peru: A Travel Survival Kit* listed nine recommended nightlife locales in Cusco's city center and advised a visit to Peña Hatuchay on Calle Media. "It's very popular with both locals and travelers and its main attraction is nonstop live *folklórico* music," the guide noted, while warning that "the toilet facilities are not for the sensitive."[116]

1988 *Caretas* cartoon showing backpacking tourism. Once scorned, adventure and countercultural tourism emerged as the backbone of tourism in the 1980s as more elite travelers avoided the perceived dangers and inconveniences of Cusco. Image reproduced with permission of Editora Novolexis.

While locals, particularly the region's youth, were able to engage with a cosmopolitan milieu largely unavailable in other provincial capitals of Peru, not all were pleased with the changes. The figure of the brichero took on greater and more controversial prominence. Instead of the "bridge man" figure of the 1970s, by the end of the 1980s the brichero had become associated with the figure of a local male who made a living from accompanying female tourists as both a guide and often a romantic partner during their time in Cusco. Some celebrated the image of the brichero as depicted by the cusqueño writer Mario Guevara as a rebellious "gringa hunter" gaining, albeit temporary, social mobility. However, cusqueños also bristled at the appearance of the brichero and his female counterpart, the brichera, as degenerate figures who flouted traditional social values while depicting Cusco's residents as decadent and lazy.[117] A former UNSAAC student recalled how, in the early 1990s, bricheros often stood out for their flashy clothes and tales of their interactions with foreigners. Yet, these same figures were often marginalized due to rumors that suggested that the bricheros were drug addicts or possessed bad characteristics.[118] Along with bricheros, concerns continued regarding the perceived social threat of backpacking tourists. When the local press reported on the appearance of AIDS in Cusco, it immediately suspected that "backpacker tourists and hippies are the carriers" of the disease.[119]

However, by the 1980s, cusqueños largely accepted and encouraged adventure tourism due to its key benefit: terrorism concerns did not discourage the arrival of backpackers and explorers. In fact, the perception of danger may have even lured some to Peru. "Mystery. And now with word of terrorism. For many these conditions . . . seem too rough (*picante*)," described the guidebook writer Peter Frost in 1983. However, Frost noted: "But there are those who still come, and it's not just Machu Picchu and the easy life that attracts them . . . thousands of tourists have arrived to explore on foot the wild highlands of Peru and travel down rivers that roar in the Andes on rafts."[120] In 1987 Lonely Planet publishers released their first edition for Peru as part of their popular series of guidebooks aimed at backpackers and independent travelers. The guide offered a remarkably positive assessment of Peru. The author mentioned the ongoing internal conflict only in a section dedicated to Ayacucho, the original base of Shining Path. Contrary to actual events, the guide assured readers that "tourists and travelers are not the target of Sendero attacks."[121] The continued appeal of Peru as a backpacking and adventure travel destination as economic and political insecurity increased baffled many, including the national press. "Beyond the recognized attractions of Peru, danger, curiously, is also an inducement to visit it," reported *Caretas* in April 1989. One U.S. backpacker interviewed expressed a certain awe at conditions in Peru. "It appears incredible that despite all the political and economic disorder, the country functions," wondered visitor Brian Kennedy. Ultimately, he confessed, "I love Peru."[122] Due to its persistence through the worst years of the tourism economy, adventure traveling also emerged as the first tourist sector to rebound after the capture of Guzmán.[123]

Boom Times

As grassroots tourism development began to change the nature of travel in Cusco, as 1990 approached, events on the national level promised major shifts for the region's tourism economy. Battered by economic chaos and increasing violence, Peruvians desperately searched for political alternatives. Anthropologist José Matos Mar denounced the inability to the state to address the needs of the "popular overflow" that flooded into shantytowns, while the economist Hernando de Soto proposed that neoliberal free markets would provide Peru the "other path" towards development.[124] In 1990, the prominent writer Mario Vargas Llosa campaigned for the presidency of Peru, leading a political coalition that promised to solve the country's woes through a rapid, neoliberal economic "shock therapy." Despite Vargas Llosa's early lead, the majority of Peruvians eventually backed a little-known agronomy professor named Alberto Fujimori who presented a more populist platform that promised reforms without harsh economic stabilization. Cusco, like most Andean regions of Peru, voted overwhelmingly in favor of Fujimori largely out of fear of the economic shocks proposed by Vargas Llosa.[125] Fujimori may have campaigned as an economic moderate, but upon becoming president he adopted an economic policy, termed the "Fujishock," that surpassed many of the neoliberal measures originally proposed by Vargas Llosa. Rapidly, the Peruvian state removed or relaxed subsidies, encouraged deregulation, and privatized its holdings in one of the most far-reaching examples of the neoliberal reforms that swept across Latin America in the 1980s and 1990s.[126]

Although the Fujishock policies initially caused economic contraction in Cusco, the new economic model developed by the government created conditions to encourage private investment in tourism. Rather than participating directly in tourism development, under Fujimori the state embraced a new role: the marketing of Cusco to attract private investors. A 1992 planning document prepared for MICTI stated the government's new policy of "reorientation of the role and action of the Vice Ministry of Tourism in order to convert itself into a promotion and advisory authority for the private sector."[127] The government dissolved FOPTUR, replacing it in 1993 with the Comisión de Promoción del Perú (Peruvian Promotion Commission, PromPerú), a new agency tasked with the promotion of Peru in international markets. Central to the mission of the new institution was the creation of the "Marca Peru" or "Peru Brand," to make the nation attractive to investors and visitors.[128] Although PromPerú's efforts promoted all of Peru's economic sectors, the need to attract private investment in tourism remained paramount.[129] PromPerú began to create extensive research on potential tourism markets to attract travelers and investors to Peru.[130]

The Fujimori government proved adept at introducing market reforms to attract international travelers while simultaneously using the subsequent growth in tourism following 1992 as evidence that the neoliberal policies were bearing fruit. Fujimori often deflected criticism of his government's authoritarianism, corruption, and human rights abuses by emphasizing improved security and economic growth.[131] Tourism growth offered Fujimori a key media opportunity to cast a positive light on his government. The

Peruvian media noted the relatively quick recovery of tourism that began in 1993.[132] Even *Caretas*, normally a critic of Fujimori, credited him with the recovery of tourism in Cusco. "Certainly, and besides the egotistical excesses of the president, things have begun to improve in the tourism sector for a time in this part," noted the magazine in 1994.[133] The *New York Times* also applauded Fujimori's reforms, citing the "American business visitors packing into Lima's hotels and tourists returning to the Inca ruins at Machu Picchu" as key evidence of Peru's economic recovery.[134] PromPerú often used the recovery of tourism as a positive indicator of Peru's attractiveness to other forms of international investment. These efforts continued under the leadership of its new director, Beatriz Boza, who oversaw the publication a bilingual periodical series, titled *Peru El Dorado*, to be distributed in international markets. The magazine featured glossy color photographs with articles on tourist attractions alongside reports of Peru's economic growth. The first edition of *Peru El Dorado*, published in 1995, featured a photograph of the PromPerú staff while proudly announcing, "A renewed climate of peace, security, and stability has transformed Peru into a country with a unique attractiveness for foreign investment, and it is recognized as one of the countries with the greatest tourism potential in the world."[135]

Many expressed delight as tourist arrivals began to recover. International tourist visits to Cusco during the high tourism season of June through August increased by 50 percent in 1993.[136] The return of tourism was more than just an economic asset, as it represented a perceived return to normality for the nation. An article published in November 1993 in *El Suplemento del Expreso* concluded on an optimistic note by declaring that "the nightmare has passed . . . this year the future appears to have turned the roulette wheel in our favor."[137] For the 1993 celebration of Inti Raymi, *El Comercio del Cusco* happily reported that "after many months of partial inactivity, once again hotels and lodges have been totally full."[138] *Caretas* magazine also reported on Cusco's positive change of fortune, noting in August 1993 that "the visits return, Cusco becomes happy, there is good news." By September 1993, adventure tourism in the Sacred Valley had expanded beyond the scope of hiking to include activities such as hang gliding.[139] In addition to an expansion in adventure travel, the 1990s also saw rising demand for mystic tourism in Peru. "After achieving a certain level of material comfort, human beings at the end of the twentieth century desperately are looking for solutions to a series of spiritual questions not yet resolved," observed *Caretas* in November 1994 as it reported on the potential for Peru's archeology to attract a new wave of travelers.[140] Increased demand for hiking in the Sacred

Valley prompted officials to add a second access point to the Inca Trail, permitting a less strenuous one-day hike to Machu Picchu in 1995.[141]

Most importantly, by 1995 observers reported that much-sought elite tourists had returned to Cusco. *Caretas* noted, "Others, more cautious and conservative, chased away during various years, now have returned in glory." PromPerú's statistics indicated that 60 percent of tourists visiting Cusco "are more than thirty years old, looking for better accommodations than the wholesome charm of sleeping in a tent."[142] However, after a decade of divestment, tourism interests in Cusco had to face the challenge of meeting increased demands of elite travelers. One hotel representative commented, "The hotels [in Cusco] are the great survivors of the crisis and now find themselves in a period of recuperation." As a result, new international tourists often arrived to find less-than-perfect lodging conditions. Other areas of tourism infrastructure, ranging from the Inca Trail to the Santa Ana Railroad, also struggled to cope with the challenge of serving a tourist population that featured increases in numbers as well as higher expectations. Many observers felt that tourism in Cusco needed to rise to the challenge in order for the area to emerge as a site for international travel. "For each satisfied tourist, three more arrive and for every unsatisfied traveler, seven decide not to come," warned one article appearing in *Caretas* in September 1994.[143] A study completed by the Monitor Company for PromPerú that surveyed international tourists confirmed the need to improve levels of service in Peru. Of the visiting tourists, 63 percent expressed dissatisfaction with the lack of reliable hot water, 42 percent were unsatisfied with hotel cleanliness, and 86 percent were unsatisfied with informational material.[144]

To meet the demands of an increasingly elite tourist demographic, the Fujimori government promoted a quick infusion of private capital into Cusco's hotel economy. In June 1994, the government announced plans to privatize the state-owned ENTURPERU hotels in Cusco by August of that same year.[145] Plans to divest the state from tourism resources met with mixed responses. *El Comercio del Cusco*'s editorial page generally opposed the Fujishock of rapid market reforms. However, even the paper acknowledged that facilities of ENAFER railways and ENTURPERU hotels had fallen into disrepair. Many observers saw the selling of the state-owned hotels, especially the Hotel Cusco, as marking a fundamental shift in national policy. When President Prado inaugurated the Hotel Cusco in 1944 to great fanfare and civic pride, it symbolized to many cusqueños the important role tourism played in elevating their region's heritage in Peruvian politics and national identity. Fifty years later, as Fujimori looked to hand the building over to private developers, many cusqueños sensed that they had arrived at another critical turning point in their region's relationship to the national state. *El Comercio de Cusco* expressed its hope that a new model of operation would "serve justice" to "this hotel so loved by cusqueños."[146]

As the Hotel Cusco was transferred to private hands, the government envisioned much grander privatization plans for other state-owned hotels. One of the marquee projects involved the San Antonio Abad monastery in the city of Cusco. COPESCO planners had selected the monastery, abandoned since the 1950 earthquake, as a potential hotel location and began renovations on the historic structure in 1974.[147] Budget cuts during the Morales Bermúdez government left the project, dubbed the Hotel Monasterio, abandoned until ENTURPERU acquired the property and recommenced renovations in 1987.[148] Once again, financial and political crises had prevented completion of the project. In January 1995, Lima-based Peru Hotel S.A. purchased a thirty-year commission of several ENTURPERU properties, including the Hotel Monasterio, the Machu Picchu Lodge, and the Hotel Isla Esteves on Lake Titicaca. Sleek advertisements for Peru Hotel announced, "We are the new hotel chain of Peru."[149] As the opening of the Monasterio approached, reports on the hotel lauded it as a new standard for luxury cultural tourism in Cusco. "[One] can not only pass by interiors finely decorated with art from the Cusco school, but also enjoy service in the five-star restaurant, 123 rooms, interior heating in all locations . . . and even a sauna and Jacuzzi," stated one report appearing in a September 1995 issue of *Caretas*.[150] After an initial investment of $11 million, the hotel opened its doors in May 1996. Fujimori attended the inauguration of the new hotel, declaring it "the best in South America."[151]

If most cusqueños accepted the new policy of the state in regard to hotel divestment, objections emerged when cultural institutions of Peru appeared to become complicit in the march toward privatization. By April 1994, the INC began to explore the possibility of offering private concessions on land and archeological sites under its control. Although the initiative was supported by CANATUR, many observers believed that the proposal went too far. *Caretas* dubbed the measure "Machu Picchu, Inc."[152] That same year, the INC decided to permit a proposed expansion of the Libertador Hotel. The project previously was prevented due to the lodging's proximity to the Coricancha archeological site. When the INC refused to acknowledge petitions from Cusco municipality to block the hotel expansion, Daniel Estrada, once again serving as mayor, looked to nonstate actors for aid in protecting the region's cultural patrimony.[153] Estrada also reached out to UNESCO to pressure the INC against approving proposed hotel construction adjacent to Cori-cancha.[154] In August, UNESCO officials arrived in Cusco as guests of the municipality to assess the Hotel Libertador site and to support city claims against construction.[155] *El Comercio de Cusco* applauded the arrival of UNESCO, arguing that it "has the unavoidable duty to come at the request of cusqueños and Peruvians."[156] Two decades earlier, UNESCO advisers and cusqueños had allied to push for hotel development in the Plan COPESCO against the objections of Lima-based preservationists. Now, with limeño investors pushing for development, the transnational institution and locals were united against hotel expansion.

Despite the pressures from local authorities and UNESCO, the Lima-based Brescia investment group, which controlled the Hotel Libertador, argued that its actions were legal. Lobbying from opponents of the hotel project did not prevent the owners from demolishing two Inca walls for the expansion by the end of August 1994, an act categorized by the local press as a "case of the insolence of economic power."[157] Despite ongoing legal disputes and pressure from the local press, work at the Hotel Libertador progressed through 1996 as the Cusco city government and the INC admitted that they lacked the legal power to block the project.[158] The Hotel Libertador was far from the only major restoration project unfolding in Cusco in the mid-1990s. Along with the Hotel Monasterio, Lima-based investors purchased and renovated multiple structures in Cusco. For example, Banco Weise took over and renovated the locale on the former palace of Inca Túpac Yupanki on Calle Maruri. While many of these restorations helped save historic structures, the inability of the INC and city authorities to keep pace with the rush of development meant that it was nearly impossible to confirm if these projects conformed to preservationist policies.[159] Lamenting the lack of oversight over the rapid development, *El Comercio del Cusco* remarked in February 1996 that "here [in Cusco] the only thing that matters is money."[160]

Preservationist efforts were also hampered by ongoing disputes between local authorities and the INC. In 1993 Mayor Estrada introduced proposals to renovate Cusco's Plaza de Armas to unearth Incaic structures hidden or built over by colonial- and republican-era construction. Once again, these proposals placed city officials in conflict with the INC, which opposed altering the Plaza de Armas. The INC's opposition was based on preservationist policies to maintain the historic colonial environment of the Plaza de Armas. However, it appeared to observers that the fight over the Plaza de Armas reflected a larger political dispute between the municipality and the INC over which entity would enforce planning and preservation in the historic city.[161]

Other observers, however, complained that the Plaza de Armas proposal, along with several other monumental — or, according to some critics, pharaonic — public works erected by Estrada in the 1990s stemmed from the mayor's own egotism rather than from a sense of patrimonial protection.[162] Disputes between the INC and Cusco's city government did not disappear with the election as mayor in 1996 of Raúl Salizar, who also clashed with the central government over preservation policy.[163] The city government also found itself in regulatory conflicts with its own citizens as well. As tourism traffic in the historic center of Cusco and its markets increased, so did conflicts over the quantity of merchants who could sell to travelers. Often informal vendors, many of them women and campesinos hoping to participate in the growing tourist economy, met opposition from the municipality, which stressed the need to maintain a clean and orderly city to maintain tourism. Some disputes, especially efforts by the city to forcibly remove vendors, turned violent.[164]

The negative effects of booming tourism also began to create conflict at Machu Picchu. As early as 1989, preservationists warned that tourism at Machu Picchu, if not managed properly, could become an "eventual aggressive factor" against the ruins.[165] By 1992 the INC reported on the potential threat of overuse by tourists at Machu Picchu. "We know very well that Machupicchu is the principal and famous motivator of touristic demand towards Peru to the point of converting itself into uncontainable, indispensable, and problematic flow, due to its negative effects on the ecosystem," noted the INC. The report concluded that "tourist activity was and will be a motive for worry."[166] However, the state appeared to value access and development at Machu Picchu over preservation. As early as 1992, the Peruvian government considered the construction of a cable car at Machu Picchu to be a "priority project," and formally began accepting bids to reboot the project abandoned in the early 1980s.[167] Simultaneously, the government approved helicopter flights to ferry tourists to and from Machu Picchu, operated by, in the words of *El Comercio del Cusco*, "a group of capital [limeño] entrepreneurs mainly composed of former Peruvian Air Force commanders and a group of cusqueño entrepreneurs whose agency was going to represent the predatory action against the Machu Picchu Historical Sanctuary."[168] By the end of the 1990s, UNESCO would be called on again to denounce tourist development practices at Machu Picchu.[169]

Private management of the Machu Picchu Lodge by Peru Hotel S.A. also proved controversial to locals. This criticism reached new levels when the corporation submitted plans to expand the Machu Picchu Lodge in 1994.[170]

The artist Fernando de Szyszlo, who had expressed his opposition to the COPESCO-approved Machu Picchu Hotel project under Velasco, published an editorial in *Caretas* to bring attention to the threat of private development at Machu Picchu.[171] Other conflicts erupted over rumors of mistreatment of locals by the private hotel ownership. "The transnational corporation Peru Hotel . . . has converted [Machu Picchu] into its own feudal estate, guarded by watchmen, strictly prohibiting any national or foreign person from using its bathroom," reported *El Comercio del Cusco* regarding the new management policies in June 1995. The article featured a subheading condemning the company's policies that read "Cusqueños we are strangers in our own homeland."[172] By the end of the month, rumors circulated through Cusco that the government planned to privatize the management of the Machu Picchu archeological complex outright. Although *El Comercio del Cusco* could not find hard evidence to suggest any such plans, one unnamed local official cryptically predicted that "with the Fujimori regime, anything could happen; we already have examples like the Amnesty Law [which absolved military leaders accused of human rights violations from human rights prosecution] and that is sufficient to suggest that now it is trying to strip the legacy of our ancestors from us."[173]

Conclusion: Cracks in the "Golden Egg"?

Many were surprised with the rapid pace at which tourism in Cusco not only recovered after years of crisis, but emerged more economically and politically influential than ever before. On the other hand, Cusco's recent tourism boom appeared to confirm the critiques of Naomi Klein, who has argued that neoliberal economic reforms are often implemented at moments of crisis when civic and democratic institutions are too weak to resist the "shock doctrine" of neoliberalism.[174] It is certainly true that the Fujimori government took advantage of Peru's deep economic crisis and internal war to implement far-reaching free-market reforms that opened Cusco's tourism market to global investment. However, the case of Cusco's neoliberal tourism boom is more complex. It is important to note that many of the changes in tourism were not mandated from the top down by the Peruvian state or global finance during the Fujishock, but were begun a decade earlier by independent entrepreneurs, many of them locals and countercultural figures. These actors created new tourism strategies and offerings that eventually were adopted by more powerful groups in the marketing of Cusco in a globalized era.

Yet, as soon as tourism in Cusco reached new heights, many of the original travel entrepreneurs expressed regret over its unforeseen consequences on the region. Many questioned if efforts to make Cusco marketable to international travelers had eventually erased its true character. "At sunset, the Plaza de Armas appears more like Amsterdam with some bricheros conducting tourism, and by night there are pubs that are totally British where little Spanish is spoken," observed one *Caretas* article from September 1995. The article noted greater threats to the region's character and appeal: "The Inca Trails are threatening to become just another road: trash and abuse are distorting what were nearly virgin passages. And there is a horrifying establishment of slot machines facing the cathedral. Helicopters too large are landing in Aguas Calientes, their noise booming on the surrounding stones."[175] By 1996 UNESCO placed Cusco on a list of endangered historic sites, citing bad planning and construction in the historic city center. Reacting to the runaway development, some even looked back to the "bad old days" with a degree of nostalgia. "Free of tourists, the city looked clean and ordered," stated one commentator in June 1996.[176]

Besides the negative cultural consequences of tourism, many locals expressed outrage at the increased stratification of the region's economy. Especially concerning to cusqueños was the emergence of highly profitable tourism venues owned by outside interests. When Rothman examined touristic development in the western United States, he noted that "when tourism creates sufficient wealth, it becomes too important to be left to the locals."[177] Increasingly, cusqueños shared his observations. One 1998 economic study on the effects of tourism in Cusco concluded, "We find that the great beneficiaries are large international investors and, after that, the few Peruvian investors." The report went on to detail that: "Middle class and lower class economic actors participate in tourism activities only through small companies, or in the informal economy."[178] Although cusqueños continued to find opportunities to participate in tourism, as the market became more international and elite, local investors lacked sufficient capital to invest in the high-end infrastructure demanded by these new arrivals. New restaurants serving international cuisine, but at prohibitively expensive prices, became a common sight in central Cusco.[179] Tourism trade also increasingly fell under the management of limeño transplants. By July 1999, *Caretas* noted the phenomenon of how "limeños that arrived planning on tourism without thinking of it much found their true calling in Cusco, leaving behind the capital's hustle for the cosmopolitan haven of the imperial city."[180] Increases in land value near historical sites and along trekking routes also became a source of local discontent. "It was shocking to us," recalled adventure travel pioneer Wendy Weeks when she discovered Lima-based agents engaging in land speculation in the Sacred Valley.[181]

As early as 1994, *El Comercio del Cusco* published a scathing editorial against the new tourism economy encouraged by the policies of Fujimori. The paper called for locals to "kill the goose that lays the golden egg." The editors marveled how "the time of slim pickings (*vacas flacas*) is only a memory, the tourism *boom* once again has become present in our city." Yet, "all have opened their eyes to the irresponsible and mercenary attitude" that had come to define the new tourism economy. The editorial concluded that, due to tourism, "here reigns the most savage economy, and the one who pays the price, or picks up the pieces (*los platos rotos*), as one says, is the '*pueblo* cusqueño' that now sees itself limited to agricultural products, while others become rich." Meanwhile, "the others, the most poor, become the miserable ones" thanks to "the political economy of '*Fujimorato señor*.'"[182] The Cusco press, once an enthusiastic backer of tourist development, now protested its effects in language that echoed the critiques of observers like Jamaica Kincaid, who depicted tourism as a neocolonial force in her native Caribbean Antigua.[183] As tourism began to be viewed as a force of displacement rather than development, it is easy to see why local opinion began to turn against it. However, local outrage did not prevent an acceleration of international tourism. In December 1996, PromPerú and government officials celebrated the milestone of the arrival of 600,000 tourists in Peru.[184]

The following year, the state privatized the Santa Ana Railroad leading to Machu Picchu. The new railroad company, PeruRail, featured joint ownership by the Lima-based Peruvian Trains & Railways, S.A. and the multinational tourism company Orient-Express Hotels, Ltd. (now named Belmond). Quickly, Orient-Express purchased Peru Hotel's holdings in the Machu Picchu Lodge, the Hotel Machu Picchu Inn, and the Hotel Monasterio, creating a near-complete vertical integration of Cusco's most-elite tourism transport and lodging. Under private ownership, service and rolling stock on the Santa Ana Railroad increased in quantity and quality. However, the designation chosen for the new luxury tourism service offered to Machu Picchu by PeruRail, for many cusqueños, has proved to be "an awful name . . . but well worth remembering"—the Hiram Bingham Train.[185]

Epilogue
The Synthesis of All Things Peruvian, 2011

In July 2011, the Peruvian state commemorated the centennial of Hiram Bingham's arrival at Machu Picchu. The celebration marked the culmination of Machu Picchu's rise from an obscure archeological complex into an almost singular national symbol of Peru and the center of a booming international tourist industry. The multiday celebration included a concert by the Chilean progressive rock band Los Jaivas, who performed one of their most famous hits, a musical rendition of Pablo Neruda's poem praising Machu Picchu.[1] The official ceremony took place on July 7, 2011, and featured a concert, a nighttime light show, and even a sky dive over the ruin to represent a condor. The spectacular event, paid for mainly by private tourism interests, was attended by President Alan García and broadcast on national television.[2] At the celebration García proclaimed Machu Picchu "the synthesis of all things Peruvian."[3] Tourists apparently shared the president's sentiment. In 2011 visits to Machu Picchu surpassed the one million mark for the first time in history.[4]

Not everyone applauded the ceremony. For example, *Caretas* magazine critiqued the ceremony as kitsch.[5] The magazine was correct in noting that the ceremony valued spectacle over fact. The date picked for the ceremony, July 7, was several weeks earlier than the actual centennial of the day that Bingham ascended to Machu Picchu, July 24, 1911. More concerning, the centennial celebrations once more validated the false narrative that proclaimed Bingham as the discoverer of Machu Picchu. In 2000 President Alejandro Toledo (who also was fond of exploiting the imagery of Machu Picchu for political gain) began to pressure Yale University to return artifacts it still held on loan from the Bingham expeditions.[6] These demands were continued by García after he returned to the presidency in 2011. Although the dispute between Yale and Peru centered on the question of legal ownership, the debates surrounding the petition made it impossible to ignore the legacy of Bingham's expeditions as well as the false historical narrative surrounding the explorer.[7] Although the press made mention of the ongoing legal dispute, at the centennial celebrations the national media continued to credit Bingham for discovering a lost city. For example, *El Comercio de Lima* described Bingham as the person who "arrived for the first time to this archeological site to later make the Incan archeological complex's architectural marvels known to the world."[8]

Perhaps of more immediate concern to the centennial organizers, cusqueños used the event to draw attention to ongoing grievances in regard to tourism policy in the region. Visitors to Cusco for the centennial were met with protest signs posted in the Plaza de Armas claiming that tourism had done little to provide opportunities for locals. One sign proclaimed, "Tourism shouldn't live off your poverty."[9] As the actual centenary date of July 24, 2011, approached, residents of nearby Urubamba municipality threatened to block the rail line to Machu Picchu in order to protest the lack of state response to devastating floods that had recently damaged the region. "We cannot celebrate one hundred years of Machu Picchu when the Sacred Valley is destroyed," observed regional councilman Marcos Concha.[10]

Tourism officials did have to confront protests at Machu Picchu in late July 2011. Ironically, the leaders of these protests were not locals, but the tourists themselves. The wave of tourists arriving to celebrate the centennial overwhelmed the Ministry of Culture's ticketing system as well as rail services, leaving many tourists unable to access Machu Picchu. On July 25, 300 angry tourists set up a road blockade to Machu Picchu to vent their frustrations. That same day, an angry Brazilian tourist fought his way into the office of Cusco's regional office of the Ministry of Culture to confront officials with claims that his vacation was ruined due to their mismanagement.[11] As a response, authorities raised the daily limit of visitors allowed into Machu Picchu. Although this did resolve visitors' anger, it also prompted objections from preservationists who claimed that the Ministry of Culture had prioritized tourism interests over protecting the structural and historical integrity of the site.[12]

The events in July 2011 illustrated both the tremendous successes and lingering paradoxes that have accompanied Machu Picchu's twentieth-century transformation. On one hand, tourism aided Machu Picchu's emergence as an iconic symbol of Peru that represented an embrace of indigenous-influenced national identity. On the other hand, the conflicts surrounding the centennial celebrations also highlighted the ongoing disconnect between Machu Picchu's fame and the expectations of the tourism economy so central to its rise. That the highly nationalistic ceremonies of July 2011 celebrated a false narrative of discovery undertaken by a citizen of the United States and that they revolved around a historical site with origins that predated the declaration of a Peruvian nation-state by several centuries illustrate how Machu Picchu's symbolism is just as problematic as it is powerful.

Themes in the Modern History of Machu Picchu

In order to understand Machu Picchu's contemporary fame, we must look to history and, in particular, the role of tourism. Understanding them helps explain Machu Picchu's modern rise. At the same time, the transformation of Machu Picchu also raises new questions regarding how we view the impact of tourism development and its place in the imagination of regional as well as national identity. It is worth revisiting some of the more important themes and factors uncovered in this book.

In the first place, the history of Machu Picchu in the twentieth century highlights the importance of considering tourism in the creation or reimagination of Machu Picchu as a national symbol. The bulk of scholarship on Machu Picchu has focused on investigating its archeological past and exploring the events and legacies of Bingham's expeditions. However, in order to fully explain how Machu Picchu became such an important national symbol, we must examine the political and economic actors invested in the site's transformation into a tourism destination during the twentieth century. Bingham's expeditions, which certainly played an important role in Machu Picchu's modern history, did not alone guarantee the site's transformation into a global symbol of Peru. Instead, Bingham and the symbolism of Machu Picchu itself were framed and defined by a diverse set of cultural, economic, and political actors who sought to develop tourism in Cusco.

Second, this book calls us to examine how tourism development occurs on a regional level. As we have seen, some of the most important actors in the modern history of Machu Picchu were locals. Regional leaders who viewed international travel as a tool to raise Cusco's cultural and political standing in Peru were some of the first backers for tourism development. The backing of Cusco's elites also proved critical in framing the tourism narrative at Machu Picchu by linking it to the region's distinct indigenismo folklore movement, which promoted a nostalgic and idealized imagining of the Inca and Andean culture. Locals also discovered that tourism could pose risks if the region's social and economic conditions failed to match the glossy descriptions in travel brochures. Tourism transformed Cusco into a showcase of Peru. However, tourism has also made Cusco into a place where, in the words of Claudio Lomnitz, "nationalism's dirty linen can be exposed."[13] If tourism can promote Cusco and Machu Picchu as iconic national symbols, it can also transform them into representations of modern Peru's blemishes as well.

Third, if tourism began as a regional project, it also reflected the shifting politics of the national state. The ebb and flow of the state in regard to tourism policy has often reflected larger changes in Peruvian national politics. The initial regional promotion of tourism in the 1920s was a reaction to the policies of the Leguía government, which sought to erode the power of the traditional elite in favor of a powerful central state. Tourism initiatives of the 1930s and 1940s reflected the growth of populism in Peru as the national state employed tourism to celebrate indigenismo and developmentalism. The abandonment of these populist policies after 1948 marked Peru's return to conservative economic programs and politics centered in Lima. The return of large state investment in tourism in the 1960s and 1970s, especially under Velasco's military rule, promised a new era in social and economic reform for Cusco, just as the abrupt abandonment of these policies in 1975 illustrated the limits of the Peruvian experiment in state capitalism. Under Fujimori in the 1990s, the Peruvian state once again returned to play a prominent role. Rather than using state spending to spur development, Fujimori's neoliberal policies used the power of government to guide and encourage private investment in Cusco's tourism economy as part of a larger embrace of free-market policies.

Fourth, the story of modern Machu Picchu calls attention to the importance of the historical tension between Cusco and Lima. Ironically, it was exactly the lack of interest of national elites in developing tourism that opened a window of opportunity for cusqueños to promote their region as the nation's primary travel attraction. Tourism, especially when backed by alliances between cusqueños and transnational forces, helped promote Machu Picchu and signs of Cusco's history as the "true" Peru instead of Lima. This largely explains why Peru's national tourism economy remains uniquely regionally focused on Cusco. However, when Cusco's traditional economy began to collapse in the 1950s, local elites increasingly turned to the state to provide investment through tourism development. Eventually, this alliance proved detrimental for the traditional local elites as the Velasco government's agrarian reform and tourism policies expropriated their economic and political power and replaced it with the national state. When state investment withered in the 1980s, Lima-based and global capital, encouraged by Fujimori's neoliberal reforms, entered the scenario to develop tourism. On one hand, this investment brought Cusco and Machu Picchu to unprecedented heights of fame. On the other hand, outside interests largely displaced cusqueños from the region's most lucrative tourism investments. By the start of the twenty-first century, if Cusco could claim cultural ownership over Peruvian national identity, then Lima could simultaneously claim ownership over the region's lucrative tourism economy.

Fifth, this book has analyzed the central role played by transnational actors. Beyond the region and the nation, transnationalism proved critical in influencing Machu Picchu's rise. Albert Giesecke and Cusco's indigenistas skillfully employed their transnational scholarly and cultural connections to promote Machu Picchu in the first half of the twentieth century. During the Good Neighbor era, new transnational networks also played a crucial role in establishing economic and cultural links between Peru and the United States. Transnational businesses that included hotel investors, film studios, and airlines all promoted travel to Machu Picchu. The rise of transnational cultural institutions after World War II also influenced the rise of tourism at Machu Picchu. UNESCO had a particularly important role, as it influenced the earthquake recovery of the 1950s, the COPESCO program in the 1960s and 1970s, and the creation of Machu Picchu and Cusco as World Heritage sites in 1983. The current wave of transnational investment in Cusco's tourism economy has also influenced the region. Not only have cusqueños interacted with these transnational forces; they have influenced them as well, often to assert regional political or cultural goals.

Sixth, this book has examined how cultural change has altered how local and global actors have interpreted Machu Picchu's meaning over time. In its first era, tourism promotion in Cusco emphasized the modernity of the region and its indigenismo folklore movement. The narratives created for tourism consumption helped define an indigenismo amenable to Cusco, and later, to national elites. In the following decades, the site reflected efforts to bolster feelings of Pan-Americanism. Machu Picchu was elevated, by both the United States and leftist figures, in calls for hemispheric unity. Later, starting in the 1960s and 1970s, Machu Picchu represented an antimodern, static imagination of the past that was increasingly appealing to travelers, many of them from the global north. While countercultural celebration of a mystic vision of Machu Picchu was viewed warily by many in Cusco, the region's youth welcomed the new social connections. By the end of the twentieth century, the shift to adventure travel, ecotourism, and luxury tourism continued to promote the Andes and indigenous culture as unchanged, naturalist, and purist links to an Inca past.

Seventh, this book underscores the role technological change has played in Machu Picchu's rise. Bingham's use of portable cameras in 1911 permitted him to take hundreds of detailed images that could be easily reproduced in newspapers and mass-culture magazines marketed in North America and Europe. John Urry has highlighted the connection between photographic images and the creation of the "tourist gaze" for global consumption.[14] The cusqueño photographer Martín Chambi and the indigenistas also understood the importance of photography in promoting tourism in the region. Now, tourists armed with selfie sticks, smartphones, and social media continue to disseminate images of Machu Picchu to an almost limitless audience. Advances in transportation also proved critical to the promotion of the site. Despite the site's rustic imagery, Machu Picchu's rise is closely connected to its proximity to the Santa Ana Railroad. Although designed with agriculture in mind, the railway's ability to deliver travelers to Machu Picchu with relative ease has proved critical in the promotion of the ruin over rival and more historically important archeological sites such as Vilcabamba that have lacked the same level of access. Aviation technology, especially the introduction of long-range flights following World War II, permitted cusqueños to lobby the state to invest in Peru's tourism. The arrival of jet aircraft revolutionized travel to Cusco and ushered in the region's first tourism boom by the late 1960s.

Eighth, this book has investigated how all of these factors created a transnational contact zone centered on Cusco that influenced concepts of Peruvian national identity. This book has examined how tourism influenced the late twentieth-century emergence of a Peruvian state nationalism that promoted the image of Peru as an Andean, indigenous nation directly linked to the Inca past. Usually, Peru has served as a case study for failed or limited postcolonial nationalism.[15] In general, these studies have looked to domestic factors in determining the success or failure of nationalism while overlooking the influence of transnational factors. Other scholars have viewed transnational forces as threats to established state nationalism in Latin America.[16] Instead, this book underscores the importance of transnational forces in the construction of national identity in Latin America. When Bingham first announced his discovery of Machu Picchu to the world, Peruvian elites promoted their nation as mestizo, coastal, and modernizing. The comments of President García a century later illustrate the degree to which the Peruvian state now embraces Machu Picchu as part of a nationalism that celebrates Andean identity and indigeneity. It also invites new scholarship on the influence of tourism on nationalism in the developing and postcolonial world. How has tourism forged transnational contact zones and defined national identity in the archeological complexes of Southeast Asia, the striking landscapes of Africa, or the multitude of historical and cultural sites across Latin America?

Finally, the making of Machu Picchu shows us that if tourism and transnationalism can offer alternate paths to the creation of nationalism, the

Contemporary tourism at Machu Picchu. Now over 1.5 million annual visitors arrive at Machu Picchu. Disseminating images of Machu Picchu in an age of social media, many of them (consciously or not) reproduce the same popular images taken by cusqueño photographer Chambi nearly a century earlier. Reproduced with permission of Reuters.

imagery that they produce is no less imagined; in the words of tourism scholar Dean MacCannell, such imagery represents a "staged authenticity."[17] From its origins, the imagery of tourism in Cusco has remained an elite-oriented cultural project constructed to serve the outside gaze. The case of Machu Picchu illustrates how transnational cultural interactions involve a mutual, but not necessarily equal, negotiation. It is true that the unique history and culture of Cusco have attracted international visitors and attention. However, it is also important to note that, in search of tourism development, cusqueños and Peruvians have sought to create narratives they believed would appeal to outside travelers and consumers. One result of these efforts is the continued propagation of a false understanding of the history of Machu Picchu and Bingham's expeditions. Another consequence of these efforts is the promotion of an idealistic narrative of Peru's indigenous past and present that does not reflect political and social realities in the Andes.

The transnational cultural and economic character of tourism has bypassed traditional domestic obstacles in Peru to elevate Machu Picchu as an icon of Peru. However, in doing so Machu Picchu has emerged as an influential, but also somewhat empty, national symbol. Lacking traditional domestic connections to the nation, Machu Picchu's validity is mainly based on its appeal to outsiders. This dichotomy is exacerbated when one considers the consistent failure of the Peruvian state to address the social demands of Andean regions while increasingly heralding Machu Picchu as a national symbol. The historian Cecilia Méndez, analyzing debates over Peruvian national identity, identified the tendency of elites since the nineteenth century to adopt a position of "Incas sí, Indios no" (Incas yes, Indians, no).[18] The influence of tourism at Machu Picchu has certainly encouraged the Peruvian state to celebrate the nation's Inca past. However, it remains to be seen if this global promotion of Machu Picchu will translate into the meaningful inclusion of grassroots indigenous culture in debates on Peru's national identity.

The contemporary Peruvian state's celebration of Andean representations deployed for tourism narratives also stands in contrast to the actual demographic shifts that have seen Peru become less indigenous and less Andean. If the Peruvian elite's celebration of mestizo nationalism at the start of the twentieth century proved anachronistic in a largely indigenous and rural nation, its contemporary embrace of Inca Machu Picchu appears equally artificial, or at least nostalgic, in twenty-first-century Peru, where nearly a third of its inhabitants live in Lima and where popular culture has centered on the figure of the *cholo*, a citizen of indigenous descent participating in an increasingly urbanized, mestizo, and coastal nation.[19]

Machu Picchu Tourism Enters Its Second Century

It is tempting to review the conflicted legacy of tourism in Cusco and deem it a failure; it is clearly not. The contemporary tourism boom that began in the mid-1990s shows no signs of relenting. Now, annual international tourism arrivals to Cusco regularly top 1.5 million, while total annual tourism visits to the region have surpassed 2.7 million. The largest group of international tourists, comprising a quarter of all arrivals, originate from the United States. Entering its second century of tourism, the Province of Cusco, which includes the capital city of the region, boasted 783 hotels, 5 of which are considered to be five-star quality. Aguas Calientes, the previously tiny village at the base of Machu Picchu, now features 124 hotels of its own.[20] It is true that tourism has not alleviated Cusco's challenges of rural underdevelopment and conflicts over extractive industries. However, at the risk of going down the rabbit hole of counterfactual history, a Cusco without Machu Picchu would likely resemble the neighboring Andean regions of Apurímac or Puno, which face the same economic challenges but do not receive the benefits of a robust tourism economy. Additionally, although its effects are not quantifiable, tourism has also provided Cusco with a cultural influence unrivaled by other areas in Peru. It is a cultural capital that is increasingly enjoyed by Peruvians themselves. Of the 1.4 million visitors to Machu Picchu in 2016, nearly 425,000 were Peruvian citizens.[21]

However, if tourism has brought economic benefits to Cusco, the popular imagery of tourism serving as the region's "golden egg" is overstated, especially in Lima's press. An economic survey from 2012 found that only 11.61 percent of the region's gross domestic product originated from the tourism-oriented sectors related to restaurants, lodging, and services.[22] Other studies, claiming tourism's large multiplier effect on other economic sectors, estimate its influence in Cusco being as high as 39 percent.[23] However, the Peruvian state's own statistical surveys from 2016 indicate that mining and other extractive industries contribute the largest portion— 50 percent—of Cusco's regional gross domestic product, while agriculture continues to absorb the largest proportion of the region's labor.[24] It is more important to note that many of the most lucrative elements of the tourism economy remain under the control of companies or individuals based in Lima or abroad. Nowhere is this clearer than when one looks at the holdings of the Belmond Ltd., a company that specializes in luxury travel. Founded in 1976, the company has its administrative offices in London but is incorporated in the Bahamas. Belmond owns six luxury hotels in Peru, four of which are located in Cusco. These holdings include the Hotel Monastario as well as the Machu Picchu Lodge adjacent to the ruin. Belmond also has a 50 percent share in PeruRail, which operates the Santa Ana Railroad to Machu Picchu as well as the Peruvian Southern Railway connecting Cusco to Lake Titicaca and the Arequipa region. With the exception of air travel, it is now possible to visit Lima, Cusco, and Machu Picchu while traveling, sleeping, and eating in facilities entirely controlled by Belmond.[25]

Employment in the most lucrative areas of Cusco's tourism economy often requires a college-level degree and fluency in multiple languages. In a strange reversal of Peru's recent history, which had seen a steady migration out of the Andes toward the coast, now many Lima residents are moving to Cusco to participate in the tourism economy. This means that, while tourism employment is available to many cusqueños, the types of tourism jobs accessible to locals can be much more limited. In 2011 I was struck by a con-versation I had with a young cusqueña waitress who wanted to work in tour-ism. Lacking a formal degree and ability to speak English, she planned to leave Peru's travel capital to work as a maid on a cruise liner in the Carib-bean in order to pursue a job in tourism. I continue to meet cusqueños working at the lower rungs of the tourism and service sectors who have ex-pressed similar challenges, highlighting the lingering frustration held by many locals regarding the unequal nature of Cusco's tourism economy. Yet, when local social movements block rail lines and protest tourism in Cusco, they are denounced in the Lima press as demonstrating local ignorance of the supposed benefits of tourism development.[26] In reality, protest move-ments that affect tourism are actually calculated measures taken by cusque-ños who understand that by threatening economic activity controlled by Lima, they can raise grievances against a national state that remains largely uninterested in the social conditions of the region.[27]

Cusco's rapidly increasing tourism levels have also placed strains on the environment surrounding Machu Picchu. Conditions reached a breaking point in 1999 when the Fujimori government pushed to construct a cable car to access Machu Picchu. Although locals and preservationists stopped the project, fears persisted that the government favored development over pres-ervation at Machu Picchu.[28] Concerns regarding the commercial exploita-tion of Machu Picchu increased in September of the following year when the filming of a beer commercial (ironically, for the Backus and Johnston–owned Cusqueña Beer) damaged the Intihuatana stone in the ruin, perhaps the site's most important archeological feature.[29] In 1999 the UNESCO-administered World Heritage Committee sent a mission to Machu Picchu to assess dan-gers to the site. The commission discovered serious environmental risks posed by tourism at Machu Picchu and focused on the unregulated growth of hotels, businesses, and infrastructure in Aguas Calientes, many of which sat in landside-prone areas of the Sacred Valley. Failure to address these risks in the early 2000s led to UNESCO threatening to rescind Machu Picchu's status as a World Heritage site.[30]

As tourism becomes more lucrative in Cusco, clashes between compet-ing interest groups regarding the region's development and historical heri-tage show no signs of abating. Renewed efforts to build the long-promised Chinchero International Airport have emerged as one of the most dramatic flash points of conflict. Running for president in 2011, Ollanta Humala prom-ised to restart work on a new airport at Chinchero. After winning the elec-tion aided by support in Cusco and southern Peru, Humala's government formally approved plans to begin work at the site in 2015.[31] However, when a new government led by Pedro Pablo Kuczynski was elected in 2016, it reviewed the Chinchero project and found evidence of corruption in the awarding of the airport's construction and management concession to the Kuntur Wasi group. As a result, Kuczynski suspended the project with the goals of renegotiating the agreement and investigating any wrongdoing.[32] In 2018 it was Kuczynksi who found himself suspended as he resigned from the presidency under accusations of corruption and mismanagement. The man who replaced him, Martín Vizcarra, was coincidentally forced from his leadership of the Ministry of Transportation and Communication in 2017 over congressional opposition to his handling of the Chinchero Airport negotiations. Despite this, Vizcarra has pledged to move forward with construction of the new airport.[33] The perilous status of the airport project and the economic opportunities it promised have raised the ire of cusqueños who argue that once again their region's future unjustly depends on decisions in Lima. The swirling of these debates did nothing to stop the larger cultural and ecological damage the airport project had already caused in Chinchero. Natalia Majluf, the director of the Museo de Arte de Lima, noted that the slew of gray concrete buildings appearing on the highway to the new airport were "the visible face of a complex project of an impertinent modernization undertaken without guidelines, without planning and without criteria."[34]

Positive trends have also emerged in recent years. Responding to pressure from national preservationists and UNESCO, the Peruvian state backed the Programa Machu Picchu (Machu Picchu Program, PMP). Created in 1995 with funds from the government of Finland as part of a debt forgiveness policy, the PMP sought to reduce institutional conflict between the INC, INRENA, the local municipality, and other institutions tasked with management of Machu Picchu and to implement urban planning in Aguas Calientes.[35] While local residents of Aguas Calientes often chafed at the top-down decisions of the PMP, between 1997 and 2000 the program helped start infrastructure investments that renovated the village's streets, built new tourist markets, and introduced improved sanitation services.[36] Daily visitors to Machu Picchu are limited to 2,500, and visitor activities to the ruin as well as the Inca Trail are more closely monitored. These reforms, including better planning agreements for Aguas Calientes, have earned the approval of UNESCO monitors, who now no longer threaten to list Machu Picchu as a World Heritage Site in Danger.[37] Due to Bingham's dubious methods, it is very likely that Peruvian artefacts improperly exported during his expeditions remain scattered in public and private collections around the world. However, in 2011 Yale University finally agreed to return Machu Picchu artefacts it held in its collections. These artefacts are now on public display in a museum in the city of Cusco.[38] Improvements are ongoing in addressing the social effects of tourism as many NGOs and businesses encourage sustainable tourism programs that aid rural communities while supporting indigenous artisan production and cultural survival. Despite uneven development, many cusqueños have found safe, stable employment in the expanding service sector of restaurants, transportation, and lodging linked with the regional tourism economy.

Inequalities and tensions have always defined the modern rise of Machu Picchu and Cusco. Much work remains be done to resolve the disconnect between the idealized symbolism of Machu Picchu and the real promise of inclusive national identity and social development in Cusco and Peru. To do so, we must have a greater understanding of the place of tourism in the modern creation of Machu Picchu. This book has explored the fascinating story of the transformation of Machu Picchu and Cusco and their place in Peruvian national identity. This book has also shown how cusqueños adeptly negotiated and influenced the politics of tourism in the twentieth century. Hopefully, as awareness of tourism's complex history in Cusco increases, the many transnational and local actors involved in its growth will be able to create policies that employ the region's rich cultural heritage as a source of more inclusive development.

Notes

Introduction

1. YPEP, box 15, folder 239, "Speech Copy with Corrections," Washington, DC, January 11, 1913. The speech and the gala's events were published in "Honors to Admundsen [sic] and Peary," *National Geographic Magazine* 23, no. 1 (January 1913): 133–30. For more details on the event, see Heaney, *Cradle of Gold*, 163–66; A. Bingham, *Portrait of an Explorer*, 291–92.

2. Ministerio de Cultura, Dirección Desconcentrada de Cultura, Cusco, "Cusco: Llegada de visitantes al Santuario Histórico de Machu Picchu," Cusco, 2017. Thanks to Roger Valencia for providing this document. World Travel and Tourism Council, *Travel & Tourism Economic Impact 2017, Peru*.

3. D. Brown, *Inventing New England*, 205.

4. Rothman, "Selling the Meaning of Place," 526.

5. Burger and Salazar, *Machu Picchu*; Cox Hall, *Framing a Lost City*; Shullenberger, "That Obscure Object of Desire"; Tamayo Herrera, *El enigma de Machupicchu*.

6. Seigel, "Beyond Compare," 63.

7. Burga and Galindo, *Apogeo y crisis de la república aristocrática*; Drinot, *The Allure of Labor*; Kristal, *The Andes Viewed from the City*.

8. Pratt, *Imperial Eyes*, 6.

9. Anderson, *Imagined Communities*; Hobsbawm, *Nations and Nationalism since 1780*.

10. Centeno and Ferraro, *State and Nation Making in Latin America and Spain*; Chatterjee, *The Nation and Its Fragments*.

11. Cotler, *Clases, estado y nación en el Perú*; Mallon, *Peasant and Nation*; Thurner, *From Two Republics to One Divided*.

12. Lomnitz, *Deep Mexico, Silent Mexico*, 125–44; Tenorio-Trillo, *Mexico at the World's Fairs*.

13. Bourdieu, "Identity and Representation."

14. Comaroff and Comaroff, *Ethnicity Inc.*

15. Flores Galindo, *In Search of an Inca*.

16. For example, see Fondo de Promoción de las Áreas Naturales Protegidas del Perú, *Recopilación bibliográfica del Santuario Histórico Machu Picchu*. The bibliography, now over fifteen years old, lists roughly 1,140 scholarly publications on Machu Picchu. The bibliography excludes the more extensive uses of Machu Picchu in guides, propaganda, and commercial publications.

17. Cox Hall, *Framing a Lost City*; Heaney, *Cradle of Gold*; Mould de Pease, *Machu Picchu y el código de ética*; Salvatore, *Disciplinary Conquest*, 75–104.

18. For a recent "bad" example of this narrative, see Adams, *Turn Right at Machu Picchu*.

19. Boorstin, *The Image*, 77–117; Fussell, *Abroad*.

20. MacCannell, *The Tourist*.

21. Smith, *Hosts and Guests*; Urry and Larsen, *The Tourist Gaze*.

22. For an introduction to the growing field in Latin America, see Wilson, "The Impacts of Tourism in Latin America"; and Babb, *The Tourism Encounter*.

23. Gascón, *Gringos como en sueños*; Luciano, *Neoliberal Reform in Machu Picchu*; Hill, "Contesting Patrimony"; Maxwell, "Tourism, Environment, and Development on the Inca Trail"; Seligman, "Market Places, Social Spaces in Cuzco, Peru"; Silverman, "Touring Ancient Times"; van den Berghe and Flores Ochoa, "Tourism and Nativistic Ideology in Cuzco, Peru"; Zorn, *Weaving a Future*.

24. Berger, *The Development of Mexico's Tourism Industry*; Berger and Wood, *Holiday in Mexico*; Cocks, *Tropical Whites*; Fonda Taylor, *To Hell with Paradise*; Merrill, *Negotiating Paradise*; Ruiz, *Americans in the Treasure House*; R. Schwartz, *Pleasure Island*; Skwiot, *The Purposes of Paradise*; Strachan, *Paradise and Plantation*.

25. D. Brown, *Inventing New England*; Capó, *Welcome to Fairyland*; Cox, *Destination Dixie*; Gassan, *The Birth of American Tourism*; Norkunas, *Politics of Public Memory*; Revels, *Sunshine Paradise*; Rothman, *Devil's Bargains*.

26. Covert, *San Miguel de Allende*.

27. Applebaum, *Muddied Waters*; Romo, *Brazil's Living Museum*; Vergara, *La danza hostil*; Weinstein, *The Color of Modernity*.

28. Glave, *La república instalada*; Walker, *Smoldering Ashes*.

29. de la Cadena, *Indigenous Mestizos*; López Lenci, *El Cusco, paquarina moderna*; Mendoza, *Creating Our Own*.

30. Rénique, *Los sueños de la sierra*; Tamayo Herrera, *Historia regional del Cuzco republicano*.

31. For an example of bringing transnational analysis to Andean history, see Gootenberg, *Andean Cocaine*.

32. Endy, *Cold War Holiday*.

33. Wright and Valencia Zegarra, *Machu Picchu*, 2–4.

34. Tamayo Herrera, *El enigma de Machupicchu*, 41. The name is likely a combination of the Quechua words "willka," which is identified with the Urubamba River valley, and "llaqta," which translates to sacred site.

35. H. Bingham, "The Discovery of Machu Picchu," 709–19; H. Bingham, "The Story of Machu Picchu," 172–86, 203–17; H. Bingham, "In the Wonderland of Peru," 387–573; H. Bingham, "Further Explorations in the Land of the Incas," 431–73; H. Bingham, *Inca Land*; H. Bingham, *Machu Picchu*; H. Bingham, *Lost City of the Incas*.

36. Amado Gonzales, "Evolución histórica de la tenencia de tierras"; Luciano, *Neoliberal Reforms in Machu Picchu*, 17–37; Reinhard, *Machu Picchu*; Rowe, "Machu Picchu a la luz de documentos de siglo XVI"; Salazar, "Machu Picchu"; Wright and Valencia Zegarra, *Machu Picchu*, 1–7.

37. Greer, "Machu Picchu before Bingham"; Heaney, *Cradle of Gold*, 83–96; Mould de Pease, *Machu Picchu y el código de ética*.

38. For an excellent overview of Bingham's life and expeditions, see Heaney, *Cradle of Gold*. Analysis of Bingham's life and influence is also found in A. Bingham, *Portrait of an Explorer*; Salvatore, *Disciplinary Conquest*, 75–104.

39. Walker, *Smoldering Ashes*.

40. Tamayo Herrera, *Historia regional del Cusco republicano*, 1–158.

41. A. Giesecke, *El censo*, 12, 25–27.

42. Instituto Nacional de Estadística, "Censos Nacionales de Población y Vivienda."

43. Smith, Introduction to *Hosts and Guests*, 1.

Chapter 1

1. H. Bingham, "Cuzco and Sacsahuaman," 234.

2. Burga and Flores Galindo, *Apogeo y crisis de la república aristocrática*; Klarén, *Peru*, 203–40.

3. Rothman, *Devil's Bargains*, 10–28.

4. Schantz, "Behind the Noir Border"; R. Schwartz, *Pleasure Island*, 16–53.

5. The most notable denunciation of tourism's commercialization and invention is Boorstin, *The Image*, 77–117. Two notable studies that analyze the power of tourism in the creation of regional identity include Koshar, "'What Ought to Be Seen'"; and D. Brown, *Inventing New England*.

6. Earle, *The Return of the Native*, 184–212.

7. For the connection between indigenismo and modernity, see Coronado, *The Andes Imagined*; Hiatt, "Flying 'Cholo'"; López Lenci, *El Cusco, paqarina moderna*. For the tension between grassroots and official indigenismo, see de la Cadena, *Indigenous Mestizos*; Lauer, *Andes imaginarios*.

8. A key exception to this is the wonderful work of Mendoza, *Creating Our Own*, 65–91.

9. Endy, "Travel and World Power"; Ruiz, *Americans in the Treasure House*.

10. Morner, *Perfil de la sociedad rural del Cuzco a fines de la colonia*, 63–108; Escandell-Tur, *Producción y comercio de tejidos coloniales*, 251–351.

11. Stavig, *The World of Túpac Amaru*, 207–36; Escandell-Tur, *Producción y comecio de tejidos coloniales*, 253–317; Walker, *The Tupac Amaru Rebellion*, 23–29.

12. The first histories to revisit the rebellion often emphasized it as a proto-national movement; they include Lewin, *La rebelión de Túpac Amaru y los orígenes de la emancipación americana*; and C. Valcárcel, *Túpac Amaru, precursor de la independencia*. A later group of scholars would emphasize the rebellion's Andean origins, which made it distinct from Peruvian nationalism. For example, see Burga, *Nacimiento de una utopia*; and Szeminski, *La utopía tupamarista*. Other historians examined the social and economic origins and consequences of the rebellion in works such as Flores Galindo, *Túpac Amaru II — 1780*; Golte, *Repartos y rebeliones*; and O'Phelan Godoy, *Rebellions and Revolts in Eighteenth Century Peru and Upper Peru*.

13. Serulnikov, *Revolution in the Andes*, 135–38; Walker, *The Tupac Amaru Rebellion*, 267–78.

14. Tamayo Herrera, *Historia regional del Cusco republicano*, 27–43. Tamayo estimates that between the Túpac Amaru II revolt and 1900, the city of Cusco's population had decreased by 65 percent. Cusco's underdevelopment did not signify inactivity. For information on political culture in nineteenth-century Cusco, see Walker, *Smoldering Ashes*.

15. For analysis of the Aristocratic Republic, see Burga and Flores Galindo, *Apogeo y crisis de la república aristocrática*. The growing notion of the Andes as "backwards" during the "Aristocratic Republic" is found in Cotler, *Clases, estado, y nación en el Perú*, 139.

16. Hiatt, "Indians in the Lobby"; Krüggeler, "Indians, Workers, and the Arrival of 'Modernity'"; Tamayo Herrera, *Historia regional del Cuzco republicano*, 107–11.

17. Tamayo Herrera, *Historia regional del Cuzco republicano*, 87–95. Documentation of rubber exploitation east of Cusco found in M. Brown and Fernández, *War of Shadows*, 57–78; Stanfield, *Red Rubber, Bleeding Trees*.

18. Rénique, *El Centro Científico del Cuzco*; Rénique, *Los sueños de la sierra*, 45–47; Tamayo Herrera, *Historia regional del Cuzco republicano*, 93.

19. Tamayo Herrera, *Historia regional del Cuzco republicano*, 100.

20. Kristal, *The Andes Viewed from the City*, 44–54.

21. Kristal, *The Andes Viewed from the City*, 93–161.

22. The limited reach of early indigenismo is documented in Kristal, *The Andes Viewed from the City*, 1–25; Lauer, *Andes imaginarios*; Tamayo Herrera, *Historia regional del Cuzco republicano*, 70–75.

23. Tamayo Herrera, *Historial regional del Cuzco republicano*, 116–22.

24. Oral History Research Office, Columbia University, "The Reminiscences of Albert A. Giesecke," 31–32. Giesecke completed his undergraduate studies at the University of Pennsylvania and also completed graduate studies at Cornell University. The Peruvian ambassador to the United States asked Leo Rowe, Giesecke's adviser at the University of Pennsylvania, to recommend a candidate for the position of rector. Giesecke arrived in Lima in 1909 and in Cusco in 1910. .

25. Tamayo Herrera, *Historial regional del Cuzco republicano*, 123–26.

26. A. Bingham, *Portrait of an Explorer*, 124–57; Heaney, *Cradle of Gold*, 79–82.

27. Giesecke recounted prior knowledge of the site on the fiftieth anniversary of Bingham's first visit to Machu Picchu; see AG-D-033, "50th Anniversary Speech," folios 1–3.

28. Researchers have extensively documented the existence of Machu Picchu and ruins at the site in geographical studies that predated Bingham's 1911 expedition. Greer, "Machu Picchu before Bingham"; Thomson, *The White Rock*; Mould de Pease, *Machu Picchu y el código de ética*.

29. A. Bingham, *Portrait of an Explorer*, 3–16; Heaney, *Cradle of Gold*, 79–89.

30. Salvatore, *Disciplinary Conquest*, 77.

31. Bingham, "In the Wonderland of Peru"; for more information on the publication and reception of the article, see Cox Hall, *Framing a Lost City*, 88–101; Heaney, *Cradle of Gold*, 166.

32. On the mythification of Machu Picchu and Bingham, see Cox Hall, "Collecting a 'Lost City' for Science"; Shullenberger, "That Obscure Object of Desire."

33. Heaney, *Cradle of Gold*, 166–67. See also Appleton, *Tom Swift and His Big Tunnel, or The Hidden City of the Andes*; Hayne, *The City in the Clouds, or A Tale of the Last Inca*; Leroux, *The Bride of the Sun*.

34. "Lost City in the Clouds Found after Centuries," NYT, June 15, 1913, SM1.

35. For analysis of the Peruvian press reaction, see Cox Hall, *Framing a Lost City*, 103–10.

36. YPEP, box 8, folder 109, Javier Prado Ugarteche to Hiram Bingham, August 19, 1913.

37. Cosío, "Una excursión a Machupiccho"; Cosío, "Una excursión a Machupiccho (conclusión)."

38. Matos Mendieta, "Peru: Some Comments," 104–23; Tantaleán, *Peruvian Archaeology*, 24–41.

39. For specific details on the agreements between Bingham and the Peruvian government for each expedition, as well as Bingham's violations, see Heaney, *Cradle of Gold*, 75–77, 115–16, 127–30, 155–56, 165–66, 171–73.

40. A. Bingham, *Portrait of an Explorer*, 304–13; Heaney, *Cradle of Gold*, 189–98; Salvatore, *Disciplinary Conquest*, 75–104; Valcárcel's personal memories of the incident are found in L. Valcárcel, *Memorias*, 187.

41. H. Bingham, *Inca Land*.

42. YPEP, box 17, folder 292, 9886, Hiram Bingham to F. H. Allen, June 12, 1922; YPEP, box 17, folder 292, 9889, Hiram Bingham to Ferris Greenslet, June 15, 1922. Bingham wrote to Grosvenor of the *National Geographic* that *Inca Land* would primarily deal with the 1911 expeditions and that a second book would recount the 1912 and 1915 expeditions. See YPEP, box 17, folder 296, 9903, Hiram Bingham to Gilbert Grosvenor, October 2, 1922.

43. A. Bingham, *Portrait of an Explorer*, 325–37; Heaney, *Cradle of Gold*, 199–207.

44. "Climbed Andes on the Way to the Governor's Chair," *Boston Daily Globe*, December 7, 1924, A10.

45. AG-0140, folio 25, Hiram Bingham to Albert Giesecke, May 6, 1926.

46. HBNP, "Machupicchu," ECL, September 10, 1926, 3.

47. Salvatore, *Disciplinary Conquest*, 101.

48. L. Valcárcel, "Sinopsis de Machupijchu."

49. Sociedad de Propaganda del Sur del Perú, *Guía general del sur del Perú*, 45.

50. AG-D-209, folios 1–2, Albert Giesecke to Luis J. García, PANAGRA, February 13, 1961.

51. Dell, *Llama Land*, 200.

52. López Lenci, *El Cusco, paqarina moderna*, 36–79; Poole, "Landscape and the Imperial Subject"; Poole, *Vision, Race, and Modernity*, 58–84; Pratt, *Imperial Eyes*; Salvatore, *Disciplinary Conquest*; Salvatore, "Local versus Imperial Knowledge."

53. Markham, *Cuzco*, 95.

54. Squire, *Peru*.

55. Marham, *Cuzco*, 238.

56. Squire, *Peru*, 455.

57. Squire, *Peru*, 460.

58. Squire, *Peru*, 461.

59. Squire, *Peru*, 505.

60. Squire, *Peru*, 459.

61. Franck, *Vagabonding down the Andes*, 439.

62. Chalmers Adams, "Cuzco, America's Ancient Mecca," 670–71.

63. Peck, *The South American Tour*, 114.

64. H. Bingham, "Cuzco and Sacsahuaman," 234.

65. Franck, *Vagabonding down the Andes*, 427–28.

66. Peck, *The South American Tour*, 112.

67. Robison Wright, *The Old and the New Peru*, 403.

68. Robison Wright, *The Old and the New Peru*, 453.

69. H. Bingham, *Inca Land*, 157–58.

70. Franck, *Vagabonding down the Andes*, 431, 433.

71. Franck, *Vagabonding down the Andes*, 473.

72. Gänger, *Relics of the Past*, 114–44; Méndez, "Incas Sí, Indios No."

73. Klarén, "The Origins of Modern Peru," 587–640; Larson, *Trials of Nation Making*, 195–201. The failure of the Peruvian state to incorporate Andean communities in the second half of the nineteenth century is a central argument in Mallon, *Peasant and Nation*, 176–219; and Thurner, *From Two Republics to One Divided*, 99–136.

74. Franck, *Vagabonding down the Andes*, 426.

75. Fuentes, *El Cuzco y sus ruinas*, 186–87.

76. de la Riva-Agüero, *Paisajes peruanos*, 225.

77. For analysis on Riva-Agüero's thought, see Drinot, "Entre el imperio y la nación"; and Vich, "Vicistudes trágicas." For a good synopsis of the Mexican state's embrace of mestizaje, see Knight, "Racism, Revolution, and *Indigenismo*." For cusqueño opposition to mestizaje, see de la Cadena, *Indigenous Mestizos*, 20–29.

78. Klarén, *Peru*, 250–51.

79. HBNP, CCC, no. 26, February 1927, cover.

80. HBNP, CCC, no. 31, July 1927, 19.

81. Mendoza, *Creating Our Own*.

82. A. Giesecke, "El Cuzco," *Mercurio Peruano*.

83. A. Giesecke, "El Cuzco," *Revista Universitaria*, 3.

84. A. Giesecke, "El Cuzco," *Revista Universitaria*, 5.

85. Koshar, "'What Ought to Be Seen,'" 323–39.

86. Mendoza, *Creating Our Own*, 21–34.

87. Cosío, *El Cuzco histórico y monumental*, 3.

88. A. Giesecke, "El Cuzco," *Revista Universitaria*, 9–10.

89. IRA, A. Giesecke, *Guía del Cuzco*, 14.

90. U. García, Valcárcel, and Giesecke, *Guía histórico-artística del Cuzco*, 7.

91. U. García, Valcárcel, and Giesecke, *Guía histórico-artística del Cuzco*, 68.

92. U. García, Valcárcel, and Giesecke, *Guía histórico-artística del Cuzco*, 41.

93. U. García, Valcárcel, and Giesecke, *Guía histórico-artística del Cuzco*, 48.

94. HBNP, CCC, no. 31, July 1927, 17.

95. Urry and Larsen, *The Tourist Gaze*, 155–56.

96. Cox Hall, Framing a Lost City, 69–85.

97. The use of photography in the formation of an official Cusco indigenismo is noted by Poole, *Vision, Race and Modernity*, 168–97.

98. Scorer, "Andean Self-Fashioning," 383–88.

99. Coronado, *The Andes Imagined*, 134–62.

100. A. Giesecke, "El Cuzco," *Revista Universitaria*, 6.

101. Cosío, *El Cuzco histórico y monumental*, 30.

102. Cosío, *El Cuzco histórico y monumental*, 56.

103. L. Valcárcel, *Cuzco*, 12.

104. Sociedad de Propaganda del Sur del Perú, *Guía general del sur del Perú*, 49.

105. *Guía general del Cuzco*, Cusco: Hersct & Flores, 1937, 18.

106. Sociedad de Propaganda del Sur del Perú, *Guía general del sur del Perú*, 20.

107. Sociedad de Propaganda del Sur del Perú, *Guía general del sur del Perú*, 14, 16, 58.

108. *Guía general del Cuzco*, 131.

109. *Guía general del Cuzco*, 133–43.

110. Coronado, *The Andes Imagined*; Kristal, *The Andes Viewed from the City*; Tamayo Herrera, "Prólogo," 9–19.

111. Rénique, *Los sueños de la sierra*, 31–42; Tamayo Herrera, *Historia regional del Cuzco republicano*, 95–102. One of the first studies evaluating the negative effects of the railroad on rural communities was L. Valcárcel, "La cuestión agraria en el Cuzco," 16–38.

112. For studies on the millenarian aspects of the Tawantinsuyo movement, see Manuel Burga, "Las profetas de la rebellion, 1920–1923," 463–517; Kapsoli, *Allyus del sol*; Kapsoli, *Los movimientos campesinos en el Perú, 1879–1965*. Revisionist studies that have highlighted the political goals of the uprisings include de la Cadena, *Indigenous Mestizos*, 86–130; Heilman, *Before the Shining Path*, 42–70; and Jacobsen, *Mirages of Transition*, 337–53.

113. Arroyo, "La experiencia del Comité Central Pro-Derecho Indígena Tahuantinsuyo," 1–24; Leibner, "Radicalism and Integration," 1–23.

114. de la Cadena, *Indigenous Mestizos*, 88–89; Lauer, *Andes imaginarios*, 107–10.

115. The concept of the "New Indian" was first proposed by the indigenista and travel guide writer José Uriel García in *El Nuevo Indio*. Proponents of this theory were often called neo-indigenistas. See Tamayo Herrera, "Prólogo," 9–19. Lauer terms this next generation of indigenista thought "indigenismo 2" in *Andes imaginarios*, 107–10. For more on the rise of neo-indigenismo and conflict between neo-indigenistas and Indians, see de la Cadena, *Indigenous Mestizos*, 44–176. For the relationship between neo-indigenismo and tourism, see Mendoza, *Creating Our Own*, 65–91.

116. de la Cadena, *Indigenous Mestizos*, 131–35.

117. Sociedad de Propaganda del Sur del Perú, *Guía general del sur del Perú*, 59.

118. *Guía general del Cuzco*, 23.

119. *Guía general del Cuzco*, 23–25.

120. *Guía general del Cuzco*, 15.

121. For example, see the discussion of the commemoration of the 400th anniversary of the foundation of São Paulo in Weinstein, *The Color of Modernity*, 221–95.

122. Klarén, *Peru*, 268–76.

123. de la Cadena, *Indigenous Mestizos*, 131–32; Kláren, *Peru*, 276–80; Tamayo Herrera, *Historia regional del Cuzco republicano*, 149–50; Tantaleán, *Peruvian Archaeology*, 67–68.

124. de la Cadena, *Indigenous Mestizos*, 73–74.

125. de la Cadena, *Indigenous Mestizos*, 128.

126. HBMC, "El congreso constituyente y el IV centenario del Cuzco," ECC, August 24, 1933, 2.

127. BCP, Ley 7798, September 13, 1933.

128. HBNP, "El turismo, riqueza que debe beneficiarnos," *La Crónica*, October 29, 1933, 2nd sec., 3.

129. HBNP, "El porvenir del Cuzco," *La Crónica*, October 29, 1933, 2nd sec., 3.

130. HBNP, "Las fiestas del cuarto centenario de la fundación espanola del Cuzco," ECL, March 9, 1934, morning edition, 1.

131. HBNP, "La celebración del IV centenario del Cuzco," *Revista del Touring Club Peruano* 8, no. 81 (October 1933): 7–10.

132. AMC, Legajo 98, Consejo Provincial del Cuzco to Senor Director de Ensenaza i Exámenes, August 29, 1933.

133. AMC, Legajo 97, Robert A. Burns to Alcalde Provincial del Cuzco, May 8, 1934; Legajo 98, James McGrady to Alcalde Provincial del Cuzco, March 9, 1934.

134. AMC, Legajo 98, Moises Ponce de León to Senor Presidente de la Comissión Organizador de las Fiestas Pro-Centenario del Cuzco, March 3, 1934.

135. HBNP, "Comisión Central de Propaganda y Turismo," ECL, March 16, 1934, morning edition, 3.

136. HBNP, "Comisión Propaganda y Turismo IV Centenario Cuzco," ECL, March 22, 1934, morning edition, 3.

137. HBNP, "Comisión de Propaganda y Turismo del IV Centenario del Cuzco," ECL, April 3, 1934, morning edition, 4.

138. HBNP, "El fomento del turismo," ECL, April 4, 1934, morning edition, 1.

139. AMC, Legajo 97, Luis E. Valcárcel to Presidente del Consejo Municipal del Cuzco, March 16, 1934.

140. AMC, Legajo 97, "Informe preliminar sobre el Plan Regular para la ciudad del Cuzco," 6.

141. AMC, Legajo 97, "Informe preliminar sobre el Plan Regular para la ciudad del Cuzco," 7.

142. AMC, Legajo 97, Sub-Comisión de Alojamiento to Alcalde del Consejo Provincial del Cercado, March 6, 1934. The letter outlines the cooperation agreement between the subcommission and the municipal lodging inspector.

143. AMC, Legajo 97, Sub-Comisión del Alojamiento, Hoteles i alojamiento de la ciudad del Cuzco, March 1934.

144. AMC, Legajo 98, Ferrocarilles del Sur del Perú to Señor Presidente del Sub-Comisión de Alojamiento para el IV Centenario del Cuzco, February 20, 1934.

145. AMC, Legajo 97, Sub-Comisión de Alojamiento, January 29, 1934.

146. AMC, Legajo 98, Presidente del Comité Central del IV Centenario del Cuzco to Sub-Comisión de Alojamiento, March 15, 1934.

147. AMC, Legajo 98, "Bases a las que se sijetaran [sic] los préstamos para la instalación de casas de alojamientos i hoteles," April 28, 1934.

148. AMC, Legajo 98, Sr. Camillo to Presidente de la Comité del IV Centenario del Cuzco, February 3, 1934.

149. AMC, Legajo 98, Humberto Gil to Sub-Comisión de Alojamiento, February 2, 1934.

150. AMC, Legajo 98, Manuel Ávila to Senor Presidente del Comité Ejecutivo-Pro IV Centenario, March 3, 1934.

151. AMC, Legajo 98, Enrique Santos to Presidente de la Comisión de Alojamiento, March 22, 1934.

152. AMC, Legajo 98, Hermoza Santos to Comité Central Pro-IV Centenario, January 24, 1934.

153. AMC, Legajo 98, Wenceslao Cano to Senores Miembros de la Sub Comisión de Alojamiento para el Centenario del Cuzco, February 8, 1934.

154. HBNP, "El arreglo de alojamiento en el Cuzco," ECL, March 12, 1934, morning edition, 1.

155. HBNP, "La celebración de IV Centenario del Cuzco," ECL, March 23, 1934, morning edition, 1.

156. HBNP, "Comezaron ayer las fiestas en el Cuzco," ECL, March 23, 1934, morning edition, 11.

157. Mendoza, *Creating Our Own*.

158. AMC, Legajo 98, Programa Municipal para la conmemoración del IV Centenario de la fundación española de la ciudad del Cuzco; HBNP, "Las fiestas del cuarto Centenario del Cuzco," ECL, March 23, 1934, morning edition, 13; for more information on the significance of the Centro Qosqo de Arte Nativo, see Mendoza, *Creating Our Own*, 76–91.

159. HBMC, "Podría establecerse el servicio aero," ECC, May 19, 1934, 1.

160. Hiatt, "'Flying Cholo.'"

161. HBMC, "Se inaguró ayer el Instituto Arqueológico," ECC, August 31, 1934, 2.

162. AMC, Legajo 98, Programa Municipal para la conmemoración del IV Centenario de la fundación española de la ciudad del Cuzco.

163. HBMC, "Las alumas del Colegio de las Mercedes excursionaron a Machupichu," ECC, September 11, 1934, 5.

164. "Cuzco Celebrates Fourth Centenary," NYT, March 24, 1934, E8.

165. HBNP, editorial, ECL, March 23, 1934, morning edition, 22.

166. HBNP, "Sigue Afluyendo gran número de turistas a la población del Cusco," ECL, March 27, morning edition, 1934, 11.

167. HBNP, "El Cuzco frente al IV centenario de su fundación española," ECL, March 22, 1934, morning edition, 4.

Chapter 2

1. Heaney, *Cradle of Gold*, 212–13; HBMC, "Las ceremonias en la histórica Machu-Picchu," ECC, October 18, 1948, 2.

2. Babb, *The Tourism Encounter*, 1–13; Berger and Wood, introduction to *Holiday in Mexico*, 1–20; Sears, *Sacred Places*.

3. Sadlier, *Americans All*.

4. Joseph, LeGrand, and Salvatore, *Close Encounters of Empire*.

5. Berger, "Goodwill Ambassadors," 107–29.

6. Lomnitz, *Deep Mexico, Silent Mexico*, 125–44; Pratt, *Imperial Eyes*, 6.

7. Drinot, *The Allure of Labor*; Stein, *Populism in Peru*.

8. MacCannell, *The Tourist*, 91–107.

9. Klarén, *Peru*, 262–67.

10. HBNP, "Chan-Chan: Capital del Gran Chimú," CCC, March 1927, 25.

11. Klarén, *Peru*, 275–76.

12. For analysis of the 1932 APRA uprising and its historical legacy, see García-Bryce, "A Revolution Remembered, a Revolution Forgotten"; M. Giesecke, *La insurrección de Trujillo*.

13. Tamayo Herrera, *Historia regional del Cuzco republicano*, 149–50.

14. de la Cadena, *Indigenous Mestizos*, 135; Klarén, *Peru*, 276–80.

15. Tantaleán, *Peruvian Archaeology*, 67–68; L. Valcárcel, *Memorias*, 262–64.

16. HBMC, "Homenaje de americanismo merecido a la ciudad del Cuzco, la milieneria capital de los Incas," ECC, January 27, 1933, 2.

17. HBNP, "Homenaje al Cuzco, la ciudad imperial," *La Crónica*, October 29, 1933, sec. 1.

18. HBNP, "El turismo, riqueza que debe beneficiarnos," *La Crónica*, October 29, 1933, sec. 3.

19. HBNP, "Leyes en favor del turismo," *Revista del Touring Club Peruano* 7, no. 77 (October–December 1932): 2.

20. HBNP, "Editorial: Se fomentará el turismo oficialmente en el Perú," *Revista del Touring Club Peruano* 7, no. 77 (October–December 1932): 5.

21. CBC, Miguel Angel Nieto, "Conferencia," *Revista Universitaria* 23, no. 66 (March 1934): 17–18.

22. HBMC, "La inauguración de la carretera Machupicchu-Quillabamba," ECC, July 6, 1933, 2.

23. HBNP, Eduardo Dibos Dammert, "Se inaguró con todo éxito el Aeródromo del Cuzco," *Revista del Touring Club Peruano* 7, no. 79 (April–June 1933): 21; HBMC, "El Aeródromo Velasco Astete," ECC, May 14, 1933, 2; Hiatt, "Flying 'Cholo,'" 339–44.

24. HBNP, Albert Giesecke, "Auto Trip from Cuzco to Lima via Ayacucho," *Turismo*, October 1940.

25. HBMC, "Excursión de maestros y alumnos del colegio San Francisco a Machupicchu," ECC, June 21, 1933, 5; "Hacia Ollanta y Machu-Picchu: Excursión del 29 de julio; Conferencias e incidentes," ECC, August 8, 1933, 2; "Las alumnas del Colegio de las Mercedes excursionaron a Machupicchu," ECC, September 11, 1934, 5.

26. HBNP, "En un tren especial cedido por el gobierno se efectuó ayer la excursión hacia Machupicchu," ECL, August 2, 1934, morning edition, 13; "Los alumnos de Colegio de Ciencias excursionaron a las ruinas de Machupicchu y Huaynapicchu," October 6, 1934, 4.

27. Alida Malkus, "To a 'Lost' City of the Incas," NYT, November 13, 1938, 197.

28. Heany, *Cradle of Gold*, 201–11; H. Bingham, *Machu Picchu: A Citadel of the Incas*.

29. Philip Ainsworth Means, "An Ancient City of the Incas: Dr. Bingham Sums Up the Results of the Machu Picchu Expedition," NYT, May 4, 1930, BR6.

30. A. Bingham, *Portrait of an Explorer*, 337.

31. di Leonardo, *Exotics at Home*, 145–98; Salvatore, *Disciplinary Conquest*.

32. Douglas Naylor, "South America Calls to the Explorer," NYT, November 1, 1931, 82.

33. D. P. Aub, "Jungle, Mountain and Plain Diversify Delights of Travel," *Washington Post*, January 28, 1934, SA3.

34. James Powers, "Finding the Lost Inca City That Cradled the Potato," *Daily Boston Globe*, July 21, 1931, 16.

35. Richard Halliburton, "The Place Where the Sun Is Tied," *Ladies' Home Journal* 46 (September 1929): 16–17, 179; Richard Halliburton, "Halliburton Climbs to Hidden Refuge of 100 Inca Priestesses," *Daily Boston Globe*, September 23, 1934, B5.

36. AG, 1095, Blair Niles to Albert Giesecke, December 4, 1935.

37. Niles, *Peruvian Pageant*; Hudson Strode, "The Legend and Drama of Peru," NYT, April 4, 1937, 101.

38. Wilder, *The Bridge of San Luis Rey*; "Wilder Novel Wins Pulitzer," NYT, May 8, 1928, 4.

39. *The Bridge of San Luis Rey*, 1929; *The Bridge of San Luis Rey*, 1944; for critical reviews of the 1944 film, see "At the Capitol," NYT, March 3, 1944, 19.

40. Sims Malkus, *The Citadel of a Hundred Stairways*.

41. "For the Young Reader's Bookshelf," NYT, May 12, 1946, 133.

42. Hergé, "Le temple du soleil."

43. Sadlier, *Americans All*, 7–21; Dozer, *Are We Good Neighbors?*, 10–15; Wood, *The Making of the Good Neighbor Policy*, 128.

44. Dallek, *FDR and American Foreign Policy, 1932–1945*; Gellman, *Good Neighbor Diplomacy*; Pike, *FDR's Good Neighbor Policy*; Wood, *The Making of the Good Neighbor Policy*.

45. Rowland, *History of the Office of the Coordinator of Inter-American Affairs*.

46. USNA, RG 59, box 4347, 823.00/1646, U.S. Embassy Lima to U.S. Department of State, comment regarding the political sympathies of various Peruvian officials and leaders, June 2, 1943.

47. Ciccarelli, "Fascism and Politics in Peru during the Benavides Regime."

48. Thorp and Bertram, *Peru, 1890–1977*, 178.

49. AG-1013, folio 13, Philip Ainsworth Means to Albert Giesecke, July 4, 1938.

50. "La fundación del Instituto Cultural Peruano-Norteamericano," ECL, morning edition, June 2, 1938, 5, HBNP; AG-D-063, speech about history of the institute given August 1960.

51. Klarén, *Peru*, 281–82.

52. USNA, RG 229, Entry 1, box 202, Peru—Country Study, "Office of Coordinator of Inter-American Affairs, Press Division."

53. HBNP, "En la mañana de ayer, el vicepresidente de los Estados Unidos llego a Cuzco," ECL, April 11, 1943, 3.

54. USNA, RG 229, box 399, OEM-CR 1, 3—Education Teaching Aids, *Latin America Today: A Study for Junior High Schools*, September 1, 1941, 65.

55. USNA, RG 229, box 399, OEM-CR 1, 3—Education Teaching Aids, *People Who Live in Thin Air: A Study of Life in the Andes Mountains of South America*, October 1, 1941.

56. USNA, RG 229, Entry 1, box 14, AIA-4186, 0—Educational Programs, "Project Authorization: Exhibits of Materials on Other American Republics."

57. USNA, RG 229, Entry 1, box 14, AIA-4186, 0—Educational Programs, "Project Authorization: Exhibits of Materials on Other American Republics."

58. USNA, RG 229, box 351, Letter P-444, Arthur Dewey, Chair, Coordination Committee for Peru to Nelson Rockefeller, November 21, 1942.

59. USNA, RG 229, box 255, B-RA 1515, 3—Radio Programs—Dramatic, Walter E. Krause, Assistant Director, Radio Division to Mr. Robert C. Wells, Chairman, Coordination Committee for Argentina, Subject: Local Programs, March 15, 1943; see also "Hello Americans: The Andes," Paley Center for Media, November 22, 1942, accessed February 9, 2013, http://www.paleycenter.org/collection/item/?q=orson+welles+radio&p=8&item=R88:0193; "Radio Reviews: Hello Americans," *Variety*, December 16, 1942, 30.

60. Original proposal found in RG 229, box 352, 3 Peru—Radio Scripts & Material, Background Material, Letter P-943, John W. G. Ogilvie, Associate Director, Radio Division to Arthur Dewey, Chairman, Coordination Committee for Peru, January 13, 1943; project cancellation in RG 229, box 352, Memorandum, October 14, 1942.

61. RG 229, box 352, Letter P-1378, Stuart Ayers, Principal Radio Field Representative, to John W. G. Ogilvie, Director, Radio Division, July 7, 1944.

62. RG 229, box 352, Peru Radio Materials—Musical, Letter P-1961, Stuart Ayers, Principal Radio Field Representative, to Wallace K. Harrison, Director, August 24, 1945.

63. USNA, RG 229, box 399, OEM-CR 1, 3—Educational Teaching Aids, *People Who Live in Thin Air: A Study of Life in the Andes Mountains of South America*, October 1, 1941, 26–27.

64. USNA, RG 229, Entry 1, OIAA, box 217, "Contract Number NDCar-86."

65. USNA, RG 229, Entry 1, OIAA, box 218, Motion Picture Society for the Americas, "Weekly Report Ending May 14, 1942," and Motion Picture Society for the Americas, "Weekly Report Ending August 26, 1942."

66. *Heart of the Inca Empire*.

67. *Saludos Amigos*. For a more critical interpretation of this film as a tool of U.S. empire, see Croce, "Walt Disney's Latin American Tour."

68. HBNP, "Touring Club Peruano," ECL, March 7, 1934, morning edition, 1; *Turismo*, January 31, 1937.

69. HBNP, "Llegaron hoy al Callao 450 turistas que viajan al bordo del 'Gripsholms,'" ECL, February 10, 1938, 6; "Los turistas del 'Columbus' en Lima," ECL, February 16, 1938, 7; "Los turistas norteamericanos del transatlantico 'Rotterdam,'" ECL, February 18, 1938, 12; "Llegada de turistas británicos que viajen en el 'Reina del Pacífico,'" ECL, February 28, 1938, 2.

70. HBNP, "El fomento del turismo," ECL, July 16, 1938, morning edition, 2.

71. HBNP, "El desarrollo de los servicios de aviación," ECL, June 3, 1938, morning edition, 2.

72. HBNP, "Visitad el Cusco!," *Revista de Touring Club Peruano* 9, no. 83 (May 1934): 14. Before 1940 the TACP was named the Touring Club Peruano.

73. HBNP, Eduardo Dibos Dammert, "Palabras del Presidente," *Turismo*, July 1936.

74. HBNP, Phyllis Snyder, "Cusco," *Turismo*, July 1936.

75. HBNP, Louis Pierard, "Tierra de los Indios," *Turismo*, February 1937; Carlos Rios Pagaza, "El Valle Sagrado de los Incas," *Turismo*, June 1937; "Tourist Guide," *Turismo*, October 1937; Carlos Martínez Hague, "Vision y esbozo del Cusco," *Turismo*, October 1938.

76. HBNP, "Nuestra riqueza arqueológica," ECL, January 18, 1938, morning edition, 1.

77. AG-D-71, folio 1, Ministerio de Relaciones Exteriores del Perú to Giesecke, March 14, 1936.

78. AG-D-071, folios 26–27, "Informe," July 24, 1936, 18–19.

79. AG-D-071, folio 4, "Informe," 1.

80. AG-D-071, folio 19, "Informe," 15.

81. HBNP, "Entrevistas," *Turismo*, March 1937.

82. For an analysis of the Benavides government and its role in debates over social reform in Peru, see Drinot, *The Allure of Labor*.

83. Baranowski, *Strength through Joy*; Koenker, *Club Red*; Shaffer, *See America First*.

84. HBNP, "Defensa de la vida, salud, y alegría de los trabajadores es el seguro social," *Turismo*, June 1937.

85. HBNP, "Editorial," *Turismo*, November 1937.

86. USNA, RG 229, Entry 40, box 657, Ministerio de Fomento y Obras Públicas, *Nuevos Hoteles del Perú para el Turismo* 2, no. 4 (September 1941): 4.

87. HBNP, "Editorial," *Turismo*, August 1938.

88. USNA, RG 229, Entry 40, box 657, Ministerio de Fomento y Obras Públicas, *Nuevos Hoteles del Perú para el Turismo* 2, no. 4 (September 1941): 24.

89. Endy, *Cold War Holidays*.

90. Philip Ainsworth Means, "Archeology as a Reason for 'Visiting the Americas,'" *Pan American Union Bulletin* 72, no. 2 (February 1938): 63–69.

91. José Tercero, "Practical Pan Americanism: The First Inter-American Travel Congress and Latin American Good Will Tour," *Pan American Union Bulletin* 73, no. 3 (March 1939): 137–41; USNA, RG 229, Entry 40, box 656, *Final Act: Second Inter-American Travel Conference, Mexico, DF, September 15–24*, Washington, DC: Pan-American Union Travel Division, 1941; USNA, RG 229, Entry 40, box 657, Dorothy Lack, "Suggested Program for the Development of Inter-American Tourist Travel for the Office of Inter-American Affairs," 3.

92. Julia MacLean Vinas, "A Sentimental Journey in Peru," *Pan American Union Bulletin* 47, no. 3 (March 1940): 123–36; *Pan American Union Bulletin* 75, no. 7 (July 1941): cover.

93. USNA, RG 59, decimal file 1930–1939, 823.11/87, "Regarding Decree of March 1937 Designating a Special Commission to Prepare the Draft of a Tourist Law," March 5, 1937; and USNA, RG 59, decimal file 1930–1939, 823.111/102, U.S. Embassy Lima to Washington, Subject: Encouragement of Tourist Traffic by the Government of Peru, December 20, 1937.

94. USNA, RG 229, Entry 1, OIAA, box 202, F. D. Rugg to Mr. J. Stanton Robbins, "Transmittal of Report of Transportation Survey of Peru," October 23, 1944, 22.

95. USNA, RG 229, Entry 1, box 202, 2 — Peru, Economic Dev., Tourists, Dorothy Lack to Juan Chávez D., Commercial Councilor, July 26, 1943.

96. USNA, RG 229, box 656, Nelson A. Rockefeller to Wallace K. Harrison, Director, Office of Inter-American Affairs, April 20, 1945.

97. USNA, RG 229, Entry 40, box 657, Suggested Program for the Development of Inter-American Tourist Travel, May 1945, 11.

98. Hanson, *The New World Guide to Latin American Republics*, 71, 89.

99. BNP, Cassinelli and Santillana, *Lima*, 3.

100. HBNP, "Editorial," *Turismo*, November 1943.

101. HBNP, Ayax, "Preparemonos para la invasión," *Turismo*, January 1944.

102. USNA, RG 229, Entry 40, box 657, "Hoteles para turistas en el Perú."

103. USNA, RG 229, Entry 40, box 657, Ministerio de Fomento y Obras Públicas, *Nuevos Hoteles del Perú para el Turismo* 2, no. 4 (September 1941): 20.

104. USNA, RG 229, Entry 40, box 657, Ministerio de Fomento y Obras Públicas, *Nuevos Hoteles del Perú para el Turismo* 2, no. 4 (September 1941): 22.

105. HBNP, "El Día del Cusco," *La Crónica*, June 24, 1944, 2.

106. de la Cadena, *Indigenous Mestizos*, 152.

107. HBMC, "Día del Cusco," *El Sol*, June 26, 1944, 1.

108. For analysis on Inti Raymi, see Dean, *Inka Bodies and the Body of Christ*, 200–218; de la Cadena, *Indigenous Mestizos*, 152–62.

109. HBNP, "El Comite Pro-Celebración del Día del Cuzco," *La Crónica*, June 24, 1944, 21.

110. HBNP, "El presidente de la república continuó su jira ayer," ECL, June 24, 1944, morning edition, 7.

111. HBNP, Elodoro Ventocilla, "Sentido del Cusco en la peruanidad," *La Crónica*, June 24, 1944, 20.

112. HBMC, "Días de fervoroso peruanismo ha vivido el Cuzco en torno a Manuel Prado celebrando el Día de la Ciudad," *El Sol*, June 26, 1944, 2.

113. Klarén, *Peru*, 289; Portocarrero Maisch, *De Bustamante a Odría*, 103–86.

114. HBNP, "Notas y comentarios," *Turismo*, November 1945.

115. HBNP, "Notas y comentarios," *Turismo*, February 1946.

116. HBNP, "Notas y comentarios," *Turismo*, April 1946.

117. AGN, Fondo Ministerio de Hacienda, H-6, lejado 2444, "Memoria de la Corporación Nacional de Turismo, correspondiente al ano 1946" (Lima: Imprenta Torres Aguirre, 1947), 9.

118. HBNP, "El gobierno regleamenta la Corporación Nacional de Turismo," *Turismo*, June 1946. The national tourism still exists as the Centro de Formación en Turismo (CENFOTUR).

119. HBNP, "Benjamín Roca Muelle," *Turismo*, June 1946.

120. For a complete transcript of the president's address, see "Discurso del Doctor José Luis Bustamante y Rivero, Presidente de la República," 63–69.

121. HBNP, "Primer Congreso Nacional de Turismo," ECL, June 9, 1947, 2.

122. HBNP, "Primer Congreso Nacional de Turismo," ECL, June 7, 1947, morning edition, 3.

123. HBNP, "El Primer Congreso Nacional de Turismo," *La Prensa*, June 9, 1947, 5.

124. BNP, "Se clausuró ayer el Congreso de Turismo," *La Prensa*, June 16, 1947, 4.

125. HBNP, "Plan vacacional," *Turismo*, October 1946.

126. Elena, *Dignifying Argentina*, 123–34; Skiwot, *The Purposes of Paradise*, 146–47.

127. AGN, Lima, Fondo Ministerio de Hacienda, H-6, legado 2444, "Memoria de la Corporación Nacional de Turismo, correspondiente al ano 1946," 17.

128. AGN, Lima, Fondo Ministerio de Hacienda, H-6, legado 2444, "Memoria de la Corporación Nacional de Turismo, correspondiente al ano 1946," 18.

129. HBMC, "El Congreso Nacional del Turismo," ECC, May 21, 1947, 2.

130. HBNP, "Recomendaciones sobre nuestro patrimonio artístico aprobados por el I Congreso Nacional del Turismo," ECL, June 12, 1947, afternoon edition, 8.

131. HBMC, "Corporación Nacional del Turismo: Boletín Informático," ECC, May 7, 1947, 3; "Corporación Nacional del Turismo: Boletín Informático," ECC, May 23, 1947, 3.

132. AINC, 08.01.01-04-1, folder "Zona Monumental—Informes en General—Cusco—anos 1941–1968," Benjamín Roca Muelle to Presidente del Consejo Nacional de Conservación y Restauración de Monumentos Historicos, May 2, 1947.

133. HBNP, "Los planos turísticos del Cusco," La Crónica, March 8, 1948, morning edition, 2.

134. HBNP, "Serán ejecutadas trabajos de reparación urgentes en las ruinas de Machu Picchu," La Crónica, May 18, 1948, morning edition, 4.

135. HBNP, "Necesidad de financiar la Semana del Cuzco," La Jornada 8, no. 81 (June 27, 1948): 1.

136. HBNP, "El Segundo Congreso Indigenista Interamericano debe ser celebrado en el Cuzco el 24 de Julio," La Prensa, January 2, 1948, 2.

137. Original intent of the highway defined in AGN, Lima, Fondo de Asuntos Indígenas, Legajo, 3.13.2.9, año 1948, folio 123, "Resolución Suprema, 15 de Mayo de 1948."

138. HBNP, "El turismo en Cusco," ECL, May 23, 1948, 2. No mention of Bingham is made in this article. The stated goal for the construction of the highway was the expected Indigenista Congress.

139. HBNP, "Las ruinas de Machu-Pichu abiertas al turismo mundial," ECL, March 4, 1948.

140. Heaney, Cradle of Gold, 189–98.

141. Salvatore, "Local versus Imperial Knowledge," 67–80.

142. AG-0140, folio 26, Hiram Bingham to Albert Giesecke, August 9, 1941.

143. AG-0521, folio 3, Albert Giesecke to John Clifford Folger, May 17, 1948.

144. AG-0140, folio 31, Hiram Bingham to Albert Giesecke, September 29, 1948.

145. HBNP, "Cuzco, Imperial Incaland, the Greatest Goal of Students and Tourists," Turismo, October–November 1948.

146. AG-0521, folio 8, Albert Giesecke to John Clifford Folger, November 22, 1948.

147. HBNP, "No hay nada comparable a Machu-Picchu," ECL, October 7, 1948, morning edition, 3.

148. BMI, Felipe Cosio del Pomar, "Machupijchu," Revista del Instituto y Museo Arqueológico, no. 12 (1948): 138.

149. A. Bingham, Portrait of an Explorer, 343; Heany, Cradle of Gold, 212–14.

150. HBMC, "Machupicchu es la antigua Vilcabamba y en esa importante ciudad estuvo Manco II," ECC, October 16, 1948, 2.

151. HBNP, "Interesante relato del doctor Hiram Bingham, descubridor de Machu Picchu," ECL, October 7, 1948, morning edition, 5.

152. HBNP, "El Camino a Machupicchu," ECL, October 19, 1948, afternoon edition, 3.

153. HBNP, "La Ciudad Perdida de los Inca," Turismo, August–September 1948.

154. AG-D-209, folio 2, Albert Giesecke to Louis J. Garcia, PANAGRA, February 13, 1961.

155. HBMC, "Las ceremonias en la histórica Machu-Picchu," ECC, October 18, 1948, 2.

156. HBNP, "Fué inagurada la carretera Hiram Bingham que conduce a las ruinas de Machupicchu," *La Crónica*, October 20, 1948, 7.

157. HBNP, "La carretera 'Bingham' une el Cuzco y Machupicchu," ECL, October 20, 1948, afternoon edition, 3.

158. HBNP, Manuel E. Cuadros E., "El camino a la ciudad de Machupicchu aumentará el turismo hacia el Cuzco," ECL, October 27, 1948, morning edition, 15.

159. "Highway to Antiquity: Carretera Hiram Bingham to Open Machu Picchu to the World," *Newsweek* 32, no. 1 (November 1948): 45.

160. AG-0140, folio 32, Hiram Bingham to Albert Giesecke, November 2, 1948.

161. Bingham, *Lost City of the Incas*.

162. Bingham, *Lost City of the Incas*, 160–67.

163. Orville Prescott, "Books of the Times," NYT, November 5, 1948, 23.

164. Victor W. Von Hagen, "Machu Picchu," NYT, December 5, 1948, BR18.

165. Endy, *Cold War Holidays*, 72–80.

166. USNA, RG 59, decimal file 1940–1949, box 4362, 823.43, Instituto Cultural Peruano Norteamericano/4, PS/9, George C. Vaillant, Cultural Relations Attaché, to U.S. Secretary of State, Subject: Report on cultural relation activities for the month of January 1944, February 1, 1943 [*sic*], 3.

167. Poole, "Landscape and the Imperial Subject," 107–38.

168. Feinstein, *Pablo Neruda*, 173–76.

169. Neruda, "Poem XII," 67.

170. Drinot, "Awaiting the Blood of a Truly Emancipating Revolution."

171. Guevara de la Serna, *The Motorcycle Diaries*, 111.

172. Shullenberger, "That Obscure Object of Desire."

173. USNA, RG 59, box 15, 032/1817, Report covering activities of Pablo Neruda, Chilean poet who recently visited Peru, November 10, 1943.

174. Klarén, *Peru*, 289–99; Portocarrero Maisch, *De Bustamante a Odría*, 187–207; Thorp and Bertram, *Peru, 1890–1977*, 201.

175. Skiwot, *The Purposes of Paradise*, 169–76.

Chapter 3

1. "Some of Damage Caused by Earthquake in Peru," NYT, May 24, 1950, 3.

2. Kubler, *Cuzco*, 5.

3. GAKP, box 1, folder 3, Junta de Reconstrucción y Fomento Industrial, *Su obra* (Cusco: n.p., 1952–53), 1.

4. Carey, *In the Shadow of Melting Glaciers*, 12.

5. Clarke, "Revolutionizing the Tragic City"; Healey, *The Ruins of the New Argentina*; S. Schwartz, *Sea of Storms*; Walker, *Shaky Colonialism*.

6. HBNP, "La visita del General Odría a la Corporación Nacional del Turismo," *Turismo*, July–August 1949.

7. HBNP, "Comisión Reorganizadora de la Corporación Nacional de Turismo," ECL, March 23, 1950, 10.

8. Mexican president Miguel Alemán Valdés vigorously used state resources to support tourism development in Mexico and Acapulco in particular in the 1940s and

1950s, as documented by Saragoza, "The Selling of Mexico," 102–4. The Cuban state's role in tourism promotion in the 1940s and 1950s is documented in R. Schwartz, *Pleasure Island*.

9. Klarén, *Peru*, 300; Portocarrero, *De Bustamante a Odría*, 103–86.

10. HBNP, "Editorial," *Turismo*, January–February 1951, 2.

11. HBNP, Juan Esteban Maguiña, "El turismo en el Perú," *La Prensa*, April 13, 1952, 2.

12. HBNP, "Serán ejecutadas trabajos de reparación urgentes en las ruinas de Machu Picchu," *La Crónica*, May 18, 1948, 4.

13. HBNP, "La reína de la belleza de Lima," *Turismo*, March–April 1949, n.p.

14. Martha Fergurson, "A Tour of Southern Peru," *Peruvian Times*, September 30, 1949, 1.

15. Collier, *Squatters and Oligarchs*; Niera, *Los Andes*, 55–62; Portocarrero, *De Bustamante a Odría*, 187–207.

16. Speech contents found in AG-D-042, folio 4, March 18, 1954; event program found in AG-1709, folio 3.

17. AG-1143, folio 3, Franklin K. Paddock to Albert Giesecke, July 7, 1958.

18. See correspondence between Giesecke and U.S. Ambassador to Venezuela Walter J. Donnelly contained in AG, legajo 0424.

19. HBNP, "Joan Fontaine y Martita Pareja," *Caretas*, September 15–30, 1953, 6–7. Correspondence between Fontaine and Giesecke is found in AG-0523, folio 4, Joan Fontaine to Albert Giesecke, September 23, 1954.

20. AG-0356, folio 3, Albert Giesecke to Harry Crocker, April 23, 1951.

21. AG-0140, folio 63, Albert Giesecke to Hiram Bingham, April 2, 1955; AG-1040, folio 64, Hiram Bingham to Albert Giesecke, April 26, 1955.

22. AG-1040, Albert Giesecke to Hiram Bingham, July 18, 1952; AG-0414, Eduardo Dibos to Albert Giesecke, August 6, 1952.

23. HBNP, "El Perú debe tener una indústria cinematográfica," ECL, May 2, 1950, 3.

24. HBMC, "En la tierra de los Incas," *El Sol*, January 18, 1952, 2.

25. *Secret of the Incas*.

26. AG, legajo 0465, Albert Giesecke to Winston Elting, October 9, 1953; AG, legajo 1438, Albert Giesecke to Adlai Stevenson, March 8, 1960.

27. Heaney, *Cradle of Gold*, 220; Deborah Nadoolman, interviewed by Mike French and Gilles Verschuere, theraider.net, September 14, 2005, accessed November 7, 2011, http://www.theraider.net/features/interviews/deborah_nadoolman.php.

28. William H. Brownell Jr., "Hollywood Digest," NYT, July 12, 1953, X5.

29. "At the Victoria," *New York Times*, May 29, 1954, 13.

30. HBNP, César Miro, "Una ciudad olvidada re resuicta," ECL, April 4, 1955, 10.

31. AG-0470, folio 19, Albert Giesecke to Mel Epstein, May 25, 1955.

32. AG-1256, folio 7, Albert Giesecke to Louis Renault, February 28, 1954.

33. HBMC, Américo Luna S., "Plan de vialidad aplicado al interés turístico," *El Sol*, January 29, 1953, 2.

34. HBMC, "Touring y Automovil Club del Perú," ECC, September 22, 1954, 2; "Reglamento y temario a los que se someterá el fórum sobre turismo en el Cuzco," ECC, December 19, 1954, 3.

35. HBNP, "Por la mejor preservación de nuestros monumentos arqueológicos," ECL, June 16, 1954, morning edition, 3.

36. Tamayo Herrera, *Historia regional del Cuzco republicano*, 168.

37. Collier, *Squatters and Oligarchs*; Klarén, *Peru*, 300–301.

38. HBNP, "Tres Comités de Auxilio Constituyó el Presidente de la Junta Militar de Gobierno en el Cuzco," ECL, May 24, 1950, 3.

39. Tamayo Herrera, *Historia regional del Cuzco republicano*, 177.

40. HBNP, "Reconstruyamos la capital arqueológica de la América," ECL, May 23, 1950, 3.

41. HBNP, "Cuzco," *La Prensa*, July 28, 1950, 2.

42. HBNP, "Sobre la ayuda de su gobierno a la reconstrucción del Cuzco, nos habla el embajador de España," ECL, May 26, 1950, 1.

43. HBNP, "Los monumentos del Cuzco y su perdurabilidad a través de las edades," ECL, May 31, 1950, 3.

44. HBNP, "Se ha procedido a demoler varios edificios del Cuzco para evitar acidentes," ECL, May 26, 1950, 3; Tamayo Herrera, *Historia regional del Cuzco republicano*, 167.

45. This style was controversially used in the modernization of Lima's Plaza de Armas in the 1930s and 1940s, as examined by Ramos, "La reforma neocolonial de la Plaza de Armas."

46. HBNP, "Conversando con el doctor Luis E. Valcárcel sobre la reconstrucción del Cuzco," ECL, May 26, 1950, 4.

47. L. Valcárcel, *Memorias*, 378.

48. HBNP, "Conversando con el doctor Luis E. Valcárcel sobre la reconstrucción del Cuzco," ECL, May 26, 1950, 4.

49. HBNP, "Propuestas para que UNESCO ayude a la reconstrucción del Cuzco," ECL, May 28, 1950, 1.

50. Greaves, Bolton, and Zapata, *Vicos and Beyond*; Carey, *In the Shadow of Melting Glaciers*, 67–96.

51. GAKP, box 1, folder 3, "Memoria de la Junta de Reconstrucción y Fomento de Cuzco," 1953.

52. Tamayo Herrera, *Historia regional del Cuzco republicano*, 178; Rénique, *Los sueños de la sierra*, 153.

53. AG, legajo 1277, Benjamín Roca Muelle to Albert Giesecke, May 31, 1950.

54. HBNP, Rafael Aguilar Paéz, "El terremoto del Cuzco," ECL, August 9, 1950, 4.

55. AG, legajo 0768, "Informe preliminar," 10–11.

56. Enríquez Verdura, "Torres Bodet y la UNESCO."

57. Kubler, *Cuzco*, 1–2.

58. GAKP, box 1, folder 3, Junta de Reconstrucción y Fomento Industrial, *Su obra* (Cusco: 1952–53).

59. D. Brown, *Inventing New England*, 105–34; Covert, *San Miguel de Allende*; Rothman, *Devil's Bargains*, 81–112.

60. AMC, Legajo 97, Emilio Harth-Terré, "Informe preliminar sobre el Plan Regular para la ciudad del Cuzco."

61. GAKP, box 1, folder 8, "Plantamiento general," 1952, 1–5.

62. GAKP, box 1, folder 8, "Plantamiento general," 1952, 1–2.

63. GAKP, box 1, folder 8, "Plantamiento general," 1952, 2.

64. HBMC, "La ciudad de Machu-picchu, require seria labor de conservación," ECC, October 20, 1948, 2.

65. HBNP, "Inspección completa de las ruínas de Machupicchu hará una Comisión del Patronato," ECL, December 6, 1952, morning edition, 14.

66. JM-285, folio 33, "Sobre conservación de monumentos arqueológicos— Memorandum para el Ministro de Educación," October 7, 1953.

67. JM-285, folios 67–70, "Dirección de arqueología e historia," June 25, 1954; JM-285, folios 81–87, "Anteproyecto de reorganización de la dirección de arqueología e historia," December 4, 1954.

68. HBNP, "Fallas en cobro de derechos para visitor Machu Picchu," ECL, September 21, 1954, morning edition, 14.

69. JM-299, folio 2, César A. Soto to Luis Felipe Paredes, December 15, 1952.

70. HBNP, "Restos arqueológicos en plena destrucción," *La Prensa*, January 7, 1953, 3.

71. HBNP, "Machu-Picchu," *La Prensa*, January 11, 1953, 5.

72. HBNP, "Se restaura la ciudadela del Machu-Picchu," ECL, September 10, 1953, morning edition, 3.

73. Brading, *Mexican Phoenix*; Earl, *The Return of the Native*.

74. HBNP, "Para restaurar Machu-Picchu se ha presupuesto solo 600 dólares," ECL, January 11, 1953, 13.

75. HBMC, "Ruinas que se arruinan," *El Sol*, January 12, 1953, 2.

76. HBNP, "En estado de abandon se hallan ruinas arqueológicas del Cuzco," ECL, March 4, 1954, morning edition, 11; "Falta dinero para la limpieza de ruinas en el Cuzco," ECL, June 14, 1954, morning edition, 3.

77. HBNP, "Photos de Machu Picchu," *La Prensa*, December 16, 1954, 1.

78. JM-210, folio 2-4, "Informe del arqueólogo Mr. Lawrence Roys sobre las ruinas de Machupicchu."

79. HBNP, "No se presta la debida atención a Machu Picchu," ECL, February 7, 1955, morning edition, 11.

80. HBNP, "Machu Picchu corre peligro de desaparecer," *La Prensa*, February 7, 1955, 5.

81. JM-210, folio 11, "Informe de la visita de inspección a las ruinas de Machupic-chu," April 2, 1955.

82. JM-210, folios 16–19, "Machupicchu—Base del Intihuatana por la sección oesta, lado del Puente de 'San Miguel,'" 4.

83. JM-210, folio 11, "Informe de la visita de inspección a las ruinas de Machupic-chu," April 2, 1955.

84. HBMC, "Restauración de Machu-Picchu demandará de la ejecución de dos planes: 6 milliones de soles," ECC, July 18, 1955, 4.

85. HBNP, "Diputaos acordó pedir a fomento obras de defensa de Machupicchu," *La Prensa*, February 15, 1955, 2; HBMC, "La ciudad de Machupicchu merecerá opor-tuna ayuda estatal," ECC, February 15, 1955, 1.

86. HBNP, "Harían una colecta pública pro-ruinas de Machupicchu," *La Prensa*, February 16, 1955, 1.

87. Manuel Mujica Gallo, "Machu Picchu: Un mendigo," *Caretas*, July 10–24, 1955, 25–27, 30.

88. HBMC, "La reconstrucción del Cuzco," *El Sol*, January 7, 1952, 2.

89. HBMC, "Autonomia en la reconstrucción del Cuzco," *El Sol*, January 10, 1952, 2.

90. HBMC, "La Catedral del Cuzco y su restauración," *El Sol*, December 19, 1952, 2.

91. HBMC, "Ano perdido," ECC, February 5, 1954, 2.

92. CBC, Junta de Reconstrucción y Fomento Industrial del Cuzco, *Memoria 1953–1954*, 8.

93. HBMC, "Estado de las obras de recontrucción del Cuzco," *El Sol*, December 6, 1954, 2.

94. AGN, Fondo Hacienda H-6, Legajo 2398, "Cámara de Comercio de Cusco Memoria de 1951," 69.

95. Anavitarte Núñez, *Algo acerca del problema de la vivienda en el Cuzco*, 18.

96. HBNP, "Raúl Porras denuncia el absoluto abandono en que está el Cuzco," *La Prensa*, November 24, 1954, 1.

97. Gabriel Amaro, "La redestrucción del Cuzco," *Caretas*, April 20, 1954, 12.

98. Joe Tobruck, "Y el Cuzco?," *Caretas*, January 3, 1955, 9.

99. HBMC, "Odría y el Cuzco," *El Sol*, December 8, 1955, 1; "Huespedes distinguidos del Cuzco," *El Sol*, December 11, 1955, 2.

100. HBNP, "3,533 turistas en 6 meses visitaron la ciudad de Cuzco," *La Prensa*, July 25, 1955, 3. The article reported that the first half of 1955 saw an increase of only fifty-six tourist arrivals in Cusco over 1954.

101. JM-026, folio 187, "Informe Bimestral: Febrero-Marzo, 1957," 5; 4,030 entries were recorded in 1955, and 4,911 entries were recorded in 1956.

102. HBMC, "Bajó el número de turistas que anualmente ingresan al Perú," *El Sol*, December 15, 1955, 3.

103. AGN, Fondo Ministerio de Hacienda, H-G, legajo 2398, Cámara de Comercio de Cusco, "Memoria de 1951," 39–41.

104. HBMC, "Resolver el problema del ferrocarril del Cuzco a la Convención," ECC, September 10, 1954, 3.

105. HBNP, "El aeropuerto del Cuzco," ECL, March 15, 1951, morning edition, 2.

106. HBMC, "Cree la Corpac que el aeródromo del Cuzco debe construir en Anta," ECC, January 30, 1954, 3; "Resulta problemática la construcción del Terminal Aéreo de Anta: Corpac," ECC, July 8, 1955, 4.

107. HBMC, "Forum sobre el turismo en el Cuzco," *El Sol*, December 17, 1954, 2.

108. HBMC, Manuel Francisco Llosa Paredes, "Ante un nuevo intento nacionalista: El fórum de turismo en el Cuzco," *El Sol*, December 20, 1954, 2.

109. AG, legajo D-048.

110. AGN, Fondo Ministerio de Hacienda, H-6, Legajo 2424, "Corporación de Reconstrucción y Fomento del Cuzco," Ministerio de Fomento y Obras Públicas, Lima, 1957, 22.

111. HBMC, "La corporación del Cuzco en marcha desde hoy," ECC, February 12, 1956, 2.

112. AGN, Fondo Ministerio de Hacienda, H-6, Legajo 2424, "Corporación de Reconstrucción y Fomento de Cuzco," Ministerio de Fomento y Obras Públicas, Lima, 1957, 22.

113. HBNP, "Con 350 mil iniciarán obras en Machupicchu," *La Prensa*, November 20, 1955.

114. JM-026, folio 86, "Informe Bimestral: Agosto-Septiembre de 1956," 8.

115. JM-026, folio 152, "Informe Bimestral: Octubre-Noviembre, 1956," 6.

116. JM,-026, folio 200, "Informe Bimestral: Abril-Mayo 1957," 2.

117. HBNP, "Conservación de restos arqueológicos," *La Prensa*, January 10, 1953, 6.

118. JM-026, folio 153, "Informe Bimestral: Octubre-Noviembre, 1956," 7-8.

119. HBMC, "Se insiste en la restauración de Machu Picchu," *El Sol*, December 1, 1952, 2.

120. JM-026, folio 153, "Informe Bimestral: Octubre-Noviembre, 1956," 7.

121. JM-026, folio 153, "Informe Bimestral: Octubre-Noviembre, 1956," 7-8.

122. HBNP, "Técnica moderna se está empleando para restaurar la ciudadela de Machu Picchu," ECL, March 23, 1957, 13.

123. HBNP, José María Arguedas, "El estado actual de las reconstrucciones en el Cuzco," *La Prensa*, November 10, 1957, 8.

124. JM-026, folios 153-154, "Informe Bimestral: Octubre-Noviembre, 1956," 7-8.

125. JM-026, folio 168, "Informe Bimestral: Octubre-Noviembre, 1956," 22.

126. JM-026, folio 186, "Informe Bimestral: Febrero-Marzo, 1957," 4.

127. JM-026, folio 186, "Informe Bimestral: Febrero-Marzo, 1957," 12.

128. HBNP, "Machupicchu, ciudadela encantada," *La Crónica*, January 9, 1955, 2.

129. AG-0465, folio 2, Albert Giesecke to Winston Elting, October 9, 1953.

130. AG-0465, folio 8, Albert Giesecke to Winston Elting, October 18, 1955. Planned budgetary changes also outlined in HBNP, "Restauración de la ciudad arqueológica de Machupicchu," *El Peruano*, September 28, 1955, 1.

131. AG-0140, folio 60, Albert Giesecke to Hiram Bingham, March 14, 1955.

132. The Junta constructed a diesel power plant for the city of Cusco and began planning for construction of a hydroelectric plant on the Urubamba River as early as 1953, as reported in GAKP, folder 3, Junta de Reconstrucción y Fomento Industrial, *Su obra*, 28-30; GAKP, box 1, folder 5, Junta de Reconstrucción y Fomento Industrial del Cuzco, *Memorandum sobre el problema de energia eléctrica e industrialización de la cuidad del Cuzco y zonas de influencia en el departamento* (Lima, January 1956); see also HBMC, "Central Hidroeléctrica en el Cuzco," ECC, March 14, 1955, 3.

133. Tamayo Herrera, *Historia regional del Cuzco republicano*, 188-89; Tamayo Herrera, *El enigma de Machupicchu*, 96-97.

134. CBC, CYRF, *Hidroelectrica de Macchupichu [sic] Cuzco*.

135. Engineering and planning reports for the project reprinted in CBC, CYRF, *Historial cronológico de la Central Hidroelectrica de Machupijchu, 1957-1962*.

136. Alfonsina Barrionuevo, "Hidroeléctrica en Machu-Picchu," *Caretas*, September 15-29, 1958, 16-18.

137. HBMC, "Problema eléctrico," *El Sol*, November 24, 1957, 12; "La inauguración de las obras del Machupicchu," *El Sol*, February 4, 1959, 3.

138. HBMC, "El turismo en el Peru y en el Cuzco, principalmente," ECC, November 6, 1957, 2.

139. Speech text found in AG-D-050, "Aspectos sobre el turismo," 3; event program found in AG-1709, folio 4.

140. HBNP, "En 1958 se evitó destrucción masiva de grupos arqueológicos de M. Pichu," *ECL*, January 1, 1959, 13.

141. HBNP, "Turistas contarán desde el domingo 15 con modernizado Hotel en Machupicchu," *La Crónica*, February 12, 1959, 2; HBMC, "Fue inagurado Hotel de Machupijchu," *ECC*, February 18, 1955, 1.

142. AG-D-033. This legajo contains Giesecke's correspondence promoting the fiftieth anniversary in 1961.

143. GAKP, box 2, folder G, "Report," July 24, 1956.

144. Rénique, *Los suenos de la sierra*, 153, 161–64.

145. Rénique, *Los suenos de la sierra*, 187–88; Tamayo Herrera, *Historia regional del Cuzco republicano*, 195.

146. Hobsbawm, "A Case of Neo-feudalism."

Chapter 4

1. CBC, Chávez Ballón, *Informe Machupijchu*, 15.

2. CBC, Chávez Ballón, *Informe Machupijchu*, 5.

3. CBC, Chávez Ballón, *Informe Machupijchu*, 9.

4. Caballero, *Economía agraria de la sierra peruana antes de la reforma agraria de 1969*; Fioravanti, *Latifundio y sindicalismo agrario en el Perú*; Guillet, *Agrarian Reform and Peasant Economy in Southern Peru*; Handelman, *Struggle in the Andes*; Mayer, *Ugly Stories of the Peruvian Agrarian Reform*; Niera, *Los Andes*. For studies on the Velasco military government, see McClintock and Lowenthal, *The Peruvian Experiment Reconsidered*; Philip, *The Rise and Fall of the Peruvian Military Radicals*; Walter, *Peru and the United States*.

5. "La era de los 'jets,'" *Caretas*, February 28–March 14, 1960, 45.

6. See advertisement in *Caretas*, May 25–June 8, 1960; "Hilbck y los aeropuertos," *Caretas*, November 10–24, 1960, 39.

7. HBNP, "PANAGRA gana el trofeo Frye," *ECL*, January 4, 1953, 1.

8. AM, DGTUR, EET VII–XIII, Box 4, Jorge Merino Silva, COPESCO, *Estudio general del trabajo (Parte I): El turismo en Sud América con especial énfasis en el Perú* (June 1971), gráfico no. 4, n.p.

9. AM, DGTUR, EET VII–XIII, Box 4, Silva, COPESCO, *Estudio general del trabajo (Parte I)*, gráfico no. 2.

10. Eunice T. Juckett, "Sunday Is a Red-Letter Day in South America," NYT, September 11, 1960, XX21.

11. HBMC, "Aeropuerto Quispiquilla," *ECC*, July 14, 1961, 1.

12. ". . . Inclusive por el aire," *Caretas*, August 23–30, 1965, 49; HBMC, "Aeropuerto del Cuzco en Quispiquilla," *ECC*, March 6, 1964, 2; HBMC, "Construcción edificio en Aeropuerto Quispiquilla," *ECC*, October 6, 1965, 1; and "Aeropuerto Quispiquilla será Velasco Astete," *ECC*, October 9, 1965, 1. Faucett advertisement, *Caretas*, May 7–20, 1968, n.p.; see advertisement in HBMC, ECC, June 7, 1968, 5.

13. Zuelow, *A History of Modern Tourism*, 149–64.

14. Alfonsina Barrionuevo, "Cuzco y turismo," *Caretas*, September 28–October 12, 1961, 31.

15. "El Perú: País oculto," *Caretas*, September 12–27, 1963, 40–43; "¿Cómo se permite?," *Caretas*, April 25–May 9, 1963, 8; "Las maniobras del TACP,'" *Caretas*, May 9–24, 1963, 12–13.

16. AG, 0671, Albert Giesecke to Victor von Hagen, February 26, 1963. Giesecke noted in his communication that Ambassador Carlos Vásquez Ayllón headed the commission. Giesecke solicited von Hagen for help in determining the tourist potential of the Inca road system; HBNP, "Informe de la Comisión Gubermental sobre creación de una entidad para la promoción del turismo en el Perú," *Boletín de la Corporación de Turismo del Perú*, March–April 1964, 18–20.

17. Klarén, *Peru*, 319–22.

18. See Levinson and de Onís, *The Alliance That Lost Its Way*; Rogers, *The Twilight Struggle*; Scheman, *The Alliance for Progress*.

19. Handelman, *Struggle in the Andes*, 85.

20. AGN, Lima, Fondo de Hacienda, H-6, Legajo 2396, Cámara de Comercio de Lima, *Boletín Semanal*, no. 726 (March 16, 1964). The state hotel chain also was placed under the supervision of COTURPERU.

21. HBNP, "Promulgación de la Ley de Creación de la Corporación de Turismo del Perú," *Boletín de la Corporación de Turismo del Perú*, March–April 1964, 26.

22. CBC, "Turismo, una industria de gran porvenir en el Perú," *Boletín de la COTURPERU*, no. 15 (December 1965): 26–29; CBC, Checchi and Company, *La perspectiva para el turismo en el Perú: Informe presentado por Checci y Compania bajo contrato con la Organización de Estados Americanos* (Washington, DC: Checchi and Company, 1965), 48–49, 64–82. The report recommended that the national state spend $102 million on tourism infrastructure by 1974, including the creation of 2,700 new hotel rooms.

23. HBNP, "Turismo, una industria de gran porvenir en el Perú," *Boletín de la COTURPERU*, no. 15 (December 1965): 27–29.

24. HBNP, "Turismo, una industria de gran porvenir en el Perú," *Boletín de la COTURPERU*, no. 15 (December 1965): 28.

25. HBMC, "La ley de turismo debe ser revisada," ECC, March 31, 1964, 2.

26. HBNP, "Más Hoteles Precisa la Ciudad de Cusco," *Boletín de la COTURPERU*, no. 2 (May–July 1964): 29–30; "Oficina Departamental en la Ciudad Imperial," *Boletín de la COTURPERU*, no. 3 (August–October 1964): 24–25, HBMC; "Los problemas del Cuzco," ECC, December 24, 1964, 1; HBMC, "COTURPERU sesiona hoy: Lima," ECC, December 28, 1964, 1.

27. HBNP, "Presupuesto de COTURPERU para 1965," *Boletín de la COTURPERU*, no. 5 (January 1965): 4–6; "El Valle Sagrado de los Incas," *Boletín de la COTURPERU*, no. 5 (January 1965): 18–22; HBMC, "5 millones: Pavimentación carretera 'Valle Sagrado,'" ECC, December 30, 1964, 1. The funding went to paving of the Carretera del Valle Sagrado de los Incas, expansion of the Cusco Hotel, illumination of the Cathedral and the Compania Church, restoration of the Casona of Garcilaso de la Vega, and the purchase of two new rail cars and two new buses to transport tourists to and from Machu Picchu.

28. AINC, 08.01.01-04-1, folder "Zona monumental—Informes en general, Cusco—Ano 1970-1990," "Bases para una política de conservación y desarrollo del Centro Histórico del Cusco," 9–10.

29. CBC, Checchi, *La perespectiva para el turismo en el Perú*, 3.

30. CBC, Checchi, *La perespectiva para el turismo en el Perú*, 13–14. The report justified the focus on U.S. travelers based on 1963 statistics. In that year, 62,500 people arrived in Peru. Of these, 17,200 were U.S. tourists, 10,000 were business travelers, 26,500 were international tourists from countries other than the United States, and 8,800 were probable immigrants and/or nontourist arrivals.

31. CBC, Checchi, *La perespectiva para el turismo en el Perú*, 35–38.

32. CBC, Checchi, *La perespectiva para el turismo en el Perú*, 54–57.

33. HBNP, "La COTURPERU en la Feria de Berlin," *Boletín de la COTURPERU*, no. 3 (August–October 1964): 20–21.

34. HBNP, "Llamado a todos los sectores para que colaboren en la magna empresa de promoción turística . . . ," *Boletín de la COTURPERU*, no. 2 (May–July 1964): 6–7.

35. Cahn and Van Heusen, "Come Fly with Me."

36. Edward C. Burks, "Magic Land of the Incas," NYT, February 23, 1964, XX47.

37. HBMP, "Diez millones de personas han admirado hasta ahora la colección, 'Oro del Perú,'" ECL, May 4, 1964. The exhibit visited Mexico, Japan, Brussels, Copenhagen, Madrid, New York, San Francisco, and São Paulo.

38. "Peru Treasures Begin U.S. Tour," NYT, October 17, 1965.

39. "Peruvian Gold Treasures Go on Display Here Today," *Washington Post*, October 14, 1965, 1.

40. HBMP, "Inaugurarán en E.U. muestra de Arte Pre-Colombino," *Expreso*, February 20, 1966.

41. AM, DGTUR, EET I–VII, Box 3, J. Krippendorf, *El mercado turístico europeo para viajes a la América del Sur y en particular el Perú*, May 1971, 43–45; AM, DGTUR, EET VII–XIII, Box 4, Silva, *COPESCO, Estudio general del trabajo (Parte I)*, gráfico no. 4, n.p.

42. AM, DGTUR, EET VII–XIII, Box 4, Silva, *COPESCO, Estudio general del trabajo (Parte I)*, chart no. 9, 20. The second-largest group, tourists from South America, accounted for 31.8 percent of arrivals.

43. Cesar Villanueva (photographer), "Vicunas nordicas invaden Machu-Picchu," *Caretas*, November 8–21, 1963, 44–47.

44. "El primer paso para conocer el mundo," *Caretas*, July 25–August 13, 1964, n.p.

45. See, for example, "El Perú de moda," *Caretas*, June 11–23, 1966, 43–46.

46. "Las ñustas, que Lima mandó al Cuzco," *Caretas*, June 26–July 8, 1965, 55.

47. Horace Sutton, *Boston Globe*, Vacation Section, July 24, 1960, A5–A6.

48. "Large Inca City Found by American Explorer," NYT, August 9, 1964, 20. Savoy's announcement was covered in a short, four-paragraph article buried on page 20; Savoy, *Antisuyo*, 73–128.

49. Richard Joseph, "New Mystery in the Clouds," *Boston Globe*, February 25, 1968, 14A.

50. HBMC, "Sólo con permiso del INC se podrá ir a Vilcabamba," ECC, September 7, 1976, 1.

51. Elizabeth Winship and Thomas Winship, "Mystery at the Top of the Sky," *Boston Globe*, January 15, 1967, A9.

52. HBNP, "Faltan respeto a turistas en ingreso a 'Machu Picchu,'" ECL, February 25, 1966.

53. "Turismo a la criolla," *Caretas*, September 18–25, 1964, 10A. Bustamante criticized the decision to renovate at great expense the Casa de Oquendo in Lima to serve as the institution's headquarters.

54. HBNP, "Crisis en turismo por culpa de Benjamín Roca Muelle," *Expreso*, February 4, 1966, 3.

55. HBNP, "Benjamin Roca Muelle: Asumo la responsabilidad de mis actos," *Expreso*, February 6, 1966; "Año del turismo," *Caretas*, December 21–January 10, 1967, 33.

56. Handelman, *Struggle in the Andes*, 81–83, 101; Hobsbawm, "A Case of Neofeudalism"; Klarén, *Peru*, 320–22; Niera, *Los Andes*, 95–99; Fioravanti, *Latifundio y sindicalismo agrario en el Perú*; Tamayo Herrera, *Historia regional del Cuzco republicano*, 191–213.

57. Handelman, *Struggle in the Andes*, 113–15; Hobsbawm, "Peasant Land Occupations."

58. Klarén, *Peru*, 329–36.

59. HBMC, "Un paro como justa protesta," ECC, June 2, 1965, 1; "Huelga hotel en suspenso," ECC, November 17, 1965, 1; "COTURPERU no dá 500 mil, consejo dejará de operar," ECC, June 1, 1967, 1.

60. Otto Zausmer, "Filthy Gutter Where Gold Once Flowed," *Boston Globe*, June 1, 1960, 32.

61. Walter, *Peru and the United States*, 70.

62. HBMC, "Luminares del cine mundial llegaron hoy" and "Guerrilleros capturados," ECC, October 19, 1965, 1.

63. HBMC, "Exigen higene en hoteles del Cuzco" and "Campesinos venden a sus hijos, hambre los obliga," ECC, June 4, 1968, 1.

64. For just a sample of the voluminous scholarly work on the military government, see Aguirre and Drinot, *The Peculiar Revolution*; McClintock and Lowenthal, *The Peruvian Experiment Reconsidered*.

65. Hobsbawm, "The Peculiar Revolution."

66. Cant, "'Land for Those Who Work It,'" 1–37.

67. See illustration, BMC, "1972: Año de las grandes realizaciones," ECC, September 18, 1972, 1.

68. CGRFA, PRO-24.001, "Ley de Ministerios. Decreto Ley No. 17271," December 3, 1968.

69. BCP, Decreto Ley 17525, March 21, 1969.

70. BCP, Decreto Ley 18059, December 19, 1969.

71. AM, DGTUR, EET VII–XIII, Box 4, *Plan COPESCO, Estudio económico financiero* (Lima: January 1972), 12–35, tourist prediction on 18.

72. AM, DGTUR, EET VII–XIII, Box 4, Jean Marie Sertillange, *COPESCO, Estudio general de turismo (Parte IV), Necesidades y requerimientos en infraestructura de transportes en la Zona Cusco-Puno* (September 1971), 1–4.

73. AM, DGTUR, EET VII–XIII, Box 4, Jean Marie Sertillange, *COPESCO, Estudio general de turismo (Parte IV), Necesidades y requerimientos en infraestructura de transportes en la Zona Cusco-Puno* (September 1971), 3–4.

74. Stallings, "International Capitalism and the Peruvian Military Government," 144–80.

75. AM, DGTUR, EET VII–XIII, Box 4, *Plan COPESCO, Estudio económico financiero*.

76. AM, DGTUR, EET VII–XIII, Box 4, *Plan COPESCO, Estudio económico financiero*, 39.

77. Philip, *The Rise and Fall of the Peruvian Military Radicals*, 78; North, "Ideological Orientations of Peru's Military Rulers," 250.

78. North, "Ideological Orientations of Peru's Military Rulers," 256.

79. AM, DGTUR, EET VII–XIII, Box 4, *Plan COPESCO, Estudio económico financiero*, 305.

80. Caballero, *Economía agraria de la sierra peruana antes de la reforma agraria de 1969*, 109.

81. AM, DGTUR, EET I–VII, Box 3, José Ignacio Estévez, COPESCO, *Estudio general del turismo (Parte III), Análisis y proyecciones del turismo en el eje Cuzco-Puno* (June 1971), 50–52; AM, Unidad Orgánica: Dirección Nacional del Turismo, Serie Documental, Estudio de Estrategia Turística COPESCO I–VII, Box 3.

82. AM, DGTUR, EET I–VII, Box 3, *Plan COPESCO, Un caso de desarrollo regional en función del turismo* (1972), 3.

83. AM, DGTUR, EET I–VII, Box 4, *Plan COPESCO, Un caso de desarrollo regional en función del turismo* (1972).

84. AM, DGTUR, EET VII–XIII, Box 4, *Análisis del impacto económico de las inversiones del Plan COPESCO*.

85. AM, DGTUR, EET I–VII, Box 3, COPESCO, *Estudio general del turismo (Parte IX), Análisis beneficio-costo de las inversiones del Plan COPESCO en la Zona Cuzco-Puno* (March 1972), 151–52.

86. AM, DGTUR, EET I–VII, Box 3, COPESCO, *Estudio general del turismo (Parte IX), Análisis beneficio-costo de las inversiones del Plan COPESCO en la Zona Cuzco-Puno* (March 1972), 206.

87. AM, DGTUR, EET VII–XIII, Box 4, *Proyecto del Micro Programa P'isaq-Cuzco*.

88. AM, DGTUR, Serie Documental Fichas Inventario del Patrimonio Turístico, Box 1, file 2.1.3.2.2, "Iglesia de Marangani."

89. AM, DGTUR, Serie Documental Fichas Inventario del Patrimonio Turístico, Box 1, file 2.1.3.2, "Poblado de Quebrada."

90. AM, DGTUR, Serie Documental Fichas Inventario del Patrimonio Turístico, Box 2, file 3.6.1, "Comunidad Nativa de Kitapayara."

91. CBC, Chávez Ballón, *Informe Machupijchu*, 8.

92. CBC, Chávez Ballón, *Informe Machupijchu*, 1.

93. AM, DGTUR, EET VII–XIII, Box 4, *Plan COPESCO, Estudio económico financiero*, anexo "PER-39."

94. CBC, José de Mesa, "Prologo," in *Cusco: La traza urbana de la ciudad inca* (Cusco: Proyecto Per-39, UNESCO, 1980), 13–17.

95. The PER-39 project was led by Alfredo Valencia Zegarra, Arminda Gibaja Oviedo, and José González Corrales under the supervision of the Mexican anthropologist José Luis Lorenzo. See CBC, Alfredo Valencia Zegarra, "Historia y evaluación de las investigaciones arqueológicas en el santuario histórico de Machu Picchu," in *Seminario-Taller Internacional Aqueología del Santuario Histórico Nacional y Sitio Patrimonio Mundial de Machu Picchu: Estado de la cuestión y propuestas para un Plan Maestro* (Cusco: n.p., 1993), 100.

96. BMCC, Unidad Especial Ejecutadora, INC-Cusco, *Informe final, obra de restauración: Conjunto aqueológico de Machupicchu, 1975-1981*, vol. 1 (Cusco, 1983), section 5.00.

97. HBMC, "A quienes beneficia el turismo en el Cuzco?," ECC, June 20, 1967, 2.

98. HBMC, "Moderno hotel construirá ENTURPERU en convento San Francisco," ECC, August 20, 1970, 1; "Hotel Posada de S. Francisco tendrá 312 camas: Costo 120 mills," ECC, August 22, 1970, 1.

99. HBMC, "Cusco tendrá el hotel más lujoso y grande del Perú," ECC, June 12, 1971, 1.

100. HBMC, "Dará aceso a complejo del gran parque arqueológico," ECC, February 7, 1970, 1; "Con 360 milliones construirán carretera de Cusco a Machupijchu," ECC, August 27, 1970, 1; "Pésimo estado de ferrocarril Cusco-Santa Ana," ECC, January 27, 1972, 2.

101. HBMC, "Autopista a Machupijchu es un hecho!," ECC, September 27, 1971, 1; "Cinco trascendentes decretos," ECC, September 28, 1971, 2.

102. AM, DGTUR, EET VII–XIII, Box 4, Silva, *COPESCO, Estudio general del trabajo (Parte I)*, 41, 64–65. Although some COPESCO scenarios recommended that the national government focus on attracting more tourists from South America, the North American market remained a development goal in all tourism plans.

103. HBMC, "Productos cusquenos irán a China Popular," ECC, August 5, 1972, 1; "Soviéticos muy felices de conocer Machupijchu," ECC, June 13, 1972, 1.

104. Harmer, "Two, Three, Many Revolutions?," 72–73; Walter, *Peru and the United States*, 242–45.

105. ENTURPERU's hotel contracts discussed in Goodsell, *American Corporations and Peruvian Politics*, 162; landing rights dispute reviewed in Walter, *Peru and the United States*, 303–4; HBNP, "Marriot [*sic*] Corporation hará lujoso hotel en el Cusco," ECC, August 14, 1971, 1.

106. See front page of HBMC, ECC, January 1, 1974, 1.

107. AG-0465, folio 5, Albert Giesecke to Albert Rothschild, December 8, 1953; "Harán un gran hotel para Machu Picchu," *La Prensa*, August 22, 1956, 1.

108. AG-D-033, folios 26–27, "Hiram Bingham y la construcción de un hotel grande en Machu Picchu," December 21, 1960.

109. "Manual del turista patriótico," *Caretas*, July 25–August 11, 1966, 16–17.

110. HBMC, "En favor del turismo," ECC, June 1, 1966, 2.

111. HBMC, "Cuzco sin alojamiento," ECC, June 13, 1967, 2.

112. AM, DGTUR, EET I–VII, Box 3, José Ignacio Estévez, *COPESCO, Estudio general del turismo (Parte III)*, 184.

113. AM, DGTUR, EET VII–XII, Box 4, *Plan COPESCO, Estudio económico financiero*, 185–197.

114. AM, DGTUR, EET VII–XII, Box 4, *Plan COPESCO, Estudio económico financiero*, 206–212.

115. AM, DGTUR, EET VII–XII, Box 4, *Plan COPESCO, Estudio económico financiero*, 114.

116. BMCP, COPESCO, *Estudio de factibilidad Hotel Machu-Picchu*, vol. 2 (Lima, June 1973), II-2.

117. HBMC, "Nuevo hotel Machupijchu costará sl. 240 millones," ECC, February 4, 1972, 1.

118. BMCP, COPESCO, *Estudio de factibilidad Hotel Machu-Picchu*, vol. 2 (Lima, June 1973), gráfico no. 3, 1–32.

119. AINC, 08.01.01-04-1, folder "Zona monumental—Informes en general, Cusco—Ano 1970-1990," Resolución Ministerial 737-72 IC/DS.

120. BCP, Decreto Ley 18799, March 9, 1971. The INC replaced earlier efforts by the Prado and Belaúnde governments to consolidate cultural coordination in Peru under an institution named the Casa de Cultura. Created by Decreto Supremo 48 on August 24, 1962, the Casa de Cultura acted as the national coordinating agency for cultural affairs, museums, and preservation. At one point headed by the prominent anthropologist José María Arguedas, the institution suffered from budgetary and bureaucratic instability and was dissolved upon the creation of the INC.

121. BCP, Decreto Ley 19033, November 16, 1971.

122. CGRFA, PRO 25.002, "Aspectos legales y de procedimiento en la conservación y defensa de Machu Picchu," October 24, 1972, 1–2.

123. CGRFA, PRO 25.002, "Aspectos legales y de procedimiento en la conservación y defensa de Machu Picchu," October 24, 1972, 2–3.

124. CGRFA, PRO 25.002, "Aspectos legales y de procedimiento en la conservación y defensa de Machu Picchu," October 24, 1972, 5–6.

125. HBNP, "Del hotel en Machu Picchu," ECL, June 18, 1972.

126. HBMC, "Americanistas dicen: No al hotel de Machupijchu," ECC, August 17, 1972, 1.

127. David F. Belnap, "'Lost City' Hotel," *Los Angeles Times*, August 6, 1972, F8.

128. HBMC, "Comisión ejecutiva dirá donde se ubica hotel en Machupijchu," ECC, June 12, 1972, 1.

129. HBMC, "Hotel en Machupicchu: Esperanza que se aleja? No," ECC, August 5, 1972, 12.

130. HBMC, "Hotel en Machupicchu, tema que quema en Lima," ECC, August 22, 1972, 2.

131. JM-197, folios 5–6, "Informe de la Comisión sobre la Delimitación del Area Intangible de Machu Picchu," 5–6.

132. HBNP, "Señalan 1,400 hectáres de zona intangible: Machu Picchu," ECL, September 23, 1972, 1.

133. HBMC, "A 20 kilómetros de Machupijchu sería construido Hotel Turistas," ECC, 11 September 1972, 1.

134. HBMC, "Enemigos del Cusco, no cejan," ECC, September 6, 1972, 2.

135. HBMC, "Piden respetarse ubicación de concurso para construir hotel del Machupijchu," ECC, October 11, 1972, 1.

136. HBMC, "Cusco pidió audiencia a Velasco para exigir hotel en Machupijchu," ECC, October 12, 1972, 1.

137. HBNP, "Directora del Instituto Nacional de Cultura: 'Ahora . . . hay que defender Machu Picchu de los Cuzqueños,'" *El Correo*, October 17, 1972, 6.

138. HBMC, "Directora de cultura debe venir para ver situación del Turismo," ECC, October 18, 1972, 1.

139. HBMC, "Otra vez el centralismo limeño vuelve sus garras contra Cusco," ECC, October 18, 1972, 2.

140. HBMC, "Tabajadores con el Cusco," ECC, October 26, 1972, 1.

141. HBMC, "La hora de definiciones," ECC, October 27, 1972, 2.

142. HBNP, "Area intangible de Machu Picchu," El Correo, October 19, 1972, 13.

143. CGRFA, PRO 25.002, Martha Hildebrandt, Directora General del INC, "La política de conservación del patrimonio monumental y el caso de Machu Picchu," October 24, 1972. For an analysis of the Velasco government's use of Túpac Amaru as a symbol, see Walker, "The General and His Rebel."

144. BCP, Decreto Ley 19597, October 31, 1972; HBNP, "Definitivo: Hotel Fuera de Las Ruinas de Machu Picchu," El Correo, October 27, 1972, 19.

145. BMCP, COPESCO, Estudio de factibilidad Hotel Machu Picchu, vol. 2, VII-18.

146. HBMC, "Hotel Machupijchu inaugurarían el 28 de julio del año 1975," ECC, November 11, 1972, 1.

147. HBMC, "Grave denuncia," ECC, June 1, 1973, 2.

148. HBNP, "El hotel de Machu Picchu y el problema de su ubicación," ECL, September 25, 1973, 2.

149. Philip, The Rise and Fall of the Peruvian Military Radicals, 131–36.

150. HBMC, "Grave denuncia," ECC, June 1, 1973, 2.

151. HBMC, "Hotel de San Sebastián debe ser realizado a breve plazo," ECC, June 14, 1973, 2.

152. HBMC, "Con más de mil millones harán obras infraestructura turística," ECC, September 13, 1973, 1; "Cientos de visitantes no conocen a Machupijchu a falta de carretera," ECC, October 5, 1973, 1.

153. HBMC, "Machupicchu: Sueño irrealizable para gran mayoría de cusqueños," ECC, October 11, 1973, 2.

154. HBMC, "Se proyecta gigantesca campaña para hacer vía a Machupijchu," ECC, June 4, 1974, 1.

155. Tamayo Herrera, Historia regional del Cuzco republicano, 227. Rumors persist that the fire was actually a case of arson to eliminate documents revealing government corruption or other misdeeds.

156. HBMC, "Anunció inversión 3 mil mlls. para Cusco en infraestructura turística," ECC, October 18, 1974, 1; "Construcción paralela hotel y carretera Machu Picchu," ECC, October 21, 1974, 1.

157. AINC, 08.13.04-12-20, "Hotel de Turistas—Machu Picchu—Urubamba—Cusco—Huayractabmo," folio 17.

158. AINC, 08.13.04-12-20, "Hotel de Turistas—Machu Picchu—Urubamba—Cusco—Huayractabmo," folios 14–15.

159. Klarén, Peru, 359–60. For analysis on the economic changes of the Morales Bermúdez government, see Schydlowsky and Wicht, "The Anatomy of an Economic Failure," 121–37; and Stallings, "International Capitalism and the Peruvian Military Government," 168–73.

160. HBMC, "A costo mil mlls. se construye Hotel Machupijchu; 20 niveles," ECC, October 8, 1976, 1; "Recortan partida para hotel de Machupijchu," ECC, September 11, 1976, 1.

161. AINC, 08.13.04-03-6, "Informe—Delimitación de areas arqueológicas en los fundos de Q'ente y St. Rita de Q;ente," December 18, 1975.

162. CBC, Chávez Ballón, *Informe Machupijchu*, 12–13.

163. AINC, 08.13.04-03-6, "Informe—Delimitación de areas arqueológicas en los fundos de Q'ente y St. Rita de Q;ente," December 18, 1975.

164. AINC, 08.13.04-03-6, "Parque Arqueológico de Machupicchu," March 2, 1977.

165. HBMC, "Invaden el predio destinado a hotel," ECC, October 24, 1973, 1.

166. Koechlin, interview. Koechlin would build the Inkaterra Machu Picchu Pueblo Hotel on parcels that he purchased. For details on the agrarian reform in Aguas Calientes, see Luciano, *Neoliberal Reform in Machu Picchu*, 25–26.

167. CBC, Checchi, *Perspectiva para el desarrollo del turismo en el Perú*, 35–38.

168. AM, DGTUR, EET VIII–XIII, Box 4, Silva, COPESCO, *Estudio general del trabajo (Parte I)*, 115.

169. HBNP, "La promoción turística y la infastructura," *La Prensa*, June 10, 1972, 10.

170. HBMC, "Turismo popular," ECC, December 28, 1972, 2.

171. Thorp and Bertram, *Peru, 1890–1977*, 301–7.

172. HBNP, Luis Delboy, "Machu Picchu: La otra Tierra Prometida," ECL, July 16, 1972, n.p.

173. Weeks, interview.

174. Drinot, "Awaiting the Blood of a Truly Emancipating Revolution."

175. Alomía Robles, Simon, and Milchberg, "El Condor Pasa (If I Could)"; "Top Grammies Won by Simon-Garfunkel," NYT, March 17, 1971, 34.

176. *The Last Movie*; Biskind, *Easy Riders, Raging Bulls*, 124–37.

177. Bernadine Morris, "Norell Does It Again," NYT, August 3, 1972, 22; see also the film *Namath*.

178. Koechlin, interview. *Aguirre, the Wrath of God*. For an account of filming *Aguirre*, see Cronin, *Herzog on Herzog*, 76–94; for a comparison between Herzog's film and the actual Lope de Aguirre expedition, see Holloway, "Whose Conquest Is This, Anyway?," 29–46.

179. Zolov, *Refried Elvis*, 141–46.

180. The Velasco state was no friend to youth counterculture, as evidenced in the actions it took against Lima's budding rock 'n' roll culture as documented by Zolov, "Peru's Overlooked Place in the History of Latin American Rock."

181. HBMC, "Tourist Supplement," 3, ECC, September 5, 1973.

182. HBMC, "Tourist Supplement," 1, ECC, September 7, 1973; "Don't Miss Winay Wayna," in "Tourist Supplement," 1, ECC, October 15, 1973.

183. HBMC, "Ruins of 'Tipon' Very Little Visited," in "Tourist Supplement," ECC, October 2, 1973, 1.

184. HBMC, "Los hippies y el crimen," ECC, December 5, 1969, 2.

185. HBNP, "Hippies hacen convención," *El Sol*, July 1, 1971, 7.

186. HBMC, "Paradiso de nudistas Machupicchu: Hippis," ECC, June 1, 1971, 1.

187. HBMC, Ernesto Valdivia Pezo, "Influencia negativa en la juventud," ECC, June 22, 1971, 2.

188. HBNP, "Fuera hippies," *El Sol*, June 3, 1971, 7.

189. HBNP, "Cayeron 300 hippies," *El Sol*, June 2, 1971, 1, 4.

190. HBNP, "Fuera hippies," *El Sol*, June 2, 1971, 1–4.

191. HBMC, "El Cusco se está convertiendo . . . ," ECC, December 31, 1973, 1.

192. HBMC, "'Mercado Hippie' Plaza de Armas," ECC, June 21, 1974, 1.

193. HBMC, "'Cusco: Limpio de hippies' protest in streets and plazas," ECC, June 20, 1974, 4.

194. HBMC, "Hallan marihuana en poder de hippie," ECC, September 5, 1972, 1.

195. HBMC, "En Machupijchu descubren plantaciones de marihuana," ECC, June 5, 1973, 5.

196. HBMC, "A un 'hippie' loretano la GC. capturo volando," ECC, June 24, 1973, 23.

197. HBNP, Germán Alatrista, "Instalarán Centros de Información en las Atalayas de Machu Picchu," *La Prensa*, April 18, 1973, 26.

198. Zolov, "Introduction: Latin America in the Global Sixties."

199. Valencia, interview, January 4, 2017.

200. Milla, interview.

201. de la Cadena, *Indigenous Mestizos*, 131–76.

202. Milla, interview.

203. de la Cadena, *Indigenous Mestizos*, 177–230.

204. Milla, interview.

205. Calvo Jara, interview.

206. Lowenthal, *The Peruvian Experiment Reconsidered*, 419.

207. CBC, Arthur D. Little Co., *Estudio de orientación estratégica para inversiones en turismo en la Región Inka: Informe final—Abril de 1996* (1996), 6.

208. CBC, Oficina de Evaluación de Operaciones, Oficina del Contralor, *Una revisión interina del impacto económico y social del Plan COPESCO*, December 1981, 3–9.

209. Cotler, "Democracy and National Integration in Peru," 28.

210. Thorp and Bertram, *Peru, 1890–1977*, 305–7.

211. Lovón Zevala, "Dinámica interna de la sierra," 151–71.

212. HBMC, "Mucha desocupación hay en el Cusco," ECC, October 22, 1974, 1.

213. Lovón Zevala, *Mito y realidad del turismo en el Cusco*, 9–21.

214. Tamayo Herrera, *Historia regional del Cuzco republicano*, 220; Rénique, *Los sueños de la sierra*, 266; Vergara, *La danza hostil*, 228–34.

215. Lovón Zevala, *Mito y realidad del turismo en el Cusco*, 9–21.

216. CBC, Oficina de Evaluación de Operaciones, Oficina del Contralor, *Una revisión interina del impacto económico y social del Plan COPESCO*, 19.

217. AINC, 08.01.01-04-1, folder "Zona monumental—Informes en general, Cusco—Ano 1970-1990," "Bases para una política de conservación y desarrollo del Centro Histórico del Cusco," 11–13.

218. AINC, 08.01.01-04-1, folder "Zona monumental—Informes en general, Cusco—Ano 1970-1990," "Bases para una política de conservación y desarrollo del Centro Histórico del Cusco," 23–28.

219. Tamayo Herrera, *Historia regional del Cuzco republicano*, 280.

Chapter 5

1. Valencia, interview, January 6, 2012.
2. Schumpeter, *Capitalism, Socialism, and Democracy*, 81–86.
3. Carrión, "Conclusion: The Rise and Fall of Electoral Authoritarianism in Peru."
4. Rothman, *Devil's Bargains*, 10.
5. Schydlowsky and Wicht, "The Anatomy of an Economic Failure," 65–93; Stallings, "International Capitalism and the Peruvian Military Government," 144–80.
6. Klarén, *Peru*, 359–65.
7. BCP, Decreto Ley 21948, October 4, 1977.
8. BCP, Decreto Ley 23015, April 30, 1980.
9. BCP, Decreto Ley 2334, December 10, 1981.
10. AM, Dirección Nacional del Turismo, Planes Operativos para Desarrollar, Caja 1, "Plan operativo del Sector Turismo, 1982–1983," May 1982, 13.
11. ACC, COPESCO, *Plan de desarrollo turístico: II etapa Plan COPESCO*, November 1980, 19.
12. "La actualidad turística y el desarrollo económico y social del Perú," Un Estudio de Diagnóstico (COPESCO—UNESCO) Boletín DRIT (1996).
13. BMCP, Dirección Ejecutiva del Plan COPESCO, *Situación de los proyectos del Plan COPESCO al 29.02.80 y evaluación primer trimestre*, March 1980.
14. ACC, COPESCO, *Plan de desarrollo turístico: II etapa Plan COPESCO*, November 1980, "Proyectos Prioritarios."
15. BMCP, Alejandro Rozas Alosilla-Velasco, "Evaluación y perspectivas del turismo receptivo en el Departamental del Cusco," presentation in XI Encuentro de Economistas, Banco Central de Reserva del Perú, 1995, 3.
16. ACC, *Transporte en helicóptero entre Cusco y Machu-Picchu: Estudio de pre-factabilidad técnica-económica*, 1974, 53.
17. ACC, *Informe final: Evaluación de los propuestas para el diseño, suministro, construcción, formación de personal, y financiación del sistema "A," teleférico al hotel de Machu Picchu*, August 29, 1975; BCP, Resolución Directoral DE-076-75, May 13, 1975.
18. AINC, 08.13.04.12-11, "Proyecto Teleférico Machupicchu—1996," folios 22–116; AINC, 08.13.04.12-11, "Proyecto Telefércio Machu Picchu—1982."
19. HBMC, "Ampliación del aeropuerto, necesidad impostergrable," ECC, August 19, 1970, 2.
20. BCP, Decreto Ley 23028, May 7, 1980.
21. HBMC, "COPESCO gestiona préstamo 3.500 mil Dls., para aeropuerto," ECC, June 9, 1980, 1; AM, DNT, Planes Operativos para Desarrollar, Caja 1, Folio Contrato de Prestación de Servicios de Consultoria para el Desarrollo de los Sitios Definativos de Ingenieria del Aeropuerto International del Cusco, Resolución Ministerial 294-82 ITI/TUR, July 2, 1982.
22. HBMC, "Hoy se hará preselección estudios definativos para nuevo aeropuerto," ECC, January 17, 1981, 1; "Antes del julio del 85, Cusco tendrá su aeropuerto internacional," ECC, February 9, 1981, 1.
23. HBMC, "Cusco, sus angustias," ECC, July 4, 1986, 2.

24. HBMC, "Cusco espera nuevo aeropuerto para su promoción turística," ECC, June 4, 1988, 1.

25. HBMC, "22 millones de intis para el puerto aéreo del Cusco," ECC, December 16, 1988, 1; "CORPAC incumple convenio implementación aeropuerto," ECC, June 12, 1989, 1.

26. HBMC, "Mejoramiento del aeropuerto," ECC, June 29, 1993, 2.

27. CBC, Sistema Nacional de Planificación, *Sistema de planes de desarrollo de Corto Plazo, 1986: Plan departamental de desarrollo de Cusco* (Lima: Sistema Nacional de Planificación, 1986), 14–15.

28. "Tomando puntería," *Caretas*, November 28, 1983, 88–89.

29. AM, DNT, Planes Operativos para Desarrollar, Caja 2, 34.

30. Findings reprinted in CBC, MICTI, *Sistema de planes de desarrollo de Corto Plazo, 1986: Plan operativo del Sector Turismo*, 5.

31. Findings reprinted in CBC, MICTI, *Sistema de planes de desarrollo de Corto Plazo, 1986: Plan operativo del Sector Turismo*, 3.

32. HBNP, Luis Sifuentes Oré, "'Descubriendo' el pueblo de Machu Picchu," *Perspectiva*, September 12, 1982, 12.

33. HBMC, "Tragedia de Tica-Tica deja 17 muertos," ECC, June 25, 1985, 1.

34. "Peru Tourist Train Derails," NYT, April 4, 1986, A9; HBMC, "Convoy de turismo volcó en Km. 13 a Machupicchu," ECC, April 3, 1986, 1.

35. CBC, MICTI, Dirección Departamental Cusco, *Plan operativo 1987*, 13–14.

36. Frost, *Exploring Cusco*, 14.

37. Rénique, *Los sueños de la sierra*, 354–58.

38. Alberto Bonilla, "El alcade rojo del Cusco," *Caretas*, March 19, 1984, 29–30.

39. CBC, Comité de Servicios Integrados Turísticos-Cuturales del Cusco, *II informe sobre los ingresos inversiones, sistemas de operación y control del boleto turístico cultural-Cusco*, November 1983, "Introducción," 1–5.

40. "Tasa desmidida," *Caretas*, May 21, 1984, 23.

41. HBMC, "Comisión bicameral llegó para tratar problemática del turismo," ECC, February 5, 1981, 1.

42. "La vara de la ley," *Caretas*, December 26, 1984, 47–48.

43. Richard Witkin, "Dispute Hampers U.S-Peru Flights," NYT, May 25, 1984, A4; "Guerra aérea con EEUU," *Caretas*, May 21, 1984, 15, 72.

44. Alberto Bonilla, "El convenio es para Aeroperú," *Caretas*, December 22, 1986, 24–27.

45. "Encuentros cercanos con el pasado," *Caretas*, November 26, 1984, 26–28.

46. Klarén, *Peru*, 382–95; Poole and Rénique, *Peru: Time of Fear*, 126–31.

47. HBMC, "Paro de 48 horas atentatorio contra fiestas del Cusco," ECC, June 16, 1981, 1; "Ofensa al Cusco," ECC, June 17, 1981, 2; "Mayoritario es paro estatales en Cusco," ECC, June 5, 1984, 1; "Huelga ENAFER priva visitar Machupijchu," ECC, June 30, 1981, 1.

48. HBMC, "Pretender sabotear fiestas del Cusco," ECC, June 30, 1988, 1.

49. HBMC, "Salvemos al turismo," ECC, June 4, 1981, 2; "Turistas víctimas de los ladrones," ECC, February 17, 1981, 1.

50. HBMC, "Audaz asalto a bus de turistas en Ccorao," ECC, June 4, 1984, 1.

51. HBMC, "¿Y los asaltos?," ECC, June 5, 1984, 2.

52. HBMC, "Emergencia en Cusco por le delincuencia," ECC, June 21, 1985, 1.

53. Rachowiecki, *Peru: A Travel Survival Kit*, 191.

54. A complete account of the internal war is found in Comisión de la Verdad y Reconciliación, *Informe final*. Some of the best-known scholarly investigations on the internal war are Degregori, *Ayacucho 1969-1979, el surgimiento de Sendero Luminoso*; Degregori, *Qué difícil es ser dios*; Gorriti, *The Shining Path*; Heilman, *Before the Shining Path*; La Serna, *The Corner of the Living*; Poole and Rénique, *Peru: Time of Fear*; Rénique, *La batalla por Puno*; Stern, *Shining and Other Paths*.

55. Comisión de la Verdad y Reconciliación, *Informe final*, 2:91; Hinojosa, "On Poor Relations and the Nouveau Riche," 68-69; Degregori, *Qué difícil es ser dios*, 36-41.

56. The vast majority of insurgent activity in Cusco was the result of the Shining Path. MRTA only began activities in La Convención Province of Cusco in April 1991, according to Comisión de la Verdad y Reconciliación, *Informe final*, 4:265.

57. "Lo del Cuzco," *Caretas*, January 12, 1981, 24.

58. The first Shining Path attacks in urban Cusco occurred in January 1981, as documented by Comisión de la Verdad y Reconciliación, *Informe final*, 4:261. The first attack recorded in Cusco Department occurred on November 9, 1980, in Tinta in Canchis Province, according to Comisión de la Verdad y Reconciliación, *Informe final*, 4:267.

59. HBMC, "Acción terrorista en Sacsaywaman," ECC, January 12, 1981, 1.

60. HBMC, "Terrorismo, atentados demasiados sospechosos," ECC, January 19, 1981, 2.

61. HBMC, "Rechazo al terrorismo," ECC, January 28, 1981, 2.

62. HBMC, "Ola de terrorismo en Cusco disminuye venida de turistas," ECC, February 4, 1981, 1.

63. HBMC, "Rebaja de tarifas en hotels," ECC, February 13, 1981, 2.

64. HBMC, "Dinamitaron la fábrica de Coca Cola," ECC, September 12 1981, 1.

65. HBMC, "Bomba estalló en hotel Savoy," ECC, September 14, 1981, 1.

66. HBMC, "Torre destruida reparán en 10 días con 300 milliones," ECC, June 13, 1983, 1.

67. HBMC, "Cusco, ciudad desguarnecida," ECC, June 14, 1983, 2.

68. HBMC, "Atentado terrorista en la estación de San Pedro causa muertos y heridos," ECC, June 25, 1986, 1.

69. "La mochilla roja," *Caretas*, June 30, 1986, 18-20; "7 Killed and 38 Hurt in Peru by Bombing of Train for Tourists," NYT, June 26, 1986, A9.

70. HBMC, "MRTA habría cometido el atentado del 25," ECC, June 27, 1986, 1; "En busca de terroristas," ECC, June 30, 1986, 1; "Atentado del vagón fue Sendero," ECC, June 4, 1987, 1.

71. HBMC, "Turismo y antiturismo," ECC, June 27, 1986, 2.

72. N.D.K., "Tips on Transportation, Weather, and Hotels for a Trip to Peru's Inca Capital," NYT, October 5, 1986, 691.

73. HBMC, "Escalada terrorista iba a producirse en Cusco," ECC, June 11, 1987, 1.

74. Comisión de la Verdad y Reconciliación, *Informe final*, 2:122.

75. Poole and Rénique, *Peru: Time of Fear*, 9.

76. "U.S. Steps Up Travel Warning to Peru," NYT, April 12, 1987, XX3.

77. Comisión de la Verdad y Reconciliación, *Informe final*, 2:131.

78. HBMC, "El Cusco y Jersey City hermanados en dolor," ECC, December 3, 1988, 1; John T. McQuiston, "Mayor Back in Jersey City after Wife Is Killed in Peru," NYT, December 5, 1988, B3.

79. Conflicting accounts of the blame found in BMC, "Execrable crimen en el marco de paro comunista," ECC, December 3, 1988, 1; see "Peru Rebels Blamed in Death of Jersey City Mayor's Wife," NYT, January 13, 1988, A8.

80. HBMC, "Consejo demandará la total reorginación de ENAFER," ECC, December 5, 1988, 1.

81. HBMC, "Luctuoso suceso," ECC, December 3, 1988, 2.

82. HBMC, "Alerta roja en Cusco por fiestas de junio," ECC, June 19, 1989, 1; "Camino Inca a 'Machupijchu' sería vetado al turismo," ECC, June 19, 1989, 1.

83. HBMC, "Crece la delincuencia y falta control policial," ECC, June 27, 1989, 2.

84. HBMC, "Coche-bomba deja 1 muerto y 8 heridos," ECC, June 13, 1990, 1.

85. HBMC, "Machupijchu marco concierto por la paz: Sinfónica Nacional," ECC, June 22, 1990, 1.

86. Klarén, *Peru*, 407.

87. "Precio de la peste," *Caretas*, September 16, 1991, 56–67.

88. "Goodbye Peru," *Caretas*, November 25, 1991, 20.

89. "Advertencias," *Caretas*, February 11, 1993, 79.

90. HBMC, "Las tres plagas que espantan turistas," ECC, June 21, 1991, 2.

91. "Ultima llamada," *Caretas*, August 5, 1991, 2.

92. CBC, Aguilar, Hinojosa, and Milla, *Turismo y desarrollo*, 11.

93. HBNP, "¡Salvan al Cusco!," *Expreso*, April 11, 1991, 3.

94. HBNP, Aída Meza Paredes, "Hoteles del Cusco en crisis: De un total de 114 cierran 80," *Expreso*, July 6, 1991, 6.

95. HBMC, "98 turistas llegan a Cusco," ECC, April 2, 1992, 1.

96. HBMC, "Delincuentes asaltan a turistas en vía pública," ECC, April 20, 1992, 5; "5 atentados terroristas," ECC, April 20, 5.

97. AINC, 08.13.04-03-6, "Parque Arqueológico de Machupicchu," March 2, 1977.

98. CBC, Fernando Astete Victoria, "Descripción de los monumentos arqueológicos existentes en el ámbito del santuario de Machu Picchu," in *Arqueología Santuario Histórico Nacional y Sitio Patrimonio Mundial de Machu Picchu: Estado de la cuestión y propuestas para un Plan Maestro*, 1994, 31–33.

99. UNESCO, "Inscription of the City of Cuzco and the Historic Sanctuary of Machu Picchu on the World Heritage List."

100. BMCC, 36-1950A, INC Region Cusco, Parque Archeológico de Machupicchu, Unidad Especial Ejecutora del INC Cusco, folio 369, "Proyecto puesta en valor de monumentos del Plan COPESCO, Segunda Etapa, Conjunto Arqueológico de Machupicchu," folios 369, 443.

101. BMCC, 0832, INC Cusco, *Machupicchu, Programación de Obra 1984, sección 01*; BMCC, file 0832, INC Cusco, *Machupicchu, Programación de Obra 1984, sección Presupuesto Analítico*; BMCC, file 0188, INC Cusco, *Dirección de Patrimonio Cultural y Monumental, Obra: Emergencia Andenes Machupicchu (sector 1), Informe anual 1986*; BMCC,

36-1950A, Parque Arqueológico de Machupicchu: INC, Departamental Cusco, Dirección de Patrimonio Cultural y Monumental, *Informe anual 1987, Conjunto Arqueológico de Machupijchu*, folio 283; BMCC, 36-1950A, Parque Arqueológico de Machupicchu: INC, Departamental Cusco, Dirección de Patrimonio Cultural y Monumental, *Informe anual 1987, Conjunto Arqueológico de Machupijchu*, folio 308.

102. Luciano, *Neoliberal Reform in Machu Picchu*, 17–60.

103. Ángeles Vargas, *Machupijchu, enigmática cuidad inka*; early archeological and restoration efforts are also documented by Maxwell, "Tourism, Environment, and Development on the Inca Trail," 147–51.

104. HBNP, Germán Alatrista, "Limpian los Caminos del Inca en el sector de Machu Picchu," *La Prensa*, June 15, 1972, 14.

105. HBNP, "Culminó exploración del Camino del Inca hasta Ollantaytambo," ECL, September 17, 1973.

106. HBMC, "Inauguran señalización de Camino Inca a Machupijchu," ECC, June 8, 1987, 1.

107. HBMC, "Hippies invaden ciudad del Cusco," ECC, June 25, 1980, 3.

108. HBMC, "Cusco es nidal pacifico de hippies," ECC, February 6, 1981, 7.

109. Weeks, interview.

110. Valencia, interview, January 6, 2012.

111. Ferreyros, "Redescubriendo el Camino Inca a Machu Picchu."

112. Joan Ambrose-Newton, "Trek to Machu Picchu," NYT, April 15, 1984, XX26.

113. Kela Leon de Vega, "Cuando el río suena . . . ," *Caretas*, May 12, 1986, 48–50.

114. "Quillabamba: Un pueblo que surge, el valle del café," *Caretas* 1021, special supplement, 1988.

115. "El nuevo imperio," *Caretas*, June 27, 1988, 6–7.

116. Rachowiecki, *Peru: A Travel Survival Kit*, 189–91.

117. Oscar Malca, "La mala vida del imperio," *Caretas*, August 8, 1988, 44–47.

118. Calvo Jara, interview.

119. HBMC, "Cusco 2nds. ciudad del Perú en SIDA," ECC, June 2, 1987, 1.

120. Peter Frost, "Sendero pedregoso," *Caretas*, October 23, 1983, 72–74.

121. Rachowiecki, *Peru: A Travel Survival Kit*, 245–47.

122. Jocelyne Frank, "Amor serrano?," *Caretas*, April 17, 1989, 50–51.

123. HBMC, "Turismo de adventura es preferido en Cusco," ECC, June 22, 1993, 4.

124. Matos Mar, *Desborde popular y crisis del estado*; de Soto, *The Other Path*.

125. Klarén, *Peru*, 399–405; Poole and Rénique, *Peru: Time of Fear*, 148; HBMC, "Pueblo cusqueño ortogó 61.85% Alberto Fujimori," ECC, June 12, 1990, 3.

126. Klarén, *Peru*, 406–14; Poole and Rénique, *Peru: Time of Fear*, 150–66; Sheahan, "Redirection of Peruvian Economic Strategy in the 1990s"; Wise, "Against the Odds."

127. AM, Dirección Nacional del Turismo, Planes Operativos para Desarrollar, Caja 4, "Sector Turismo: Plan de desarrollo, 1992–1995."

128. Denegri, "Acerca de PromPerú," 39–63; "Imágen instamatic," *Caretas*, February 25, 1993, 21. PromPerú was created with supreme decree DS 010-93-PCM.

129. Plutt, "Strategies for Tourism Promotion," 121–63.

130. PromPerú, *Perfil de quejas y pedidos de los turistas*.

131. Carrión, "Public Opinion, Market Reforms, and Democracy in Fujimori's Peru."

132. HBNP, Ana María Mejía Rusconi, "La recuparación del turismo en el Perú ya se inició," *El Suplemento del Expreso*, July 19, 1993, 10.

133. "La pinta es lo de menos," *Caretas*, September 22, 1994, 35.

134. James Brooke, "Peru: On the Very Fast Track," NYT, January 31, 1995, D1.

135. HBNP, *Peru El Dorado*, no. 1 (July–September 1995).

136. "Turismo al aire," *Caretas*, October 14, 1993, 64.

137. HBNP, "Se avecina un *boom* turístico en el país," *El Suplemento del Expreso*, November 21, 1993, 4.

138. HBMC, "Hoteles y albergues totalmente copados," ECC, June 24, 1993, 1.

139. Marco Zileri and Diana Zileri, "Amantes de vertigo," *Caretas*, September 16, 1993, 50–53.

140. "Mística turística," *Caretas*, November 10, 1994, 48.

141. "Atajo inca," *Caretas*, December 21, 1995, 65.

142. "Oleada invocada," *Caretas*, September 21, 1995, 8–9.

143. "La pinta es lo de menos," *Caretas*, September 22, 1994, 34–36.

144. "Huésped y lustre," *Caretas*, June 22, 1995, 58.

145. HBMC, "Hoteles regionales privatizarán en Agosto," ECC, June 4, 1994, 1.

146. HBMC, "Hotel Cusco, 50 años de servicio," ECC, June 23, 1994, 1.

147. Plans to complete the project under COPESCO announced in HBMC, "A costo de 408 mlls. condicionan semenario S. Antonio para hotel," ECC, December 17, 1976, 1.

148. "Santo Remedio," *Caretas*, August 17, 1987, 77–78.

149. Peru Hotel, S.A. advertisement, *Caretas*, September 1, 1995, 33.

150. "Como Dios manda," *Caretas*, September 21, 1995, 5–6.

151. "Apostando por el turismo," *Caretas*, May 2, 1996, 49.

152. "Machu Picchu Inc.," *Caretas*, April 21, 1994, 83; "Mesa servida?," *Caretas*, May 5, 1994, 80–81.

153. HBMC, "Técnicos evaluarán daños de helicópteros Machupijchu," ECC, June 28, 1994, 1.

154. HBMC, "Alcade pidirá apoyo a UNESCO para Qoricancha," ECC, July 2, 1994, 1.

155. HBMC, "UNESCO equipará museo koricancha," ECC, August 17, 1994, 1; HBNP, "Habilitar convento para museo de Koricancha recomienda Unesco," ECL, August 19, 1994, B16.

156. HBMC, "Koricancha y la UNESCO," ECC, August 17, 1994, 2.

157. HBMC, "Demuelen muros Inkas en trabajos Hotel Libertador," ECC, August 29, 1994, 1.

158. HBMC, "H. Libertador desafía a UNESCO, y al Cusco con construcción," ECC, February 12, 1996, 2.

159. Fernando Vivas S., "Ombligo herido," *Caretas*, June 13, 1996, 48–51.

160. HMBC, "Cusco tierra de nadie," ECC, February 13, 1996, 4.

161. Helaine Silverman, "Mayor Daniel Estrada and the Plaza de Armas of Cuzco, Peru," 181–217.

162. Edmundo de los Ríos, "Ombligo roto," *Caretas*, March 14, 1994, 88–90.

163. "Con la misma vara," *Caretas*, June 3, 1996, 50–51.

164. For detailed analysis on these conflicts and their cultural meaning, see Seligmann, "Market Places, Social Spaces in Cuzco, Peru," 45–56.

165. CBC, Jean Francois Bouchard, *Machu Picchu: Aquitectura, evaluación y diagnóstico: Medidas de conservación; Misión de cooperación, septiembre 1989*, 5.

166. BMCC, file 36-1950A, Parque Arquelógico de Machu Picchu. INC, Cusco, Dirección de Patrimonio Cultural y Monumental, *Proyecto 900004: Monumentos Arqueológicos, Parque Arqueológico de Machupicchu, Informe anual de obra 1992*, folio 164.

167. AM, Dirección Nacional del Turismo, Planes Operativos para Desarrollar, Caja 4, MICTI, *Sector Turismo: Plan de desarrollo, 1992–1995*, March 1992; AM, Despacho Ministerial, *Estudio de Impacto Ambiental Proyecto Teleférico Machu Pichu*, Caja 2, Carpeta 4.

168. HBMC, "Helicópteros no aterrizarán en ciudadela Machupijchu," ECC, July 6, 1994, 1.

169. HBMC, "UNESCO recomienda al gobierno paralizar instalción teleférico y ampliación de hotel en Machupicchu," ECC, February 19, 1999.

170. HBMC, "INC devasta el Koricancha y quiere destruir a Machupijchu," ECC, June 21, 1994, 1.

171. Fernando de Szyszlo, "Las ruinas se arrunian," *Caretas*, January 30, 1997, 60.

172. HBMC, "Privatizadores convierten Machupicchu zona prohibida," ECC, June 8, 1995, 1.

173. HBMC, "Machupicchu sería privatizada cusqueños debemos defenderla," ECC, June 27, 1995, 1.

174. Klein, *The Shock Doctrine*.

175. HBMC, "Oleada invocada," *Caretas*, September 21, 1995, 8–9.

176. Fernando Vivas S., "Ombligo herido," *Caretas*, June 13, 1996, 48–49.

177. Rothman, *Devil's Bargains*, 11.

178. BMCC, Paliza Gallegos, *Volumen II: Impacto económico del turismo en el Cusco y el siglo XXI*.

179. "El sabor imperial," *Caretas*, June 18, 1998, 54–56.

180. "Tierra adoptiva," *Caretas*, July 15, 1999, 52–55.

181. Weeks, interview.

182. "Turismo: Mata a la gallina de los huevos de oro," ECC, August 8, 1994, 2.

183. Kincaid, *A Small Place*, 3–19.

184. "Bingo!" *Caretas*, December 12, 1996, 39; HBNP, "Llegó la turista número 600 mil de este año," ECL, December 10, 1996, A6; BNP, "Joven periodista es el turista 600 mil," *La República*, December 10, 1996, 15.

185. CBC, PeruRail, *Peruanos trabajando por el Perú*, 1997, 3; original quote found in YPEP, box 15, folder 239, "Speech Copy with Corrections," Washington, DC, January 11, 1913.

Epilogue

1. HBNP, "Condecoran a personas que dedicaron su vida a la ciudadela," ECL, July 7, 2011, A13.

2. HBNP, Gabriela Machuca, "Se iluminó en sus cien años," ECL, July 8, 2011, A2–A3.

3. "Alan García: Machu Picchu es la síntesis de la peruanidad," *La Republica*, July 7, 2011, accessed July 25, 2011, http://www.larepublica.pe/07-07-2011/alan-garcia-machu-picchu-es-la-sintesis-de-la-peruanidad.

4. "One Million Tourists Visit Machu Picchu in 2011," *Peruvian Times*, November 20, 2011, accessed December 15, 2011, http://www.peruviantimes.com/20/one-million -tourists-visit-machu-picchu-in-2011/14250/.

5. "Aguas Calientes y Festejos Tibios," *Caretas*, July 14, 2011, 72.

6. Vich, "Magical, Mystical."

7. Heaney, *Cradle of Gold*, 222–35; Arthur Lubow, "The Possessed," NYT, June 24, 2007, E42–49, E68, E82–83.

8. HBNP, Gabriela Machuca, "Se iluminó en sus cien años," ECL, July 8, 2011, A2– A3.

9. HBNP, "Colgaron afiches como protesta por las celebraciones," *La República*, July 8, 2011, 23.

10. "Celebraciones por centenario de Machu Picchu amenazados por protestas," ECC, July 4, 2011, accessed July 25, 2011, http://elcomercio.pe/peru/lima/cusco -celebraciones-centenario-machu-picchu-se-ven-amenazadas-noticia-839911.

11. HBNP, José Salcedo, "Caos y protestas en la ciudadela," *La República*, July 26, 2011, 22.

12. HBNP, José Salcedo, "Amplían número de ingresos a Machu Picchu por quince días," *La República*, July 27, 2011, 22.

13. Lomnitz, *Deep Mexico, Silent Mexico*, 144.

14. Urry and Larsen, *The Tourist Gaze*, 186–88.

15. Cotler, *Clases, estado, y nación en el Perú*; Mallon, *Peasant and Nation*; Thurner, *From Two Republics to One Divided*.

16. Zolov, *Refried Elvis*; Lomnitz, *Deep Mexico, Silent Mexico*, 125–44.

17. MacCannell, *The Tourist*, 105–7.

18. Méndez, "Incas Sí, Indios No."

19. Instituto de Opinión Pública, "Etnicidad, origen familiar-cultural y condicio- nes de vida en el Perú"; Degregori, *Del mito de Jnkarri al mito del progreso*.

20. Gobierno Regional del Cusco and DIRCETUR, *Boletín Estadístico de Turismo–2014*, 8, 11, 15, 95.

21. Ministerio de Cultura, Dirección Desconcentrada de Cultura, Cusco, "Cusco: Llegada de visitantes al Santuario Histórico de Machu Picchu."

22. Observatorio Turístico del Perú, "Cuzco: Participación porcentual del P.B.I. por sectores."

23. "El turismo en el Cusco crecerá 7% y moverá más de US $700 millones este año," *Gestión*, September 26, 2012, accessed October 25, 2017, https://gestion.pe/economia /desarrollo-regional-cusco-mas-alla-machu-picchu-2013198.

24. Instituto Nacional de Estadísticas e Información, "Cuadro no. 2, Cusco: Valor agregado bruto," June 2017, accessed October 25, 2017, https://www.inei.gob.pe /estadisticas/indice-tematico/pbi-de-los-departamentos-segun-actividades -economicas-9110/.

25. Belmond.com, http://www.belmond.com/, accessed May 29, 2017.

26. HBNP, "¿Así nos queremos como nos visten? Continuán los maltratos a turistas en Machu Picchu," ECL, April 16, 2004, A12.

27. For a detailed analysis of how locals evaluate protests against tourism, see Luciano, *Neoliberal Reform in Machu Picchu*, 67–81.

28. HBMC, "El teleférico no pasará dijeron en Machupijchu," ECC, June 15, 1999, 9.

29. "Lo que Backus podría pagar por los daños al Intihuatana," *La República*, March 9, 2005, accessed April 20, 2012, http://larepublica.pe/09-03-2005/lo-que-backus-podria-pagar-por-los-danos-al-intihuatana.

30. UNESCO, *Report on the Reactive Monitoring Mission to the Historic Sanctuary of Machu Picchu (Peru) from April 22 to 30th April of 2007*, 6–15.

31. "Estado aprobó estudio definitivo de ingeniería del aeropuerto internacional de Chinchero en Cusco," *Gestión*, December 11, 2015, accessed October 15, 2017, https://gestion.pe/empresas/estado-aprobo-estudio-definitivo-ingenieria-aeropuerto-internacional-chinchero-cusco-2150859.

32. "Gobierno suspende firma de adenda de aeropuerto de Chinchero," *La República*, January 30, 2017, accessed May 29, 2017, http://larepublica.pe/politica/844152-gobierno-suspende-firma-de-adenda-de-aeropuerto-chinchero.

33. "La difícil tarea de Martín Vizcarra, destrabar los proyectos del sur," *La República*, March 23, 2018, accessed April 3, 2018, http://larepublica.pe/politica/1215723-la-dificil-tarea-de-martin-vizcarra-destrabar-los-proyectos-del-sur.

34. Natalia Majluf, "Debates sobre cultura," *Poder*, May 5, 2017, accessed October 25, 2017, https://poder.pe/2017/05/05/01304-debates-sobre-cultura-la-tragedia-de-chinchero/.

35. AM, Unidad Orgánica Despacho Ministerial, Serie Programa de Manejo Integral del Santuario Histórico de Machu Picchu, Folder 122, *Informe final*, January, 2001.

36. For a detailed analysis of local politics in Aguas Calientes and the PMP, see Luciano, *Neoliberal Reform in Machu Picchu*.

37. "Machu Picchu se aleja de la lista de patrimonio en peligro," ECL, February 1, 2016, accessed February 2, 2016, http://elcomercio.pe/peru/cusco/machu-picchu-se-aleja-lista-patrimonio-peligro-noticia-1875528?flsm=1.

38. For an analysis of the museum in Cusco, see Cox Hall, *Framing a Lost City*, 171–75.

Bibliography

Archives and Collections

College Park, Maryland
  United States National Archives (USNA)
    Record Group 59, U.S. Department of State (RG 59)
    Record Group 229, Office of Inter-American Affairs (RG 229)
Cusco, Peru
  Archivo del Plan COPESCO–Cusco (ACC)
  Biblioteca del Centro Bartolomé de las Casas (CBC)
  Biblioteca del Ministerio de Cultura del Cusco (BMCC)
  Biblioteca del Museo del Inca (BMI)
  Biblioteca Municipal del Cusco
    Archivo Municipal del Cusco (AMC)
    Hemeroteca de la Biblioteca Municipal del Cusco (HBMC)
Lima, Peru
  Archivo del Ministerio de Comercio Exterior y Turismo (AM)
    Serie Documental Estudio de Estrategia Turística (EET)
  Archivo General de la Nación (AGN)
  Biblioteca del Congreso del Perú (BCP)
  Biblioteca del Pontificia Universidad Católica del Perú
    Colección Gobierno Revolucionario de las Fuerzas Armadas (CGRFA)
  Biblioteca Nacional del Perú (BNP)
    Hemeroteca de la Biblioteca Nacional del Perú (HBNP)
  Instituto Riva-Agüero
    Archivo Histórico Riva-Agüero
      Colección Giesecke (AG)
      Colección Jorge Muelle (JM)
    Biblioteca del Instituto Riva-Agüero (IRA)
  Ministerio de Cultura
    Archivo del Instituto Nacional de Cultura (AINC)
    Biblioteca del Ministerio de Cultura del Perú (BMCP)
New Haven, Connecticut
  Yale University Manuscripts and Archives
    George Alexander Kubler Papers, MS 843 (GAKP)
    Yale Peruvian Expedition Papers, MS 664 (YPEP)

Newspapers and Periodicals

Boletín de la Corporación de Turismo del
   Perú/Boletín de la COTURPERU, Lima
Boston Daily Globe
Caretas, Lima
Ciudad y Campo y Caminos, Lima (CCC)
El Comercio del Cusco (ECC)
El Comercio de Lima (ECL)
El Correo, Lima
El Peruano, Lima
El Sol, Cusco
Expreso, Lima
Gestión, Lima
La Crónica, Lima
Ladies' Home Journal
La Jornada, Cusco

La Prensa, Lima
La República, Lima
Los Angeles Times
National Geographic Magazine
Newsweek
New York Times (NYT)
Pan American Union Bulletin
Perspectiva, Lima
Peru El Dorado, Lima
Poder, Lima
Revista del Instituto y Museo Arqueológico
Revista del Touring Club Peruano, Lima
Revista Universitaria, Cusco
Turismo, Lima
Washington Post

Articles, Books, and Other Published Materials

Adams, Mark. *Turn Right at Machu Picchu: Rediscovering the Lost City One Step at a Time*. New York: Dutton, 2011.

Aguilar, Víctor, Leonith Hinojosa, and Carlos Milla. *Turismo y desarrollo: Posibilidades en la Región Inka*. Cusco: Cámara Regional del Turismo Cusco and Centro de Estudios Regionales Andinos Bartolomé de las Casas, 1992.

Aguirre, Carlos, and Paulo Drinot, eds. *The Peculiar Revolution: Rethinking the Peruvian Experiment under Military Rule*. Austin: University of Texas Press, 2017.

Amado Gonzales, Donato. "Evolución histórica de la tenencia de tierras en el Santuario Histórico-Parque Arqueológico Nacional de Machupicchu." *Revista del Instituto Americano de Arte*, no. 20 (2016): 145–64.

Anavitarte Núñez, Carlos. *Algo acerca del problema de la vivienda en el Cuzco*. Cusco: n.p., 1956.

Anderson, Benedict. *Imagined Communities*. Rev. ed. London: Verso, 2006.

Ángeles Vargas, Victor. *Machupijchu, enigmática cuidad inka*. Lima: Industrialgráfica, 1972.

Applebaum, Nancy P. *Muddied Waters: Race, Region, and Local History in Colombia, 1846–1948*. Durham, NC: Duke University Press, 2003.

Appleton, Victor (aka Howard Garis). *Tom Swift and His Big Tunnel, or, The Hidden City of the Andes*. New York: Grosset and Dunlap, 1916.

Arroyo, Carlos. "La experiencia del Comité Central Pro-Derecho Indígena Tahuantinsuyo." *Estudios Interdisciplinos de America Latina y el Caribe* 15, no. 1 (January–June 2004): 1–24.

Babb, Florence E. *The Tourism Encounter: Fashioning Latin American Nations and Histories*. Stanford: Stanford University Press, 2011.

Baranowski, Shelley. *Strength through Joy: Consumerism and Mass Tourism in the Third Reich*. Cambridge: Cambridge University Press, 2004.

Berger, Dina. *The Development of Mexico's Tourism Industry: Pyramids by Day, Martinis by Night*. New York: Palgrave Macmillan, 2006.

———. "Goodwill Ambassadors on Holiday: Tourism, Diplomacy, and Mexico-U.S. Relations." In *Holiday in Mexico: Critical Reflections on Tourism and Tourist Encounters*, edited by Dina Berger and Andrew Grant Wood, 107–29. Durham, NC: Duke University Press.

Berger, Dina, and Andrew Grant Wood, eds. *Holiday in Mexico: Critical Reflections on Tourism and Tourist Encounters*. Durham, NC: Duke University Press, 2010.

Bingham, Alfred M. *Portrait of an Explorer: Hiram Bingham, Discoverer of Machu Picchu*. Ames: Iowa State University Press, 1989.

Bingham, Hiram. "Cuzco and Sacsahuaman." *Records of the Past* 8, no. 5 (1909): 223–41.

———. "The Discovery of Machu Picchu." *Harper's Magazine* 127 (April 1913): 709–19.

———. "Further Explorations in the Land of the Incas." *National Geographic Magazine* 29, no. 5 (May 1916): 431–73.

———. *Inca Land: Explorations in the Highlands of Peru*. Boston: Houghton Mifflin, 1922.

———. "In the Wonderland of Peru." *National Geographic Magazine* 24, no. 4 (April 1913): 387–573.

———. *Lost City of the Incas: The Story of Machu Picchu and Its Builders*. New York: Duell, Sloan and Pearce, 1948.

———. *Machu Picchu: A Citadel of the Incas: Report of the Explorations and Excavations Made in 1911, 1912, and 1915 under the Auspices of Yale University and the National Geographic Society*. New Haven, CT: Yale University Press, 1930.

———. "The Story of Machu Picchu: The National Geographic Society–Yale University Explorations in Peru." *National Geographic Magazine* 27, no. 2 (February 1915): 172–86, 203–17.

Biskind, Peter. *Easy Riders, Raging Bulls: How the Sex-Drugs-and-Rock 'N' Roll Generation Saved Hollywood*. New York: Simon & Schuster, 1998.

Boorstin, Daniel J. *The Image: A Guide to Pseudo-Events in America*. 50th anniversary ed. New York: Vintage Books, 2012 [1962].

Bourdieu, Pierre. "Identity and Representation: Elements for a Critical Reflection on the Idea of Region." In *Language and Symbolic Power*, edited by John B. Thompson, 220–28. Cambridge, MA: Harvard University Press, 1991.

Brading, D. A. *Mexican Phoenix: Our Lady of Guadalupe; Image and Tradition across Five Centuries*. Cambridge: Cambridge University Press, 2001.

Brown, Donna. *Inventing New England: Regional Tourism in the Nineteenth Century*. Washington, DC: Smithsonian Books, 1997.

Brown, Michael F., and Eduardo Fernández. *War of Shadows: The Struggle for Utopia in the Peruvian Amazon*. Berkeley: University of California Press, 1991.

Burga, Manuel. "Las profetas de la rebellion, 1920–1923." In *Estados y naciones en los Andes: Hacia una historia comparativa*, edited by Jean Paul Deler and Y. Saint-Geours, 463–517. Lima: Instituto de Estudios Peruanos, 1986.

————. *Nacimiento de una utopía: Muerte y resurrección de los Incas*. 2nd ed. Lima: Universidad Nacional Mayor de San Marcos, 2005 [1988].

Burga, Manuel, and Alberto Flores Galindo. *Apogeo y crisis de la república aristocrática: Oligarquía, aprimso, y comunismo en el Perú, 1895-1932*. Lima: Ediciones Rikchay Peru, 1980.

Caballero, José María. *Economía agraria de la sierra peruana antes de la reforma agraria de 1969*. Lima: Instituto de Estudios Peruanos, 1981.

Cant, Anna. "'Land for Those Who Work It': A Visual Analysis of Agrarian Reform Posters in Velasco's Peru." *Journal of Latin American Studies* 44, no. 1 (February 2012): 1-37.

Capó Jr., Julio. *Welcome to Fairyland: Queer Miami before 1940*. Chapel Hill: University of North Carolina Press, 2017.

Carey, Mark. *In the Shadow of Melting Glaciers: Climate Change and Andean Society*. Oxford: Oxford University Press, 2010.

Carrión, Julio F. "Conclusion: The Rise and Fall of Electoral Authoritarianism in Peru." In *The Fujimori Legacy: The Rise of Electoral Authoritarianism in Peru*, edited by Julio F. Carrión, 294-318. University Park: Pennsylvania State University Press, 2006.

————. "Public Opinion, Market Reforms, and Democracy in Fujimori's Peru." In *The Fujimori Legacy: The Rise of Electoral Authoritarianism in Peru*, edited by Julio F. Carrión, 126-49. University Park: Pennsylvania State University Press, 2006.

Cassinelli, Cataline, and Pilar Lana Santillana. *Lima: The Historic Capital of South America*. English ed. Lima: Compañía Hotelera del Perú, 1943.

Centeno, Miguel A., and Agustín E. Ferraro, eds. *State and Nation Making in Latin America and Spain: Republics of the Possible*. Cambridge: Cambridge University Press, 2014.

Chalmers Adams, Harriet. "Cuzco, America's Ancient Mecca." *National Geographic Magazine* 19, no. 10 (October 1908): 669-89.

Chatterjee, Partha. *The Nation and Its Fragments: Colonial and Postcolonial Histories*. Princeton, NJ: Princeton University Press, 1993.

Chávez Ballón, Manuel. *Informe Machupijchu: De 1967 a 1971*. Cusco: Patronato Departamental de Arqueología del Cusco, 1971.

Ciccarelli, Orazio. "Fascism and Politics in Peru during the Benavides Regime, 1933-1939: The Italian Perspective." *Hispanic American Historical Review* 70, no. 3 (August 1990): 405-32.

Clarke, Nathan. "Revolutionizing the Tragic City: Rebuilding Cimbote, Peru, after the 1970 Earthquake." *Journal of Urban History* 41, no. 1 (January 2015): 93-115.

Cocks, Catherine. *Tropical Whites: The Rise of the Tourist South in the Americas*. Philadelphia: University of Pennsylvania Press, 2013.

Collier, David. *Squatters and Oligarchs: Authoritarian Rule and Policy Change in Peru*. Baltimore: Johns Hopkins University Press, 1976.

Comaroff, John L., and Jean Comaroff. *Ethnicity, Inc*. Chicago: University of Chicago Press, 2009.

Comisión de la Verdad y Reconciliación. *Informe Final*. 9 vols. Lima: Comisión de la Verdad y Reconciliación, 2003. http://www.cverdad.org.pe/ifinal/index.php.

Coronado, Jorge. *The Andes Imagined: Indigenismo, Society, and Modernity*. Pittsburgh: University of Pittsburgh Press, 2009.

Cosío, José Gabriel. *El Cuzco histórico y monumental*. Cusco: n.p., 1924.

———. "Una excursión a Machupiccho." *Revista Universitaria* 1, no. 2 (September 1912): 2–22.

———. "Una excu[r]sión a Machupiccho (conclusión)." *Revista Universitaria* 1, no. 3 (December 1912): 12–25.

Cotler, Julio. *Clases, estado y nación en el Perú*. Lima: Instituto de Estudios Peruanos, 1985.

———. "Democracy and National Integration in Peru." In *Peruvian Experiment Reconsidered*, edited by Cynthia McClintock and Abraham F. Lowenthal, 3–38. Princeton, NJ: Princeton University Press, 1983.

Covert, Lisa Pinley. *San Miguel de Allende: Mexicans, Foreigners, and the Making of a World Heritage Site*. Lincoln: University of Nebraska Press, 2017.

Cox, Karen L. *Destination Dixie: Tourism and Southern History*. Gainesville: University Press of Florida, 2014.

Cox Hall, Amy. "Collecting a 'Lost City' for Science: Huaquero Vision and the Yale Peruvian Expeditions to Machu Picchu, 1911, 1912, and 1914–15." *Ethnohistory* 59, no. 2 (Spring 2012): 293–321.

———. *Framing a Lost City: Science, Photography, and the Making of Machu Picchu*. Austin: University of Texas Press, 2017.

Croce, Marcela. "Walt Disney's Latin American Tour." Translated by Nicolas Allen. *Jacobin*, October 20, 2017. Accessed October 25, 2017. https://www.jacobinmag.com/2017/10/disney-donald-duck-carioca-latin-america-imperialism.

Cronin, Paul. *Herzog on Herzog*. London: Faber and Faber, 2002.

CYRF. *Hidroelectrica de Macchupichu [sic] Cuzco: Bases de licitación*. Cusco: n.p., 1958.

———. *Historial cronológico de la Central Hidroelectrica de Machupijchu, 1957–1962*. Cusco: H. G. Rozas, 1962.

Dallek, Robert. *FDR and American Foreign Policy, 1932–1945*. New York: Oxford University Press, 1979.

Dean, Carolyn. *Inka Bodies and the Body of Christ: Corpus Christi in Colonial Cuzco, Peru*. Durham, NC: Duke University Press, 1999.

Degregori, Carlos Iván. *Ayacucho 1969–1979, el surgimiento de Sendero Luminoso*. Lima: Instituto de Estudios Peruanos, 1990.

———. *Del mito de Jnkarr al mito del progreso*. Lima: Instituto de Estudios Peruanos, 2013.

———. *Qué difícil es ser dios: El Partido Comunista del Perú-Sendero Luminoso y el conflicto armado interno en el Perú, 1980–1999*. Lima: Instituto de Estudios Peruanos, 2011.

de la Cadena, Marisol. *Indigenous Mestizos: The Politics of Race and Culture in Cuzco, Peru, 1919–1991*. Durham, NC: Duke University Press, 2000.

de la Riva-Agüero, José. *Paisajes peruanos*. Lima: Pontificia Universidad Católica del Perú, 1995.

de Soto, Hernando. *The Other Path: The Invisible Revolution in the Third World*. New York: Harper & Row, 1989.

Dell, Anthony. *Llama Land: East and West of the Andes in Peru*. London: Geoffrey Bless, 1926.

Denegri, Guillermo. "Acerca de PromPerú: ¿Construyendo una institución?" In *El rol del estado en la labor de promoción-país: Hacia una AuditoríaAcadémica de PromPerú*, edited by Beatriz Boza, 39–63. Lima: PromPerú, 2000.

di Leonardo, Michaela. *Exotics at Home: Anthropologies, Others, American Modernity*. Chicago: University of Chicago Press, 1998.

"Discurso del Doctor José Luis Bustamante y Rivero, Presidente de la República." In *El turismo en el Perú*, edited by Luis Aylaza Paz Soldán, 63–69. Lima: Imprenta Torres Aguirre, 1947.

Dozer, Donald F. *Are We Good Neighbors?* Gainesville: University Press of Florida, 1961.

Drinot, Paulo. *The Allure of Labor: Workers, Race, and the Making of the Peruvian State*. Durham, NC: Duke University Press, 2011.

———. "Awaiting the Blood of a Truly Emancipating Revolution: Che Guevara in 1950s Peru." In *Che's Travels: The Making of a Revolutionary in 1950s Latin America*, edited by Paulo Drinot, 88–126. Durham, NC: Duke University Press, 2010.

———. "Entre el imperio y la nación: Ayacucho a comienzos del siglo XX en dos relatos de viaje." In *Entre la región y la nación: Nuevas aproximaciones a la historia ayacuchana y peruana*, edited by Roberto Ayala Huaytalla, 195–222. Lima: Instituto de Estudios Peruanos and CEHRA, 2013.

Earle, Rebecca. *The Return of the Native: Indians and Myth-Making in Spanish America, 1810-1930*. Durham, NC: Duke University Press, 2007.

"El II Congreso Indigenista Interamericano." *B.B.A.A., Boletín Biográfico de Antropología Americana* 12, no. 1 (January–December 1949): 16–23.

Elena, Eduardo. *Dignifying Argentina: Peronism, Citizenship, and Mass Consumption*. Pittsburgh: University of Pittsburgh Press, 2011.

Endy, Christopher. *Cold War Holidays: American Tourism in France*. Chapel Hill: University of North Carolina Press, 2004.

———. "Travel and World Power: Americans in Europe, 1890-1917." *Diplomatic History* 22, no. 4 (Fall 1998): 565–94.

Enríquez Verdura, Carlos. "Torres Bodet y la UNESCO." PhD diss., Colegio de México, 1997.

Escandell-Tur, Neus. *Producción y comercio de tejidos coloniales: Los obrajes y chorrillos del Cusco 1570-1820*. Cusco: Centro de Estudios Regionales Andinos, Bartolomé de Las Casas, 1997.

Feinstein, Adam. *Pablo Neruda: A Passion for Life*. New York: Bloomsbury, 2004.

Ferreyros, Alberto. "Redescubriendo el Camino Inca a Machu Picchu." E-mail to the author, April 12, 2017.

Fioravanti, Eduardo. *Latifundio y sindicalismo agrario en el Perú: El caso de los valles de La Convención y Lares (1958-1964)*. 2nd ed. Lima: Instituto de Estudios Peruanos, 1976.

Flores Galindo, Alberto. *In Search of an Inca: Identity and Utopia in the Andes*. Edited and translated by Carlos Aguirre, Charles F. Walker, and Willie Hiatt. Cambridge: Cambridge University Press, 2010.

————, ed. *Túpac Amaru II — 1780*. Lima: Retablo de Papel Ediciones, 1976.

Fonda Taylor, Frank. *To Hell with Paradise: A History of the Jamaican Tourist Industry*. Pittsburgh: University of Pittsburgh Press, 2003.

Fondo de Promoción de las Áreas Naturales Protegidas del Perú. *Recopilación bibliográfica del Santuario Histórico Machu Picchu*. Lima: Profonanpe, 2000.

Franck, Harry A. *Vagabonding down the Andes: Being the Narrative of a Journey, Chiefly Afoot, from Panama to Buenos Aires*. New York: Century Co., 1917.

Frost, Peter. *Exploring Cusco*. 4th ed. Lima: Nueva Imágenes, 1989.

Fuentes, Hildebrando. *El Cuzco y sus ruinas*. Lima: Imprenta del Estado, 1905.

Fussell, Paul. *Abroad: British Literary Traveling between the Wars*. New York: Oxford University Press, 1980.

Gänger, Stephanie. *Relics of the Past: The Collecting and Study of Pre-Columbian Antiquities in Peru and Chile, 1837-1911*. Oxford: Oxford University Press, 2014.

García, José Uriel. *El Nuevo Indio*. Cusco: Editorial Rozas, 1930.

García, Uriel, Luis E. Valcárcel, and Albert Giesecke. *Guía histórico-artística del Cuzco*. Lima: Editorial Garcilaso, 1925.

García-Bryce, Iñigo. "A Revolution Remembered, a Revolution Forgotten: The 1932 Aprista Insurrection in Trujillo, Peru." *A Contracorriente* 7, no. 3 (Spring 2010): 277-322.

Gascón, Jorge. *Gringos como en sueños: Diferenciación y conflicto, campesinos en los Andes peruanos ante el desarrollo del turismo*. Lima: Instituto de Estudios Peruanos, 2005.

Gassan, Richard H. *The Birth of American Tourism: New York, the Hudson Valley, and American Culture*. Amherst: University of Massachusetts Press, 2008.

Gellman, Irwin F. *Good Neighbor Diplomacy: United States Policies in Latin America, 1933-1945*. Baltimore: Johns Hopkins University Press, 1979.

Giesecke, Albert. *El censo de la provincia del Cuzco del 12 de septiembre de 1912*. Cusco: Imprenta del Trabajo, 1913.

————. "El Cuzco: Meca del turismo de la América del Sur." *Mercurio Peruano* 4, no. 25 (July 1920): 54-68.

————. "El Cuzco: Meca del turismo de la América del Sur." *Revista Universitaria* 10, no. 35 (August 1921): 3-17.

————. *Guía del Cuzco: La Meca de la América del Sur, en la tierra de los Incas*. Lima: Imprenta "Garcilaso," 1924.

Giesecke, Margarita. *La insurrección de Trujillo: Jueves 7 de julio 1932*. Lima: Fondo Editorial del Congreso del Perú, 2010.

Glave, Luis Miguel. *La república instalada: Formación nacional y prensa en el Cuzco, 1825-1839*. Lima: Instituto de Estudios Peruanos, 2004.

Gobierno Regional del Cusco and DIRCETUR. *Boletín Estadístico de Turismo — 2014*. Cusco: DIRCETUR, 2014.

Golte, Jürgen. *Repartos y rebeliones: Túpac Amaru y las contradicciones de la economía colonial*. Lima: Instituto de Estudios Peruanos, 1980.

Goodsell, Charles T. *American Corporations and Peruvian Politics*. Cambridge, MA: Harvard University Press, 1974.

Gootenberg, Paul. *Andean Cocaine: The Making of a Global Drug*. Chapel Hill: University of North Carolina Press, 2008.

Gorriti, Gustavo. *The Shining Path: A History of the Millenarian War in Peru*. Translated by Robin Kirk. Chapel Hill: University of North Carolina Press, 1999.

Greaves, Tom, Ralph Bolton, and Florencia Zapata, eds. *Vicos and Beyond: A Half Century of Applying Anthropology in Peru*. Lanham, MD: AltaMira Press, 2011.

Greer, Paolo. "Machu Picchu before Bingham." *South American Explorers Magazine* (May 2008): 36–41.

Guevara de la Serna, Ernesto. *The Motorcycle Diaries: A Journey around South America*. Translated by Ann Wright. New York: Verso, 1995.

Guía general del Cuzco. Cusco: Hersct & Flores, 1937.

Guillet, David. *Agrarian Reform and Peasant Economy in Southern Peru*. Columbia: University of Missouri Press, 1979.

Handelman, Howard. *Struggle in the Andes: Peasant Political Mobilization in Peru*. Austin: University of Texas Press, 1975.

Hanson, Earl Parker, ed. *The New World Guide to Latin American Republics, Sponsored by the Office of the U.S. Coordinator of Inter-American Affairs*. Vol. 2. New York: Duell, Sloan and Pearce, 1943.

Harmer, Tanya. "Two, Three, Many Revolutions? Cuba and the Prospects for Revolutionary Change in Latin America, 1967–1975." *Journal of Latin American Studies* 45, no. 1 (February 2013): 61–88.

Hayne, Coe. *The City of the Clouds, or A Tale of the Last Inca*. Elgin, IL: David C. Cook, 1919.

Healey, Mark. *The Ruins of the New Argentina: Peronism and the Remaking of San Juan after the 1944 Earthquake*. Durham, NC: Duke University Press, 2011.

Heaney, Christopher. *Cradle of Gold: The Story of Hiram Bingham, a Real-Life Indiana Jones, and the Search for Machu Picchu*. New York: Palgrave Macmillan, 2010.

Heilman, Jaymie. *Before the Shining Path: Politics in Rural Ayacucho, 1895–1980*. Stanford: Stanford University Press, 2010.

Hergé. "Le temple du soleil." *Tintin*, no. 1 (September 26, 1946).

Hiatt, Willie. "Flying 'Cholo': Incas, Airplanes, and the Construction of Andean Modernity in 1920s Cuzco, Peru." *The Americas* 63, no. 3 (January 2007): 327–58.

———. "Indians in the Lobby: Newspapers and the Limits of Andean Cosmopolitanism, 1896–1930." *The Americas* 68, no. 3 (January 2012): 377–403.

Hill, Michael D. "Contesting Patrimony: Cusco's Mystical Tourist Industry and the Politics of *Incanismo*." *Ethnos* 72, no. 4 (December, 2007): 433–60.

Hinojosa, Iván. "On Poor Relations and the Nouveau Riche: Shining Path and the Radical Peruvian Left." In *Shining and Other Paths: War and Society in Peru, 1980–1995*, edited by Steve J. Stern, 60–83. Durham, NC: Duke University Press, 1998.

Hobsbawm, Eric. "A Case of Neo-feudalism: La Convencion, Peru." *Journal of Latin American Studies* 1, no. 1 (May 1969): 31–50.

———. *Nations and Nationalism since 1780: Programme, Myth, Reality*. 2nd ed. Cambridge: Cambridge University Press, 1992.

———. "Peasant Land Occupations." *Past and Present Society*, no. 62 (February 1974): 120–52.

————. "Peru: The Peculiar Revolution." *New York Review of Books* 17, no. 10 (December 16, 1971).

Hobsbawm, Eric, and Terence Ranger, eds. *The Invention of Tradition*. New York: Cambridge University Press, 1984.

Holloway, Thomas S. "Whose Conquest Is This, Anyway?" In *Based on a True Story: Latin American History at the Movies*, edited by Donald F. Stevens, 29–46. Wilmington, DE: SR Books, 1997.

Instituto de Opinión Pública. Pontificia Universidad Católica del Perú. "Boletín no. 141: Etnicidad, origen familiar-cultural y condiciones de vida en el Perú," April 2017. Accessed May 28, 2017. http://repositorio.pucp.edu.pe/index/handle /123456789/69825.

Instituto Nacional de Estadística e Información. "Censos nacionales de población y vivienda, 1940, 1961, 1972, 1981, 1993 y 2007," 2007. Accessed May 29, 2017. http:/ /www.inei.gob.pe/estadisticas/indice-tematico/poblacion-y-vivienda/.

————. "Cuadro no. 2, Cusco: Valor agregado bruto," June 2017. Accessed October 25, 2017. https://www.inei.gob.pe/estadisticas/indice-tematico/pbi-de -los-departamentos-segun-actividades-economicas-9110/.

Jacobsen, Nils. *Mirages of Transition: The Peruvian Altiplano, 1780–1930*. Berkeley: University of California Press, 1993.

Joseph, Gilbert M., Catherine C. LeGrand, and Ricardo D. Salvatore, eds. *Close Encounters of Empire: Writing the Cultural History of U.S.–Latin American Relations*. Durham, NC: Duke University Press, 1998.

Kapsoli, Wilfredo. *Allyus del sol: Anarquismo y utopía andina*. Lima: TAREA Asociación de Publicaciones Educativas, 1984.

————. *Los movimientos campesinos en el Perú, 1879–1965*. 2nd ed. Lima: Atusparia Ediciones, 1982.

Kincaid, Jamaica. *A Small Place*. New York: Farrar, Straus and Giroux, 1988.

Klarén, Peter. "The Origins of Modern Peru." In *The Cambridge History of Latin America*, vol. 1, edited by Leslie Bethell, 587–640. Cambridge: Cambridge University Press, 1986.

————. *Peru: Society and Nationhood in the Andes*. New York: Oxford University Press, 2000.

Klein, Naomi. *The Shock Doctrine: The Rise of Disaster Capitalism*. New York: Metropolitan Books, 2007.

Knight, Alan. "Racism, Revolution, and *Indigenismo*: Mexico, 1910–1940." In *The Idea of Race in Latin America, 1870–1940*, edited by Richard Graham, 71–113. Austin: University of Texas Press, 1990.

Koenker, Diane P. *Club Red: Vacation Travel and the Soviet Dream*. Ithaca, NY: Cornell University Press, 2013.

Koshar, Rudy. "'What Ought to Be Seen': Tourists' Guidebooks and National Identities in Modern Germany and Europe." *Journal of Contemporary History* 33, no. 3 (July 1998): 323–40.

Kristal, Efraín. *The Andes Viewed from the City: Literary and Political Discourse on the Indian in Peru, 1848–1930*. New York: Peter Lang, 1987.

Krüggeler, Thomas. "Indians, Workers, and the Arrival of 'Modernity': "Cuzco, Peru (1895–1924)." *The Americas* 56, no. 2 (October 1999): 161–89.

Kubler, George. *Cuzco: Reconstruction of the Town and Restoration of Its Monuments*. Report of the UNESCO Mission of 1951. Paris: UNESCo, 1952.

Larson, Brooke. *Trials of Nation Making: Liberalism, Race, and Ethnicity in the Andes, 1810–1910*. Cambridge: Cambridge University Press, 2004.

La Serna, Miguel. *The Corner of the Living: Ayacucho on the Eve of the Shining Path Insurgency*. Chapel Hill: University of North Carolina Press, 2012.

Lauer, Mirko. *Andes imaginarios: Discuciones del indigenismo 2*. Cusco: Centro de Estudios Regionales Andinos, Bartolomé de las Casas, 1997.

Leibner, Gerardo. "Radicalism and Integration: The Tahuantinsuyo Committee Experience and the *Indigenismo* of Leguía Reconsidered, 1919–1924." *Journal of Iberian and Latin American Research* 9, no. 2 (2003): 1–24.

Leroux, Gaston. *The Bride of the Sun*. New York: McBride Nast, 1915.

Levinson, Jerome I., and Juan de Onís. *The Alliance That Lost Its Way: A Critical Report on the Alliance for Progress*. Chicago: Quadrangle Books, 1970.

Lewin, Boleslao. *La rebelión de Túpac Amaru y los orígenes de la emancipación americana*. Buenos Aires: Hachette, 1957.

Lomnitz, Claudio. *Deep Mexico, Silent Mexico: An Anthropology of Nationalism*. Minneapolis: University of Minnesota Press, 2001.

López Lenci, Yazmín. *El Cusco, paqarina moderna: Cartografía de una modernidad e identidad en los Andes peruanos (1900–1935)*. Lima: Instituto Nacional de Cultura, 2007.

Lovón Zevala, Gerardo. "Dinámica interna de la sierra." In *Estrategias para el desarrollo de la sierra*. Cusco: Universidad Nacional Agraria La Molina and Centro de Estudios Rurales Andinos Bartolomé de las Casas, 1986.

———. *Mito y realidad del turismo en el Cusco*. Cusco: Centro Bartolomé de las Casas, 1982.

Lowenthal, Abraham F. "The Peruvian Experiment Reconsidered." In *The Peruvian Experiment Reconsidered*, edited by Cynthia McClintock and Abraham F. Lowenthal, 415–30. Princeton, NJ: Princeton University Press, 1983.

Luciano, Pellegrino A. *Neoliberal Reforms in Machu Picchu: Protecting a Community, Heritage Site, and Tourism Destination in Peru*. Lanham: Lexington Books, 2018.

MacCannell, Dean. *The Tourist: A New Theory of the Leisure Class*. New York: Schocken Books, 1976.

Mallon, Florencia. *Peasant and Nation: The Making of Postcolonial Mexico and Peru*. Berkeley: University of California Press, 1995.

Markham, Clements. *Cuzco: A Journey to the Ancient Capital of Peru*. London: Chapham and Hall, 1856.

Matos Mar, José. *Desborde popular y crisis del estado: El nuevo rostro del Perú en la década de 1980*. Lima: Instituto de Estudios Peruanos, 1984.

Matos Mendieta, Ramiro. "Peru: Some Comments." In *History of Latin American Archaeology*, edited by Augusto Oyuela-Caycedo, 104–23. Aldershot: Avebury, 1994.

Maxwell, Keely. "Tourism, Environment, and Development on the Inca Trail." *Hispanic American Historical Review* 92, no. 1 (February 1992): 143–71.

Mayer, Enrique. *Ugly Stories of the Peruvian Agrarian Reform*. Durham, NC: Duke University Press, 2009.

McClintock, Cynthia, and Abraham F. Lowenthal, eds. *The Peruvian Experiment Reconsidered*. Princeton, NJ: Princeton University Press, 1983.

Méndez G., Cecilia. "Incas Sí, Indios No: Notes on Peruvian Creole Nationalism and Its Contemporary Crisis." *Journal of Latin American Studies* 28, no. 1 (February 1996): 197–225.

Mendoza, Zoila S. *Creating Our Own: Folklore, Performance, and Identity in Cuzco, Peru*. Durham, NC: Duke University Press, 2008.

Merrill, Dennis. *Negotiating Paradise: U.S. Tourism and Empire in Twentieth-Century Latin America*. Chapel Hill: University of North Carolina Press, 2009.

Morner, Magnus. *Perfil de la sociedad rural del Cuzco a fines de la colonia*. Lima: Universidad del Pacífico, 1978.

Mould de Pease, Mariana. *Machu Picchu y el código de ética de la sociedad de arqueología americana*. Lima: Consejo Nacional de Ciencia y Tecnologia; Pontificia Universidad Católica del Perú Fondo Editorial; Instituto Nacional de Cultura; Universidad Nacional San Antonio de Abad del Cuzco, 2003.

Neruda, Pablo. "Poem XII." In *Macchu [sic] Picchu*, translated by Nathaniel Tarn, 67–71. New York: Noonday Press, 1966.

Niera, Hugo. *Los Andes: Tierra o muerte*. Santiago, Chile: Editorial ZYX, 1965.

Niles, Blair. *Peruvian Pageant: A Journey in Time*. Indianapolis: Bobbs-Merrill, 1937.

Norkunas, Martha K. *The Politics of Public Memory: Tourism, History, and Ethnicity in Monterey, California*. Albany: State University of New York Press, 1993.

North, Liisa L. "Ideological Orientations of Peru's Military Rulers." In *The Peruvian Experiment Reconsidered*, edited by Cynthia McClintock and Abraham F. Lowenthal, 245–74. Princeton, NJ: Princeton University Press, 1983.

Observatorio Turístico del Perú. "Cuzco: Participación porcentual del P.B.I. por sectores." Accessed May 2, 2014. http://www.observatorioturisticodelperu.com /mapas/cuscpbip.pdf.

O'Phelan Godoy, Scarlett. *Rebellions and Revolts in Eighteenth Century Peru and Upper Peru*. Cologne: Böhlau, 1985.

Oral History Research Office, Columbia University. "The Reminiscences of Albert A. Giesecke." New York: Columbia University, 1963.

Paliza Gallegos, Luis Alberto. *Impacto económico del turismo en el Cusco y el siglo XXI*. Vol. 2. Cusco: UNSAAC, 1998.

Peck, Annie. *The South American Tour*. New York: George H. Doran, 1913.

Philip, George D. E. *The Rise and Fall of the Peruvian Military Radicals, 1968–1975*. London: Athlone Press, 1978.

Pike, Frederick B. *FDR's Good Neighbor Policy: Sixty Years of Generally Gentle Chaos*. Austin: University of Texas Press, 1995.

Plutt, Hans Michael. "Strategies for Tourism Promotion." In *Peru: A Nation in Development*, 121–63. Lima: PromPerú, 1996.

Poole, Deborah. "Landscape and the Imperial Subject: U.S. Images of the Andes, 1850–1930." In *Close Encounters of Empire: Writing the Cultural History of U.S.-Latin American Relations*, edited by Gilbert M. Joseph, Catherine C. LeGrand, and Ricardo D. Salvatore, 107–38. Durham, NC: Duke University Press, 1998.

———. *Vision, Race, and Modernity: A Visual Economy of the Andean Image World*. Princeton, NJ: Princeton University Press, 1997.

Poole, Deborah, and Gerardo Rénique. *Peru: Time of Fear*. London: Latin American Bureau, 1992.

Portocarrero Maisch, Gonzalo. *De Bustamante a Odría: El fracaso del Frente Democrático Nacional, 1945–1950*. Lima: Mosca Azul Editores, 1983.

Pratt, Mary Louise. *Imperial Eyes: Travel Writing and Transculturation*. 2nd ed. London: Routledge, 2008.

PromPerú. *Perfil de quejas y pedidos de los turistas: Memoria del Servicio de Protección al Turista, 1994–1999*. Lima: PromPerú, 2000.

Rachowiecki, Rob. *Peru: A Travel Survival Kit*. South Yarra, Victoria: Lonely Planet, 1987.

Ramos, Horacio. "La reforma neocolonial de la Plaza de Armas: Modernización urbana y patrimonio arquitectónico en Lima, 1901–1952." *Histórica* 40, no. 1 (2016): 101–41.

Reinhard, Johan. *Machu Picchu: Exploring an Ancient Sacred Center*. Los Angeles: Cotsen Institute of Archeology at UCLA, 2007.

Rénique, José Luis. *El Centro Científico del Cuzco, 1897–1907*. Lima: Pontificia Universidad Católica del Perú, 1980.

———. *La batalla por Puno: Conflicto local y nación en los Andes peruanos*. Lima: Instituto de Estudios Peruanos, 2011.

———. *Los sueños de la sierra: Cuzco en el siglo XX*. Lima: CESPES, 1991.

Revels, Tracy J. *Sunshine Paradise: A History of Florida Tourism*. Gainesville: University Press of Florida, 2011.

Robison Wright, Marie. *The Old and the New Peru: A Story of the Ancient Inheritance and the Modern Growth and Enterprise of a Great Nation*. Philadelphia: G. Barrie and Sons, 1908.

Rogers, William D. *The Twilight Struggle: The Alliance for Progress and the Politics of Development in Latin America*. New York: Random House, 1967.

Romo, Anadelia A. *Brazil's Living Museum: Race, Reform, and Tradition in Bahia*. Chapel Hill: University of North Carolina Press, 2010.

Rothman, Hal K. *Devil's Bargains: Tourism in the Twentieth-Century American West*. Lawrence: University Press of Kansas, 1998.

———. "Selling the Meaning of Place: Entrepreneurship, Tourism, and Community Transformation in the Twentieth-Century American West." *Pacific Historical Review* 65, no. 4 (November 1996): 525–57.

Rowe, John. "Machu Picchu a la luz de documentos de siglo XVI." *Historia* 16, no. 1 (1990): 139–54.

Rowland, Donald W. *History of the Office of the Coordinator of Inter-American Affairs*. Washington, DC: U.S. Government Printing Office, 1947.

Ruiz, Jason. *Americans in the Treasure House: Travel to Porfirian Mexico and the Cultural Politics of Empire*. Austin: University of Texas Press, 2014.

Sadlier, Darlene J. *Americans All: Good Neighbor Cultural Diplomacy in World War II*. Austin: University of Texas Press, 2012.

Salazar, Lucy C. "Machu Picchu: Mysterious Royal Estate in the Cloud Forest." In *Machu Picchu: Unveiling the Mystery of the Incas*, edited by Richard L. Burger and Lucy C. Salazar, 21–47. New Haven, CT: Yale University Press, 2004.

Salvatore, Ricardo. *Disciplinary Conquest: U.S. Scholars in South America, 1900–1945*. Durham, NC: Duke University Press, 2016.

———. "Local versus Imperial Knowledge." *Neplanta: Views from the South* 4, no. 1 (2003): 67–80.

Saragoza, Alex. "The Selling of Mexico: Tourism and the State, 1929–1952." In *Fragments of a Golden Age: The Politics of Culture in Mexico since 1940*, edited by Gilbert Joseph, Anne Rubenstein, and Eric Zolov, 91–115. Durham, NC: Duke University Press, 2001.

Savoy, Gene. *Antisuyo: The Search for the Lost Cities of the Amazon*. New York: Simon and Schuster, 1970.

Schantz, Eric M. "Behind the Noir Border: Tourism, the Vice Racket, and Power Relations in Baja California's Border Zone, 1938–65." In *Holiday in Mexico: Critical Reflections on Tourism and Tourist Encounters*, edited by Dina Berger and Andrew Grant Wood, 130–60. Durham, NC: Duke University Press, 2010.

Scheman, L. Ronald. *The Alliance for Progress: A Retrospective*. New York: Praeger, 1988.

Schumpeter, Joseph A. *Capitalism, Socialism, and Democracy*. New York: Harper and Row, 1976 [1942].

Schwartz, Rosalie. *Pleasure Island: Tourism and Temptation in Cuba*. Lincoln: University of Nebraska Press, 1997.

Schwartz, Stewart B. *Sea of Storms: A History of Hurricanes in the Greater Caribbean from Columbus to Katrina*. Princeton, NJ: Princeton University Press, 2015.

Schydlowsky, Daniel M., and Juan J. Wicht. "The Anatomy of an Economic Failure." In *The Peruvian Experiment Reconsidered*, edited by Cynthia McClintock and Abraham F. Lowenthal, 94–143. Princeton, NJ: Princeton University Press, 1983.

Scorer, James. "Andean Self-Fashioning: Martín Chambi, Photography and the Ruins of Machu Picchu." *History of Photography* 38, no. 4 (November 2014): 379–97.

Sears, John F. *Sacred Places: American Tourist Attractions in the Nineteenth Century*. Amherst: University of Massachusetts Press, 1989.

Seigel, Micol. "Beyond Compare: Comparative Method after the Transnational Turn." *Radical History Review* 91 (Winter 2005): 62–90.

Seligmann, Linda J. "Market Places, Social Spaces in Cuzco, Peru." *Urban Anthropology and Studies of Cultural Systems and World Economic Development* 29, no. 1 (Spring 2000): 1–68.

Serulnikov, Sergio. *Revolution in the Andes: The Age of Túpac Amaru*. Translated by David Frye. Durham: Duke University Press, 2013.

Shaffer, Marguerite S. *See America First: Tourism and National Identity, 1880–1940*. Washington, DC: Smithsonian Books, 2001.

Sheahan, John. "Redirection of Peruvian Economic Strategy in the 1990s: Gains, Losses, and Clues for the Future." In *The Fujimori Legacy: The Rise of Electoral*

Authoritarianism in Peru, edited by Julio F. Carrión, 178–200. University Park: Pennsylvania State University Press, 2006.

Shullenberger, Geoffrey. "That Obscure Object of Desire: Machu Picchu as Myth and Commodity." *Journal of Latin American Cultural Studies* 17, no. 3 (December 2008): 317–33.

Silverman, Helaine. "Mayor Daniel Estrada and the Plaza de Armas of Cuzco, Peru." *Heritage Management* 1, no. 2 (Fall 2008): 181–217.

———. "Touring Ancient Times: The Present and Presented Past in Contemporary Peru." *American Anthropologist* 104, no. 3 (2002): 141–55.

Sims Malkus, Alida. *The Citadel of a Hundred Stairways*. Chicago: John C. Winston Co., 1941.

Skwiot, Christine. *The Purposes of Paradise: U.S. Tourism and Empire in Cuba and Hawaii*. Philadelphia: University of Pennsylvania Press, 2010.

Smith, Valene L., ed. *Hosts and Guests: The Anthropology of Tourism*. 2nd ed. Philadelphia: University of Pennsylvania Press, 1989.

———. Introduction to *Hosts and Guests: The Anthropology of Tourism*, edited by Valene L. Smith, 2nd ed., 1–17. Philadelphia: University of Pennsylvania Press.

Sociedad de Propaganda del Sur del Perú. *Guía general del Sur del Perú*. Cusco: Imprenta H. G. Rozas, 1921.

Squire, E. G. *Peru: Incidents of Travel and Exploration in the Land of the Incas*. New York: Harper and Brothers, 1877.

Stallings, Barbara. "International Capitalism and the Peruvian Military Government." In *The Peruvian Experiment Reconsidered*, edited by Cynthia McClintock and Abraham F. Lowenthal, 144–80. Princeton, NJ: Princeton University Press, 1983.

Stanfield, Michael Edward. *Red Rubber, Bleeding Trees: Violence, Slavery, and Empire in Northwest Amazonia, 1850–1933*. Albuquerque: University of New Mexico Press, 1998.

Stavig, Ward. *The World of Túpac Amaru: Conflict, Community, and Identity in Colonial Peru*. Lincoln: University of Nebraska Press, 1999.

Stein, Steve. *Populism in Peru: The Emergence of the Masses and the Politics of Social Control*. Madison: University of Wisconsin Press, 1980.

Stern, Steve J., ed. *Shining and Other Paths: War and Society in Peru, 1980–1995*. Durham, NC: Duke University Press, 1998.

Strachan, Ian Gregory. *Paradise and Plantation: Tourism and Culture in the Anglophone Caribbean*. Charlottesville: University of Virginia Press, 2002.

Szeminksi, Jan. *La utopía tupamarista*. Lima: Pontíficia Universidad Católica del Perú, 1984.

Tamayo Herrera, José. *El enigma de Machupicchu: Historia, arqueología estética, ecología y prospectiva del monumento artístico-arqueológico más importante del Perú*. Lima: n.p., 2011.

———. *Historia regional del Cuzco republicano: Un libro de síntesis, 1808–1980*. 3rd ed. Lima: n.p., 2010.

———. "Prólogo." In *El pensamiento indigenista*, edited by José Tamayo Herrera, 9–19. Lima: Mosca Azul Editores, 1981.

Tantaleán, Henry. *Peruvian Archaeology: A Critical History*. Translated by Charles Stanish. Walnut Creek, CA: Left Coast Press, 2014.

Tenorio-Trillo, Mauricio. *Mexico at the World's Fairs: Crafting a Modern Nation*. Berkeley: University of California Press, 1996.

Thomson, Hugh. *The White Rock: Exploration of the Inca Heartland*. London: Weidenfeld and Nicolson, 2001.

Thorp, Rosemary, and Geoffrey Bertram. *Peru, 1890–1977: Growth and Policy in an Open Economy*. London: Macmillan, 1978.

Thurner, Mark. *From Two Republics to One Divided: Contradictions of Postcolonial Nationmaking in Andean Peru*. Durham, NC: Duke University Press, 1997.

UNESCO. "Inscription of the City of Cuzco and the Historic Sanctuary of Machu Picchu on the World Heritage List," October 17, 1985. http://whc.unesco.org /archive/1985/sc-85-conf008-inf3e.pdf.

———. *Report on the Reactive Monitoring Mission to the Historic Sanctuary of Machu Picchu (Peru) from April 22 to 30th April of 2007*. Paris: UNESCO, 2007.

Urry, John, and Jonas Larsen. *The Tourist Gaze 3.0*. Los Angeles: Sage, 2011.

Valcárcel, Carlos Daniel. *Túpac Amaru, precursor de la independencia*. Lima: Universidad Nacional Mayor de San Marcos, 1977.

Valcárcel, Luis E. *Cuzco: Capital arqueológica de Sud América, 1534–1934*. Lima: Banco Italiano, 1934.

———. "La cuestión agraria en el Cuzco." *Revista Universitaria* 3, no. 9 (June 1914): 16–38.

———. *Memorias*. Lima: Instituto de Estudios Peruanos, 1981.

———. "Sinopsis de Machupijchu." *Revista Universitaria* 18, no. 57 (1929): 89–103.

van den Berghe, Pierre L., and Jorge Flores Ochoa. "Tourism and Nativistic Ideology in Cuzco, Peru." *Annals of Tourism Research* 27, no. 1 (2000): 7–26.

Vergara, Alberto. *La danza hostil: Poderes subnacionales y estado central en Bolivia y Perú (1952–2012)*. Lima: Instituto de Estudios Peruanos, 2015.

Vich, Víctor. "Magical, Mystical: 'The Royal Tour' of Alejandro Toledo." *Journal of Latin American Cultural Studies* 16, no. 1 (March 2007): 1–10.

———. "Vicisitudes trágicas: Territorio, identidad y nación en los *Paisajes peruanos* de José de la Riva-Agüero y Osma." *Revista Andina*, no. 34 (January 2002): 123–34.

Walker, Charles F. "The General and His Rebel: Juan Velasco Alvarado and the Reinvention of Túpac Amaru II." In *The Peculiar Revolution: Rethinking the Peruvian Experiment under Military Rule*, edited by Carlos Aguirre and Paulo Drinot, 49–72. Durham, NC: Duke University Press, 2017.

———. *Shaky Colonialism: The 1746 Earthquake-Tsunami in Lima, Peru, and Its Long Aftermath*. Durham, NC: Duke University Press, 2008.

———. *Smoldering Ashes: Cuzco and the Creation of Republican Peru, 1780–1840*. Durham, NC: Duke University Press, 1999.

———. *The Tupac Amaru Rebellion*. Cambridge, MA: Belknap Press of Harvard University Press, 2014.

Walter, Richard J. *Peru and the United States, 1960–1975: How Their Ambassadors Managed Foreign Relations in a Turbulent Era*. University Park: Pennsylvania State University Press, 2010.

Weinstein, Barbara. *The Color of Modernity: São Paulo and the Making of Race and Nation in Brazil.* Durham, NC: Duke University Press, 2015.

Wilder, Thornton. *The Bridge of San Luis Rey.* New York: Albert and Charles Boni, 1927.

Wilson, Tamar Diana. "The Impacts of Tourism in Latin America." *Latin American Perspectives* 160, no. 3 (May 2008): 3–20.

Wise, Carol. "Against the Odds: The Paradoxes of Peru's Economic Recovery in the 1990s." In *The Fujimori Legacy: The Rise of Electoral Authoritarianism in Peru,* edited by Julio F. Carrión, 201–26. University Park: Pennsylvania State University Press, 2006.

Wood, Bryce. *The Making of the Good Neighbor Policy.* New York: Columbia University Press, 1961.

World Travel & Tourism Council. *Travel & Tourism Economic Impact 2017, Peru.* London: 2017. https://www.wttc.org/-/media/files/reports/economic-impact -research/countries-2017/peru2017.pdf

Wright, Kenneth R., and Alfredo Valencia Zegarra. *Machu Picchu: A Civil Engineering Marvel.* Reston, VA: ASCE Press, 2000.

Zolov, Eric. "Introduction: Latin America in the Global Sixties." *The Americas* 70, no. 3 (January 2014): 349–62.

———. "Peru's Overlooked Place in the History of Latin American Rock." *NPR Online,* April 21, 2011. Accessed August 1, 2013. http://www.npr.org/blogs /altlatino/2011/04/21/135042157/perus-overlooked-place-in-the-history-of-latin -american-rock.

———. *Refried Elvis: The Rise of the Mexican Counterculture.* Berkeley: University of California Press, 1999.

Zorn, Elayne. *Weaving a Future: Tourism, Cloth, and Culture on an Andean Island.* Iowa City: University of Iowa Press, 2004.

Zuelow, Eric G. E. *A History of Modern Tourism.* London: Palgrave Macmillan, 2016.

Films and Music

Aguirre, the Wrath of God. Produced by Werner Herzog. Directed by Werner Herzog. 94 min. Werner Herzog Filmproduktion and Hessischer Rundfunk. 1972.

Alomía Robles, Daniel, Paul Simon, and Jorge Milchberg. "El Condor Pasa (If I Could)." From *Bridge over Troubled Water.* Simon & Garfunkel. Columbia. 1970.

The Bridge of San Luis Rey. Produced by Hunt Stromberg. Directed by Charles Brabin. 86 min. Metro-Goldwyn-Mayer. 1929.

The Bridge of San Luis Rey. Produced by Rowland V. Lee and Benedict Bogeaus. Directed by Benedict Bogeaus. 107 min. United Artists. 1944.

Cahn, Sammy and Jimmy Van Heusen. "Come Fly with Me." From *Come Fly with Me.* Frank Sinatra. Capitol. 1958.

Heart of the Inca Empire. Produced by Howard Knapp, Wendell Clark Bennett, US Office for Inter-American Affairs. Directed by Howard Knapp. 25 min. 1943.

The Last Movie. Produced by Paul Lewis. Directed by Dennis Hopper. 108 min. Universal Pictures. 1971.

Namath. Produced by Rick Bernstein and Steve Sabol. 86 min. HBO Sports and NFL Films. 2012.

Saludos Amigos. Produced by Walt Disney. Directed by Norman Ferguson, Wilfred Jackson, Jack Kinney, Hamilton Luske, William Roberts. 42 min. Disney. 1942.

Secret of the Incas. Produced by Mel Epstein. Directed by Jerry Hopper. 100 min. Paramount Pictures. 1954.

Interviews

Calvo Jara, María Cristina. Interview by Mark Rice. January 18, 2017.

Koechlin, José. Interview by Mark Rice. December 3, 2011.

Milla, Carlos. Interview by Mark Rice. January 17, 2017.

Valencia, Roger. Interview by Mark Rice. January 6, 2012, and January 4, 2017.

Weeks, Wendy. Interview by Mark Rice. October 26, 2011.

Index

AeroPerú, 107, 111–12

agrarian reform, 12, 96–98, 101, 106, 108, 119–20, 141–42

agrarian revolts, 35–36, 97, 105. *See also* Comité Pro-Derecho Indígena Tawantinsuyo; Ejército de Liberación Nacional; Movimiento de la Izquierda Revolucionaria

Aguas Calientes, 21, 49, 109, 120, 133–34, 141–42, 153, 162, 164–65, 196n166

Aguirre, the Wrath of God, 122

Alejandro Velasco Astete Airport, 49, 88, 100, 132

Alianza Popular Revolucionaria Americana (APRA), 35, 47–48, 62, 71, 74, 135. *See also* García, Alan; Haya de la Torre, Victor Raúl

Alliance for Progress, 101

Alomía Robles, Daniel, 54, 122

Ancash, 79–80

Andes: global interest, 25, 50–52, 54–55, 122, 129, 157, 159; place in Peruvian nation identity, 1–2, 28–31, 44–45, 84–85, 160–62

Apurímac, 136, 163

archeology: as academic study in Peru, 20, 22, 25; Peruvian legislation of, 22–23, 114; preservation debates, 79, 81, 84–86, 91–93, 114–15; tourism appeal, 32–34, 38–39, 56, 64, 148. *See also* Archeology Council

Archeology Council (Patronato Departamental de Arqueología): budget, 83–85; Inca Trail, 142; Machu Picchu management, 82–86, 90–91, 98, 109; tourism promotion, 38, 62, 64

Arequipa, 18–19

Argentina, 31

Arguedas, José María, 91–92

Aristocratic Republic, 18–19

Arteaga, Melchor, 21, 67

aviation, 42, 55, 95, 100, 135, 160. *See also* AeroPerú; Alejandro Velasco Astete Airport; Braniff International Airways; Chinchero International Airport; Corporación Peruana de Aeropuertos y Aviación Comercial; Faucett Airlines; jet aircraft; Jorge Chávez International Airport; Pan American-Grace Airways

Ayacucho, 136, 145

Belaúnde Terry, Fernando: economic policies, 101, 133; historical preservation policies, 107, 141; political problems, 105–6, 135; tourism policies, 99, 101, 107, 133–34

Belmond, 154, 163

Benavides, Óscar R., 37, 41–42, 48, 57–58

Bingham, Hiram: archeological theories, 10, 49–50, 66–69; descriptions of Cusco, 16, 18, 27; early life, 11; expeditions to Machu Picchu, 10–11, 21–23, 32, 49–50, 157, 159; *Inca Land*, 23, 27, 49, 171n42; "In the Wonderland of Peru," 22; *Lost City of the Incas*, 68–69; *Machu Picchu: A Citadel of the Incas*, 49–50; Machu Picchu artefacts, 11, 23, 65, 155, 165–66; political career, 11, 23–24, 49–50; public image of, 22, 45–46, 50–51, 66–69, 76, 155, 157; relationship with cusqueños, 21–23, 25, 65–68; return to Machu Picchu, 45, 65–69, 71–72, 74, 83

Bingham, Suzanne, 66–67

regional politics, 35–37, 86–88,
96–97, 101, 128, 134–45, 149–51;
rivalry with Lima, 7, 28–29, 84–85,
87–88, 110, 115–18, 150, 153, 158;
transnational links, 97, 159; transportation infrastructure, 18–19, 31, 42;
urban planning, 39–40, 81–82; visitor
impressions of, 25–27; youth, 125–27,
144, 159. *See also* Cusco folklore;
Cusco press; Cusco Quadricentennial;
Cusco Week; earthquake of 1950;
tourism in Cusco
Cusco folklore: and national identity,
46, 78, 98; and tourism, 31, 36, 39, 42,
46–47, 65, 98. *See also* Centro Qosqo
de Arte Nativo; Inti Raymi
Cusco press: and Bingham, 23, 67–68;
criticism of Lima, 85–87, 115–18;
growth of, 19; and hippies, 123–25; and
tourism, 64–65, 118–19, 148–50, 154
Cusco Quadricentennial, 36–42; civic
celebrations, 41–42; and folklore, 39,
41–42; infrastructure improvements,
38–39, 42, 49; international interest,
42–43; local support for, 38–39; lodging
concerns, 40–41; and Machu Picchu,
42, 49; national support for, 38–39,
41–43, 48; and tourism, 37–39, 43
Cusco Week, 60–61, 65, 95. *See also* Inti
Raymi
Cusqueña Beer, 164

de Soto, Hernando, 145–46
Dibos Dammert, Eduardo, 56
Dirección General del Turismo
(DGTUR), 107
disaster economics, 72–73, 95–96
Disney, 55
Donald Duck, 55

earthquake of 1950: damage, 72, 79, 149;
reconstruction, 78–82, 89, 96–97;
tourism, 80–82, 89–90, 95–97. *See also*
Corporación de Reconstrucción y
Fomento del Cuzco; disaster

economics; Junta de Reconstrucción y
Fomento Industrial del Cuzco
Ejército de Liberación Nacional (ELN),
105, 108
Empresa Nacional de Ferrocarriles del
Perú (ENAFER), 107, 133, 139, 148
Empresa Nacional del Turismo (EN-
TURPERU), 107, 110–11, 134, 148–49
environmental tourism, 129
Estrada Pérez, Daniel, 134, 149–51

fascism in Peru, 33, 53
Faucett Airlines, 77, 100
Federación de Trabajadores del Cuzco, 97
Fejos, Paul, 142
Ferreyros, Alberto, 143
film, 54–55, 76–77, 122. See also *Aguirre,
the Wrath of God; Saludos Amigos;
Secret of the Incas*
Flores Galindo, Alberto, 5
Fondo de Promoción Turística
(FOPTUR), 131, 133, 140, 146
Fontaine, Joan, 76
Franck, Harry, 26–27
Frost, Peter, 145
Fuentes, Hildebrando, 28
Fujimori, Alberto: economic policies,
130, 146–47, 152, 154, 157; politics,
129–30, 139–41, 146–47, 152, 154;
tourism policies, 146, 148–49, 157, 164

García, Alan, 135, 137, 155, 160
García, José Uriel, 20, 32
gender, 126, 144
Generation of the Sierra, 20–21, 30. *See
also* Cosío, José Gabriel; García, José
Uriel; Giesecke, Albert; Tamayo,
Francisco; Valcárcel, Luis E.
Giesecke, Albert: and Hiram Bingham,
21, 65–68, 71, 76; influence, 20–21,
48, 75–76; promotion of Machu
Picchu, 24, 51, 65–68, 71, 75–77, 96;
promotion of tourism, 29–33, 39,
56–58, 65–68, 75–77, 89, 92–97; and
UNSAAC, 20–21, 31–32, 170n24

Instituto Nacional de Cultura (INC): conflicts with locals, 116–17, 119–20, 141–42, 149–51; creation, 114, 194n120; Hotel Machu Picchu, 115–17; management of Machu Picchu, 119–20, 139, 141–42, 149, 151; tourism development in Cusco, 128, 134, 139, 149–51

Instituto Nacional de Recursos Naturales (INRENA), 141–42

Inter-American Development Bank, 107, 110, 132

Inter-American Indigenista Conference, 65, 71

internal conflict, 129, 136–41, 143. *See also* Movimiento Revolucionario Túpac Amaru; Shining Path

Inti Raymi: folklore, 61; indigenismo, 61; origins, 60–61; security concerns, 136, 139; tourism, 61–62, 64–65, 89, 142, 147. *See also* Cusco Week

Jersey City, New Jersey, 139

jet aircraft, 100–101, 160

Jipis. *See* hippies

Jorge Chávez International Airport, 100

Junta de Reconstrucción y Fomento Industrial del Cuzco: creation, 80; criticism of, 86–89; economic development goals, 80, 94, 96–97; preservation efforts, 80–82, 86–87

Kincaid, Jamaica, 154

Klein, Julius, 76

Kodak, 21–22

Koechlin, José, 122, 196n166

Kubler, George A., 81, 96

Kuczynski, Pedro Pablo, 165

La Convención, 19, 97, 105, 108–9

Lake Titicaca, 31, 55, 108, 149

Leguía, Augusto: and Cusco, 29, 37, 47–48; fall from power, 37, 47; and indigenismo, 35–36; Patria Nueva

government, 29, 37; road construction, 29, 35; and UNSAAC, 20

Lima: economic power, 12, 74, 96, 110, 128, 150, 154, 158, 162, 164; support of tourism, 56; travel to, 55; views on Cusco, 16, 28–29, 38, 43–44, 56; views on indigenous culture, 16, 28–29, 43–44

Los Jaivas, 155

Luna, Américo, 77

Machu Picchu: archeological expeditions to, 21–25; cable car proposals, 164; centennial celebration, 155–56; in film, 54–55, 76–77, 122; global interest in, 22, 24, 45–47, 49–52, 68–70, 85, 104, 115, 159; and Hiram Bingham, 1, 5, 21–24, 45–47, 65–69; location, 9–10; national symbol of Peru, 1–4, 45–47, 69–70, 73, 82–85, 117, 119, 155–57, 160, 162; photography, 32–34; pre-Columbian era, 10; preservation concerns, 82–87, 94, 116, 119–20, 141–49, 151, 164–65; prior knowledge of, 21; restorations, 42, 65, 74, 90–92, 96, 110, 141; tourist destination, 1–2, 45–47, 58–60, 65–71, 82–84, 92–94, 96, 98–99, 102–4, 129, 151, 155; transnational contact zone, 159–61; transportation infrastructure, 19, 25, 49, 65, 67–68, 88, 104, 110, 118–19, 132–35, 151, 160. *See also* Hotel Machu Picchu; Huayna Picchu; Programa Machu Picchu; Supervigilancia de los Trabajos de Restauración de Machu Picchu

Machu Picchu Historical Sanctuary, 120, 141–42, 151

Machu Picchu Hydroelectric Plant, 94–96, 137

Machu Picchu Tourist Lodge: construction, 49; operations, 84, 92; privatized ownership, 149, 151–52, 154, 163; renovations and expansions, 60, 65, 95

Sumac, Yma, 77
Supervigilancia de los Trabajos de
    Restauración de Machu Picchu, 90
Szyszlo, Fernando de, 115, 152

Tamayo, Francisco, 20
Tampu Tocco, 10, 67
Tennessee Valley Authority, 80
Tiffany family, 11
Tintin, 52
Toledo, Alejandro, 155
Torres Bodet, Jaime, 80
Touring y Automovíl Club del Perú
    (TACP), 38, 56–58, 62, 74, 76–78, 83.
    See also *Turismo*
tourism: and the Cold War, 46, 58, 71;
    and the Good Neighbor policy, 46,
    58–59; and modernity, 29–32, 159;
    and nationalism, 3, 5, 7, 17, 43,
    45–47, 69, 157–58, 160–61; and
    nostalgia, 96–97; and photography,
    32–34; and regional identity, 4, 16–17,
    45–47, 69, 157; scholarship on, 1–2,
    5–7; staged authenticity, 47, 161; as
    transnational force, 2, 6, 97, 130. *See
    also* guidebooks; tourism in Cusco;
    tourism in Peru; tourists
tourism in Cusco: adventure tourism,
    129, 142–43, 145, 147; backpacking,
    98–99, 112–13, 123, 129, 132, 142–43;
    economic effects, 43–44, 108–11, 134,
    140, 152–54, 162–63; hotels, hippie
    tourism in, 121–27, 142–43; and
    indigenismo, 17, 31–35, 37, 60–62,
    69–70, 121, 157; internal conflict
    effect on, 135–43; labor, 108–11,
    127–28, 163–64; local and grassroots
    participation in, 41, 77–78, 128–30,
    142–43, 145, 151, 153, 166; local
    opposition to tourism, 123–25,
    150–54, 156, 164–65; local support for
    tourism, 16–17, 29–37, 81, 102, 110,
    115–18, 145, 157; luxury and elite
    tourism, 106, 110–13, 121, 148–49,
    153–54; national support for, 39,

41–42, 64–65, 71–74, 89–90, 99–102,
    108–11, 118–20, 127–28, 134–35,
    146–49; outsider and international
    investment in, 58–59, 128, 130, 149–54,
    158, 163; tourism infrastructure, 39–40,
    95, 101–2, 111–12, 132–34, 148–49;
    touristic descriptions of Cusco, 29–35,
    59; visitor impressions, 24–27, 40, 101,
    105–6, 148. *See also* COPESCO; Cusco;
    Hotel Machu Picchu; tourism; tourism
    in Peru; tourists
tourism in Peru: economic impact, 1;
    and nationalism, 3, 5, 7, 17, 31–32,
    43, 45–47, 61–62, 69, 98; planning,
    56–57, 62, 95, 121, 146; and populism,
    57–58, 63; state investment, 58,
    71–74, 101–3, 107, 110–11, 118–19,
    127–28, 131–35, 146–48, 157–58
tourists: Argentina tourists, 31;
    definintion of, 13; domestic tourists,
    13, 64, 119, 121, 163; hippies and
    countercultural, 98–99, 121–23, 129;
    international tourists, 13, 55, 63–64,
    74, 88, 95, 98, 100–103, 111, 121,
    128–29, 131, 135, 140, 147–48,
    153–54, 162; signs of modernity,
    31–32, 111; tourist opinions of Peru,
    105–6, 145, 148, 156; U.S. tourists,
    56, 59–60, 69–70, 100, 102, 111
transnationalism: cultural links, 46, 71,
    73, 99, 122, 159; and indigenismo,
    46–47, 159; institutions, 2–3, 73, 79,
    97, 99, 107, 150, 159; and nationalism,
    3–7, 17, 45–47, 69, 158, 160–61; and
    regionalism, 2–4, 7, 17, 44–47, 69, 71,
    73, 99, 130, 159; and tourism, 2–4,
    6, 17, 97, 130, 157, 160–162; transna-
    tional contact zone, 3, 46, 160
travel narratives: depictions of Catholi-
    cism, 26; depictions of Cusco, 25–28;
    depictions of Indians, 26–28. *See also*
    Chalmers Adams, Harriet; Franck,
    Harry; Fuentes, Hildebrando;
    guidebooks; Markham, Clements;
    Peck, Annie; Riva-Agüero y Osma,

Made in United States
North Haven, CT
25 January 2023

31522050R00152